Natural Beauty

Natural Beauty

A Theory of Aesthetics Beyond the Arts

Ronald Moore

CRITICAL ISSUES
IN PHILOSOPHY

broadview press

Library and Archives Canada Cataloguing in Publication

Moore, Ronald, 1943-
    Natural beauty : a theory of aesthetics beyond the arts / Ronald Moore.

(Critical issues in philosophy)
Includes bibliographical references and index.
ISBN 978-1-55111-503-0

    1. Nature (Aesthetics)—Textbooks. 2. Aesthetics—Textbooks. I. Title.
II. Series.

BH301.N3M65 2007   111'.85   C2007-903281-8

Broadview Press is an independent, international publishing house, incorporated in 1985. Broadview believes in shared ownership, both with its employees and with the general public; since the year 2000 Broadview shares have traded publicly on the Toronto Venture Exchange under the symbol BDP.

We welcome comments and suggestions regarding any aspect of our publications—please feel free to contact us at the addresses below or at broadview@broadviewpress.com.

North America
PO Box 1243, Peterborough, Ontario, Canada K9J 7H5
PO Box 1015, 3576 California Road, Orchard Park, NY, USA 14127
Tel: (705) 743-8990; Fax: (705) 743-8353
email: customerservice@broadviewpress.com

UK, Ireland, and continental Europe
NBN International, Estover Road, Plymouth, UK PL6 7PY
Tel: 44 (0) 1752 202300; Fax: 44 (0) 1752 202330
email: enquiries@nbninternational.com

Australia and New Zealand
UNIREPS, University of New South Wales
Sydney, NSW, Australia 2052
Tel: 61 2 9664 0999; Fax: 61 2 9664 5420
email: info.press@unsw.edu.au

www.broadviewpress.com

Consulting Editor for Philosophy: John Burbidge

Typesetting by Aldo Fierro.

This book is printed on paper containing 100% post-consumer fibre.

PRINTED IN CANADA

Contents

Preface

In one sense, natural beauty is perfectly familiar and unremarkable. It's the robin on our grass in the morning, the break of the waves along the shore, the rustle of the wind in the maple. It's just there—obvious, right at hand, and readily apprehended. And yet, in another sense, it's mysterious. Although it's easy to say that the robin, the crab nebula, the frangipani fragrance, and the maple rustle are beautiful, it's hard to say why they are beautiful. And it's harder still to explain what's going on when we engage in that peculiar mode of mental regard we often speak of as "appreciation" in finding such things beautiful.

For one thing, the considerations we have in mind when we think of various artifacts as beautiful—musical compositions, athletic feats, automobile designs, perfume fragrances—don't always apply comfortably to natural objects. For another, the independence they have from human agency imparts to them a special privilege. They are what they are in their natural environment; so their beauty must be comprehended in a way that immunizes it to some degree from our intellectual meddling. It is my aim in this book to present an account of our appreciation of natural beauty that retains both its familiarity and its mystery.

Ronald Hepburn, the father of environmental aesthetics, once remarked that "unrestricted generalizations in aesthetics are usually precarious in proportion to their attractiveness."[1] This is certainly true. They are precarious because they present such easy targets for rebuttal. One solid counterexample demolishes a universal claim. But they also are precarious in that they fail to take account of the way our thinking about topics such as natural beauty *evolves*, both historically in our culture and individually in our personal development. The process by which we grow up aesthetically—as a people and as individuals—is gradual, incremental, and necessarily incomplete.

I have, for these reasons, tried to avoid unrestricted generalizations in this

7

book. Nevertheless, I have advanced a number of general—not universal—claims about natural beauty that draw equally on historically evolved components and familiar experiential components of aesthetic experience. Because they draw upon a common stock of historical reflection in Western civilization and upon awarenesses most readers of this book will have had, I hope and expect that these claims will seem convincing. In this book I set forth a clear view of what makes our aesthetic experience of natural objects appealing and precious. This is a book about beauty in nature, rather than a book about the beauty of nature.[2] It is not, that is to say, a study in environmental aesthetics. It does, of course, consider many examples of beauty drawn from natural environments. These are often the evident, easy, and paradigmatic examples of natural beauty. But, it also takes into account non-artifactual objects divorced from natural environments—at least as these are usually understood. Waterfalls, sunsets, and grazing elk are natural things that can be and often are beautiful. But so are—in the sense of "natural" I deploy here—the grain on my coffee table, the weed in my otherwise tidy front lawn, the whorls and loops in my thumbprint, and the faint red glow of a distant star. So, while I try to avoid the precariousness of unrestricted generalization, I deliberately embrace the precariousness of nearly unrestricted scope in the topic of this study. The only beautiful things I wish to exclude from attention here are the man-made ones. This leaves me with a world (worlds, really) of quite heterogeneous subjects to be coaxed into a coherent general analysis.

What makes this task less daunting is the simple fact that, in a preliminary and rough-and-ready way, people make judgments of the kind I want to explain all the time. That is, ordinary people in all times and places have found ways of identifying certain elements, and not others, in their experience of the non-artifactual as precious and delightful. And they have generally taken these natural elements to be like artifactual elements in some ways, but importantly unlike them in others. A viewer captivated by the splashy display of vibrant colors in an autumn maple leaf is likely to be deeply mindful of the fact that this aesthetic object lies outside of human creation. But, at the same time, that viewer may recall ways in which interweavings of colors have affected him similarly in the observation of man-made objects—fabrics, paintings, lamp shades, and so on. Often—in fact typically, I think—people move quite nimbly in their sensibilities from the natural to the man-made. And the aim of their appraisal is not to make one the instructor or manager of the other, but to wring profit from their inter-relationships. People want to appreciate natural beauty as natural. But they also want to integrate the aesthetic awareness they obtain in relation to natural beauty with aesthetic awareness that informs and motivates their lives generally. My aim is to follow up on the lead these common recognitions give us and present an account that renders them as intelligible and coherent as possible. I believe that, when you look at it carefully and well, natural beauty is not just one more chip in the assorted pile of value chips we play in the game of life. It is instead the basis for forms of experience that affect the play of all the other chips, and thus makes the whole game more rewarding. Our delight in what is there, unmade and open to sensory awareness, is a fundamental value in a good life.

***

This undertaking would have been impossible without the constant help and support of my wife, Nancyanne, the thoughtful contributions from my daughter, Hollis, and the encouragement of a great number of colleagues who have, with their inspiration and criticism, helped me reach the position I take here. I want especially to acknowledge the contributions and advice of Allen Carlson, Noël Carroll, Donald Crawford, Marcia Eaton, Stan Godlovitch, and Stephanie Ross, without whose thoughtful comments, conversations, and responses to inquiries over the years this book would never have been completed.

An earlier version of portions of chapters 1 and 2 appeared in *Journal of Aesthetic Education*, Vol. 33, No. 3 (Fall, 1999), and part of chapter 5 has appeared in *Journal of Aesthetic Education*, Vol. 36, No. 2, Summer 2002. The latter was an article co-authored with Marcia Eaton, but I have tried to restrict what I include here to just the parts I contributed to the joint publication, and I use this material with Prof. Eaton's consent. A version of chapter 6 has appeared in *Ethics, Space, and the Environment*, Vol. 9, No. 3, October 2006. "This is just to Say," by William Carlos Williams, from *Collected Poems: 1909-1939*, Vol. 1, copyright ©1938 by New Directions Publishing Corp. is reprinted by permission of New Directions Publishing Corp.

NOTES

1 Ronald Hepburn, "Contemporary Aesthetics and the Neglect of Natural Beauty," in *British Analytical Philosophy*, ed. Bernard Williams and Alan Montefiore (London: Routledge & Kegan Paul, 1966), p. 291 n. 5.

2 I am indebted to Allen Carlson for suggesting this way of putting the distinction between the project of this book and work of the kind he, Hepburn, Arnold Berleant, Yi-Fu Tuan, Stan Godlovitch, Noël Carroll, Marcia Eaton and others have been pursuing over the past two decades.

Introduction

At sea stiff clouds appeared and started to color. Did natural beauty, however overdone, serve or permit anything needful? Was beauty necessary? This question she was perhaps put here to ask. Evidently she was not put here to answer it, since it called to mind only the Thurber and White title *Is Sex Necessary?*

Annie Dillard, "The Two of Them,"[1]

*I*s natural beauty necessary? Does it serve any truly fundamental purpose in our lives? Annie Dillard's protagonist, young Mrs. Maytree, hesitates to answer this question. But as soon as she asks it, the centrality of natural beauty in her world of experience is revealed in the book title that comes to mind. I think it's that way with most of us. When we ask ourselves what natural beauty is, or whether it serves needful aims, we struggle to come up with confident answers. When, instead of asking questions, we simply admire sea clouds coloring up so brilliantly that they seem almost overdone, the importance in our lives of beautiful natural objects like these seems obvious.

But what is obvious isn't always explicable. And what is important isn't always necessary. This book tackles these problems. First, it aims to provide an account of natural beauty that respects both common perceptions and philosophical theories. It regards positive aesthetic responses to natural objects, wherever and however formed, as bedrock expressions of value. It regards philosophical theories of natural beauty as efforts to explicate and elaborate these same responses. Its chief objective is to coax the responses and the explications into an intelligible accord. Second, it aims to provide an account of natural beauty that shows why its role in our lives is neither superficial nor meretricious, but essential to life goals most of us espouse. It is important to some people to have expensive jewelry, to be skillful bridge players, or to be admired by their fellow-workers. But, as even their advocates will admit, these objectives are not *necessary*, not indispensable to the leading of a good life. To ask whether natural beauty is necessary is, I think, really to ask whether the role it plays in a good and fulfilling life is *indispensable*. And this book addresses that question, too.

The account I present here makes plenty of room for taking both natural and artifactual objects as demanding features of aesthetic analysis peculiar to themselves. But it also aims to make sense of the way people properly draw upon unrestricted ranges of aesthetic capacity in their appreciation of both. It takes the broadest possible view of nature, going beyond standard concepts to encompass the entire world of the non-man-made. In my view, it is not only the leaping salmon that is natural. It is the glint of light off its surface, the microscopic features in its scales, the distant stars under which it is leaping, and everything else that can be comprehended up to the point of our own deliberate manufacture. Dust. Rainbows. Arcturus. A smile. A harmony of particles observable only in an electron microscope. Features that appear only as a result of the interplay of other features: sparkles on rippling water in the wind, the counterpoint of seabird song and surf sound, the wild play of branches and leaves swirling against a background of broken crags.

Scale is not an issue. A grove of trees might be beautiful. For different reasons, a tree within that grove might be beautiful. For yet other reasons, a leaf on that tree might be beautiful. And for yet other reasons, the pattern of colors on that leaf might be beautiful. Put before a microscope or some other sensory modification device, the leaf might yield additional, independent forms of beauty. My account deals with natural beauty at all levels of sensory awareness.

Moreover, the view I advance is deliberately noncommittal on the analysis of beauty itself. The account of beauty judgments I present is meant to be compatible with a broad range of theories. One reason I take this approach is to deflect the potential complaint that my analysis works only if natural beauty is presented in some particular way—a formalist account, say, or a phenomenalist, a non-cognitivist, or pragmatist analysis. My approach is meant to be amenable to (or at least not excluded by) all these views. But another reason is to insure that the account I give of natural beauty will work well with conceptions not tied to *any* theory—conceptions espoused by people who think of beauty judgments as personal, private, and not amenable to reform by anybody's theory.

Although my account is deliberately noncommittal, it doesn't take beauty to be just anything that pleases anyone about any object. I take beauty to be a positive aesthetic virtue found in objects or their traits when attention to their sensible features produces and sustains deep and positive satisfaction, and does so in a way that involves stages of response and distinctions among the satisfactions associated with these stages, leading to a culmination of those satisfactions. It is important to the notion of beauty I endorse that not every buzz or tingle count as a relevant aesthetic satisfaction. It is equally important that the unsophisticated, untrained apprehensions of children, early peoples, and other naïfs not be discounted. Beauty judgments, whether they pertain to natural objects or to artworks, are positive aesthetic appraisals emergent in all stages of human development and in all cultures. Like moral judgments, they amplify and mature over the course of a lifetime—a person's as well as a culture's lifetime. And they can be better or worse founded, depending on the ways in which these judgments integrate initial aesthetic responses with accounts of aesthetic experience in the context of an appreciative cultural environment.[2]

Our aesthetic consideration of the non-manmade world should be extended beyond familiar environmental values to take account of features to be savored in all manner of settings and conditions. Accordingly, nature is not to be identified with the great out-of-doors, or the wilderness, or the totality of ecosystems. To be sure, roaring waterfalls, mountain peaks, and newborn fawns are proper and secure examples of beautiful natural objects. But natural beauty can also be found in the cloud outside the office window, the moss in pavement cracks, the play of light on rain-soaked cobbles in the street, and the pattern of dust on puddles in a rutted playground.

In declaring that my focus will extend beyond environmental natural beauty, I don't want to suggest that I take environmental aesthetics lightly or that I think of the important work done in this field as peripheral to the topic at hand. Any sensible account of the aesthetics of natural beauty will have to consider beauty in the natural environment to be a central focus of attention. But by insisting that, though central, it is not the *exclusive* focus of attention, I hope to counteract the excesses of some currently influential analyses of aesthetic value in natural contexts. I intend the picture of natural beauty I present to seem plausible not only as an overview of the wider topic, but as a clarification of environmental beauty as a subtopic within it.

In one conspicuous respect, the approach I take toward beauty in the natural environment is eccentric and old-fashioned. Recent aesthetic theory is skeptical of border crossings between art and nature. The currently prevalent idea is that treating aesthetic features in natural settings as though they were pictures on a wall, scenes in movies, or elements in a musical score is demeaning and disrespectful to the natural phenomena themselves. Each mode of experience, it is argued, is owed its own respect, and hence its own analysis. What we create as an artwork is one thing, to be sized up and welcomed or dismissed according to its conception, the degree to which it realizes its objective, and its resultant station in our lives. But what we don't create—the world out there beyond our instrumentalities—is just what it is, a raw, uncontrived subject-matter to be welcomed or dismissed on entirely different grounds.

I certainly agree that it is a mistake to think of a mountain scene as beautiful just because it looks so much like the sort of thing Albert Bierstadt, for example, painted beautifully. But it is not a mistake to think that the characteristics to which our attention is drawn in the mountain scene on the one hand and the Bierstadt landscape on the other are alien to each other. The account I present here urges us to allow the experience of art to inform and inspire our experience of natural phenomena, and vice versa. I can see no reason to think that the one must contaminate or denigrate the other.

In a similar vein, I think it would be wrong to situate us, as human participants in the experience of our world, as inside or outside of nature. We are things we didn't make. We are also uniquely conscious beings that make things for our own delectation. And as conscious beings, we make experiences—some of them aesthetic experiences—out of what we find in the world with which our senses make us acquainted. When we say that we step back to see nature as nature, we must recognize that we are at the same time part of nature. It would therefore be wrong to conceive of ourselves as making judgments about natural beauty in the detached and external way that astrophysicists might make judgments about supernovas. Though we are things we didn't make, we are still part of the process that made all the rest. This insider-outsider relation might be seen as an ambiguity of perspective destined to muddle the analysis. Yet it needn't do so. We are in language and in culture, but we think about both of them through language and culture. Law shapes our culture; but we regard law through law as we change and cultivate it. Art shapes and reacts to us. We are in and out of it at the same time, unproblematically for the most part. Innumerable examples available from everyday life make it plain that we can be, in relation to a body of experience, apart, and yet a part. I do hope fervently that my daughter will grow up to be happy, but I don't want to impose my conception of happiness on her. I want my garden to reflect my decisions. Yet I want it to surprise me with its peculiar display of bounty. So I don't think that the project of understanding the aesthetic aspects of nature is complicated by the fact that we, as observers of nature, are natural.

NOTES

1   Annie Dillard, "The Two of Them," *Harper's*, Vol. 307, no. 1842 (November, 2003).

2   Beauty, as the notion is deployed in popular parlance, is either cheap or deep. It is maximally cheap if it attaches to anything at all toward which one has an emphatic positive response, no matter of what kind or for what reason. It is maximally deep if it attaches only to the most elevated or revered of objects, or to various objects for the profoundest of reasons. Natural beauty as I speak of it in this book is meant to mark a range of response that falls between these extremes. It is meant to be deep*ish* without being implausibly deep. Whether it is deep enough to handle the notions immersed in it is a question I leave to the judgment of the reader.

CHAPTER 1

Appreciating Nature as Natural

THE PROBLEM OF APPRECIATION

*P*eople who write about natural beauty are fond of reminding us that nature must be appreciated as *natural*. By this they generally mean that the norms of appreciation we use in taking the measure of beauty in man-made objects—especially artworks—are out of place in the world of natural things. After all, they argue, mountains, marmots, and monsoons are not intentional objects; their meaning is not measured against the purposes of any (mortal) creator. The aesthetic concepts we apply to paintings, plays, and poems, whose nature and value are tightly tied to the purposes organizing their creation, do not apply to them. So, to the degree that we see beauty as caught up in what we make, we are at a loss to measure the beauty of the utterly unmade. Mountains just are what they are, the evolved products of age-old geophysical forces predating and indifferent to human life. It is precisely because paintings of mountains, as opposed to mountains themselves, are products of human will that we can regard them as well- or ill-composed, belonging to this or that style, sentimental, idealized, ironic, morbid, and so on.

There is a great deal of merit in this view. It is no less foolish and distortive to look at a mountain landscape as though it really were a painting—faulting it or admiring it for its compositional balance, say—than it is to look at a painting as though it really were a mountain landscape—faulting it or admiring it for its repleteness of ecological detail. The difference in intentionality entails a host of differences in the parameters of response. We don't approach the objects of natural and artifactual beauty in the same way. We set ourselves up to enjoy a symphony by drawing upon our familiarity with other performances of the work, other works of the same or similar genre, standard techniques of classical composition, the tonal characteristics of instruments employed, and so on. When we are delighted with the unexpected power of a given passage or disappointed in the tempi, our critical awareness is tempered and guided by our knowledge of the canons, categories, and standards that apply to composition and performance of works of this type; we hear the work as similar to or different from others that are in various ways like it. By contrast, we set ourselves up to enjoy a walk along a mountain stream by doing away with many, if not most, categories of learned appreciation and by opening ourselves to a freer form of enjoyment. When we are struck with the sudden aspect of a field of fireweed and toadflax, our pleasure seems more nearly unmediated. We needn't know a lot about standard botanical characteristics of these species, differences from and similarities to other related wildflowers, their ecological niche, and so on, to gain an intense aesthetic satisfaction from the experience.

But it is easy to overstate the difference between these two modes of appreciation. The aesthetic enjoyment of artworks is not purely a matter of locating them in a field of categories and concepts; nor is the enjoyment of nature a purely unmediated concession to sense over thought. It is evident in the actual practice of appreciation that each of these modes of awareness feeds off the other. We habitually deploy concepts, techniques, ways of speaking, background assumptions, analogies, allusions, and notions of aesthetic relevance that work for us in one domain *because* they work for us in the other. It is useful to see a sea fog as reminiscent of Whistler's *Nocturne in Blue and Green* (1877) precisely because it calls our attention to features of an ambient sensory environment that come to the foreground only in light of our prior experience of the artwork. And it is useful to see a Turner sunset as particularly splendid because our eyes have been trained to see splendor in wonderful sunsets. To generalize the point, our experience in reflecting on the aesthetic qualities of artworks serves us well in regarding analogous properties throughout life, not only in thinking about the qualities and compositions of nature, but in thinking about those of interior design, automobiles, prose, politics, and the pattern of living we create daily. Likewise, our familiarity with the particularities of natural objects is a useful preparation for our enjoyment of art, but not only art; it grounds our delectation of countless analogous features and configurations of elements in all corners of our experience.

This view may seem platitudinous. Nature prepares us for art and art prepares us for nature. But the point is deeper than it appears at first. Despite the fact that the point is both simple and obvious, it has generated a substantial amount of philosophical controversy. The core of the controversy lies in the fact that, although we are reasonably confident of the critical and analytical framework

appropriate to the appreciation of artworks, we are less confident of the corresponding framework of ideas appropriate to the appreciation of natural objects.
We are generally prepared to believe that our aesthetic response to natural objects
is, despite any conceptual deficit, neither naïve nor unsuited to its objects. But,
if the appreciation of natural objects is not supported by *some* kind of cognitive
apparatus, something like—even remotely like—the conceptual scheme that
supports our judgments in the art world, how can it be anything but shallow,
subjective, and inaccessible to critical assessment? At present, philosophers are
generally inclined to respond to this question in one of two ways. Conceptualists,
like Allen Carlson and Marcia Eaton, insist that there are, after all, categories and
concepts that can be deployed to help aesthetic judgments in respect to natural objects assume the legitimacy, such as it is, of aesthetic judgments in the art
world. Non-conceptualists, like Arnold Berleant and Noël Carroll, insist that the
fundamental twist in our view of nature is a liberation of reflection from prior
conceptual frameworks, so that imagination can gain ascendancy over thought.[1]

In this chapter and the next I make the case for a view of natural aesthetics
that aims to mediate between these views. On the one hand, I want to reaffirm
nature's natural connection with our experience of art and, on the other hand,
I want to free aesthetic appreciation of nature from both of the two masters to
whom it has recently fled: science and unfettered imagination. The view I advance takes natural objects as objects of aesthetic awareness and appreciation
in a way that respects their difference from artifacts while remaining accessible
to many of the categories of analysis, criticism, and appreciation that apply to
artworks. My fundamental claim is that we approach the qualities of things we
think worthy of admiration in nature through lenses we have developed for
thinking of aesthetic qualities *at large*—not art, not literature, not music, not
politics, not urban planning, not landscape design, but all of these and more.

GLASS FLOWERS

One of the great treasures of Harvard University is the Ware Collection of
Glass Models of Plants or, as it is more simply known to its more than one hundred thousand annual viewers, the glass flowers. The glass flowers are not art,
or at least not designed to have been appreciated as art. Created in Germany
with apparently irreproducible skill between the years 1887 and 1936 by Leopold
and Rudolf Blaschka as accurate models of various species of plant life, they
were meant to be pedagogical tools for the instruction of students whose access
to botanical specimens would otherwise be constrained by the vicissitudes of

transport and the periodicity of seasons. The collection comprises more than eight hundred exquisitely fashioned models, ranging from truly exotic plants, scarcely ever seen, to common weeds. Invariably, viewers are powerfully impressed by the lifelike quality of the models. In fact, such was the skill of the Blaschkas that it would be nearly impossible to tell which was glass and which was a real flower if a model and its subject were placed side by side.

One of the specimens represented is *Chicorium intybus*, common chicory. This is a delicate roadside wildflower, familiar throughout North America. Its long, straight, striated stalks are festooned with star clusters of short, triangular leaves and compact, blue, daisy-like flowers. Providing they can resist discounting its charm by its commonness, many people regard it as a pretty, even beautiful, flower. Now suppose that, having been struck by the beauty of the glass specimen, a museum visitor were to walk outside and discover at the parking lot's edge a living chicory plant, a plant whose physical differences from that of the glass plant were visually indiscernible. Having found the man-made chicory beautiful, should the viewer, to be consistent (i.e., *aesthetically* consistent), find the live chicory equally beautiful?

If we are tempted to think otherwise, won't that be because we are implicitly counting the factors of illusion, hard work, and rarity into our assessment of the glass flower's beauty? But don't these factors contribute to the model's worth in ways other than in the respect of beauty (and other exclusively aesthetic considerations)? It is tempting to think that we should be able to discount all the background factors—including everything relating to the two objects' disparate causal histories, insurable values, age, and so on—so as to isolate the immediate, foreground sensory experience in which they are alike. After all, aesthetic regard concerns itself fundamentally with the manifold of *sensory awareness*, and not with all that causes it or is caused by it. So it would seem reasonable to conclude that if the glass chicory and the living chicory *look* the same, then, so far as the sense of sight is concerned at least, the two should be deemed equally beautiful, perhaps even aesthetically identical.

To extend the hypothesis, we might suppose that a team of latter-day super-Blaschkas, empowered with all the tools of modern simulation technology, might set about to replicate each of the other sensible characteristics of chicory in a synthetic model. The olfactory qualities would prove no problem to any modern perfumier; chicory has a very faint and unsubtle fragrance. The gustatory qualities might be more of a challenge; chicory is famous for its distinctive flavor—a flavor which many people believe (wrongly, I think) improves the taste of coffee. Still, were native chicory no longer widely available, it is a virtual certainty that chemical laboratories could soon produce an artificial chicory flavoring satisfactory to the most discerning chicory-coffee aficionado. (And perhaps they already have.) It is easy to imagine that synthetic fiber scientists could replicate the tactile qualities of all parts of the chicory plant, not only its general feel, but its malleability, ductility, tensile strength, etc. Whatever minimal sounds the plant makes in this or that atmospheric condition could be synthesized easily in any well-equipped sound studio. So, the success of such a venture in plant synthesis is certainly not beyond imagining. Let us assume, then, that we have two specimens at our disposal, a real chicory plant and an artificial chicory plant that cannot be distinguished from it on any sensory basis. Must we now accept the conclusion that the two are aesthetically identical, so that *anything* we are warranted in saying pertinent to the aesthetic status of the one we must be willing to say about the other, and any response we make to either must be made to both?

Some people will no doubt find this an easy question. They will say that the hypothesis has been forged in such a way as to exclude any basis of discrimination between the two, so that the question answers itself. They will say that just as an animal breeder who is presented with a creature and its perfect clone cannot tell them apart (for that's what it means to be a *perfect* clone), the aesthetic judge who is presented with a real plant and its perfect synthetic replica cannot, *ex hypothesi*, draw an aesthetic distinction between them.

But others will resist the pull of the hypothesis. They will answer the question in the negative because they think that, the apparent physical identity of the two plants notwithstanding, *something* is present in the natural plant and absent in the artificial plant that bears importantly on *how* the two are seen. There is an important difference, they will want to insist, between perceiving a set of characteristics in an object and perceiving that same set of characteristics as *natural* to that object. To perceive something as a product of nature is not to perceive one more thing about it; it is to change the way we perceive everything about it. This response is pretty much the one Immanuel Kant gave to the question more than two hundred years ago.

In *The Critique of Judgment* (1790), Kant commended the observer who takes an immediate interest in natural rather than artifactual beauty, and went so far as to say that the former perspective is favorable to a certain moral feeling (and is indeed "a mark of a good soul"). His way of delineating the natural and artifactual frames of mind draws him directly into our conundrum:

> He who by himself (and without any design of communicating his observations to others) regards the beautiful figure of a wild flower ... with admiration and love; who would not willingly miss it in nature although it may bring him some damage; who still less wants any advantage from

it—he takes an immediate and also an intellectual interest
in the beauty of nature. That is, it is not merely the form of
the product of nature which pleases him, but its very presence pleases him....

But it is noteworthy that if we secretly deceived this lover
of the beautiful by planting in the ground artificial flowers
(which can be manufactured exactly like real ones) ... and he
discovered the deceit, the immediate interest that he previously took in them would disappear at once, though perhaps
a different interest, viz. the interest of vanity in adorning
his chamber with them for the eyes of others, would take its
place. This thought then must accompany our intuition and
reflection on beauty, viz. that nature has produced it; and on
this alone is based the immediate interest that we take in it.[2]

Here Kant appears to be saying that it is an essential and proper part of our
aesthetic regard for natural objects to perceive them as other than collections
of sensible features. It is to perceive these features as drawn together by natural
forces (of growth, transformation, and evolution, let us say) rather than by
artifice. The attention we give to natural objects can amount to an immediate
interest, and even a form of love, only when their very presence is understood
to be predicated on processes removed from human design.[3]

But what is it, exactly, about a thing that has emanated from natural process
rather than human manufacture (which is, after all, just one more attenuated
form of natural process, if you take human participation in the great chain of
being seriously) that should render our contemplation of it so immediately
pleasing and valuable? And what is it that should lead to such disdain (or at
least "disappearance of immediate interest") when what was thought to be a
flower is ultimately discovered to be its artificial counterpart? The production
of nature look-alikes can be, in its own way, both pleasing and moving, as
the popular reaction to the Blaschka flowers demonstrates. Why should the
matter of *origin* count for so much? As Kant puts it, our experience of the
one is rendered replete with immediate pleasure, love, and even an intimation
of moral consciousness, while the other is purged of all of these. Is prejudice
about origins here anything more than an eco-sensitive analog of the social
prejudice endemic in human society that irrationally inflates or reduces our
estimate of others according to their origins—ethnic, national, or regional?

The easy answer to this question is that we value the naturalness of the
natural flower because it is full of a past and a future bound up with the rest of

nature, and therefore implicated in it. We admire and respect nature, in turn, for a host of reasons—reasons that involve a tangle of normative concerns ranging from the ecological to the theological. Many of these may be hard to tease apart from aesthetic concerns. For example, our judgments about what is morally good in nature may seem nearly inextricable from our judgments about natural beauty. As we have seen, Kant endorsed as a fundamental value in the contemplation of nature an activity he regarded as mingling aesthetic and moral virtues in the making of goodness.[4] And a fair number of recent writers have echoed Kant's sentiment, if for various non-Kantian reasons.[5] On Kant's analysis, even if the natural object and the man-made object are, in all perceptible qualities, identical, then deeming the natural as natural would impute to its object some moral weight, or at least some weight other than, and different from, whatever weight it enjoys simply as an exemplar of its type.[6]

If, however, we are not as inclined as Kant and his philosophical successors have been to affiliate the contemplation of natural beauty with moral edification, on what basis will appreciating natural objects as natural make them special, and even superior to, their non-natural counterparts? And, if we put aside not only moral features, but *all* value normative characteristics except the aesthetic, what is left that should incline us to take the chicory plant to be importantly different from, and perhaps even superior to, its glass twin just because the former and not the latter is *natural*?

WARHOL AND BLASCHKA

This puzzle about flowers and their artificial counterparts echoes a well-known example that lies at the heart of modern aesthetic theory. Andy Warhol created artifacts that mimicked their originals. It is fair to say that one of his artfully constructed Brillo Boxes was just as indistinguishable from a real Brillo box as a Blaschka chicory is indistinguishable from its natural counterpart. In a justly famous article, Arthur Danto argues that these apparent indiscernibles become non-identical when we regard them through a certain conceptual lens—a lens involving an atmosphere of theory and a knowledge of the history of art, a lens involving a special, interpretive sense of "is" that Danto calls the "is of artistic identification."[7] The Warhol Brillo Box distinguishes itself from the grocery-store Brillo box through being swept up by this theoretical mode of regard into an artworld. It is tempting to think that a parallel answer should be available in the case of the Blaschka chicory and its real-world look-alike. It is tempting, that is, to suppose that the difference between the artifact and the natural object should be, like the difference between the artwork and the quotidian artifact, resolvable by invoking the interpretive lens of theory. But is there an "is" of natural aesthetic identification? Is there, that is to say, a special mode of deeming that uniquely applies to natural objects in the appreciation of their aesthetic features?

Some philosophers seem to think there is. On their view, we implicitly invoke it when we view nature as natural. Like Danto's artworld, the natureworld, if we can call it that, becomes discernible (and properly appreciable) only in an atmosphere of history and theory—natural history and scientific theory, as it usually turns out. Underlying such a view is the conceptualist assumption that the way we come to understand things in general—the way we see them for what they are—is by invoking the right conceptual sorting devices (categories, taxonomic divisions, classes of similar types, and the like) and subsuming instances under them. Thus, the this-and-here item is made intelligible as an example of a given sort. It is by invoking the concept "sonata" that a certain form of musical composition can be heard for what it *is*, as making sense and being good, bad, or indifferent, as having features that are standard for works of its type and allow us to become aware of the *Gestalt* it shares with other relevantly similar works.[8] Warhol's Brillo Box falls away from its real-world look-alikes when, and only when, it is seen through the concept of Pop Art construction. If it weren't subsumed under the category of Pop Art artifact (or some similar *Gestalt*-indicating concept), it would fail to qualify at all as a work of art. By parity of reasoning, one might suppose that the Blaschka chicory falls apart from its real-world chicory counterpart just when the former is seen through the concept of a museum model of display and the latter is seen through the biological concepts appropriate to its species and type.

Applying the general conceptualist assumption to natural objects, the two-fold claim is first that, if the concepts and categories we have chosen are the right ones, they give us a "fix" on the nature of these objects, and thus provide us with a necessary (although certainly not a sufficient) condition for appreciating, judging, or simply contemplating them; and second that there are concepts and categories appropriate to the aesthetic contemplation of natural objects. The dominant view is that, in today's world,[9] these concepts and categories are supplied by natural history and natural science. These are what give us the true and objective account of nature and its contents.

Non-conceptualists argue that the role of theory in natural aesthetics is quite the opposite. Whereas, they insist, it is appropriate to regard man-made things as fitting into, and evaluated under, man-made categories and concepts, it is distortive and misleading to impose these same sorts of cognitive constraints on nature. After all, nature is free, unbounded by classifications in its splendid diversity, and potentially open to perceptual delight in endlessly various ways.

To burden it with categorial subsumption, or even analogy to other modes of experience, is to belie its unique charm. Just as the conceptualists urge the explanatory categories of science on natural objects on the ground that science presents things as they are, so the non-conceptualists insist that leaving natural objects as they are means leaving the artificial cognitive framing devices at home.

Part of the impetus for this view comes from Kant. Kant urged us to regard judgments of beauty (in nature as in art) as fundamentally detached from understanding, and only indirectly stimulating it. If, as Kant supposes, our regard for the beauty of a natural chicory plant is freed from the thought "chicory" and all associated taxonomic frames born in the botany laboratory, we can look admiringly at it for what it is, not as a specimen of its type. And, in doing so, we can become aware of all those features that are unique to its individual appearance in the here and now. Another part of the impetus comes from the latter-day aesthetic attitude theorists who have insisted that proper aesthetic awareness of an object demands a disinterested and sympathetic attention to it for its own sake, setting aside all the intellectual baggage we usually carry to our various life projects.[10] If contemplating natural objects for their own sake requires abandonment not only of our everyday worries, aspirations, doubts, and so on, but also of the very intellectual apparatus that we bring to our everyday world to make it manageable, then it will be imperative to experience nature a-conceptually, not just non-scientifically. This move leads (or at least seems to lead) to a position that gives something like free rein to imagination. Each item of observation in the natural context invites its own response, and each response provides its own constellation of impulses to the subject. There is no reason to suppose that these impulses correspond to categories established by prior comprehension. So the aesthetic appreciation of natural objects transcends, or eclipses, the ways we are accustomed to thinking not only about art, but about everything.

No sensible person will deny that both science and imagination inform our appreciation of nature in important ways. Nevertheless, both the conceptualist position and the non-conceptualist position I have outlined are seriously flawed. In chapter 2, I defend a view that draws lessons from their failings while it capitalizes on their admitted strengths.

NOTES

1   In "Fact and Fiction in the Aesthetic Appreciation of Nature," *Journal of Aesthetics and Art Criticism* 56 (1998), Marcia Eaton draws this distinction somewhat differently. She divides the competing positions into the

"cognitive model" and the "imaginative model." My way of framing the difference is meant to suggest that, though there is cognitive content at work on both sides of the division, classifications of the kind standardly used to identify types of natural objects by the sciences are helpful on one side and not on the other.

2 Immanuel Kant, *Critique of Judgment*, trans. J.H. Bernard (New York: Hafner Publishing Co., 1951), pp. 141-142.

3 The key remark is this: "In saying it is *beautiful* and in showing that I have taste, I am concerned, not with that in which I depend on the existence of the object, but with that which I make out of this representation in myself." *Ibid.*, p. 39.

4 See *Ibid.*, p. 141. I discuss this in chapter 4

5 See, for example, Marcia Eaton, "The Beauty that Requires Health," in *Placing Nature: Culture and Landscape Ecology*, ed. Joan Nassauer (Washington, DC: Island Press, 1997).

6 This conclusion may seem to clash with what Kant says in his famous declaration of the independence of beauty judgments from the existence of their objects (*Critique*, Bernard, ed., p. 39), but it reflects a profound sense in which Kant subscribes to the moral instructiveness of the natural order in general.

7 Arthur Danto, "The Artworld," *Journal of Philosophy* 61 (1964) pp. 580-81.

8 Many theorists inclined in this direction find support for their views in Kendall Walton's essay "Categories of Art," *Philosophical Review* 79 (1970). In this essay, Walton argues that to perceive a work of art is, typically, to perceive it in a category, and to perceive it in a category is to perceive the *Gestalt* of that category in the work. The *Gestalt* of a category is a function of what the artform has evolved to be, a basis for our expectations of perceptive awareness. So, on Walton's account, what we can comprehend in a work is always a function of what its categorial predecessors have prepared us to comprehend.

9 Aesthetic categories as well as explanatory principles are clearly time-relative. In an earlier age, theology and mythology occupied the position natural science does today as suppliers of conceptual tools for making natural objects intelligible.

10 Jerome Stolnitz develops this view in *Aesthetics and the Philosophy of Art Criticism* (New York: Houghton Mifflin, 1960), pp. 32-42.

CHAPTER 2

Conceptualism and Non-conceptualism

CONCEPTUALISM AND ITS PROBLEMS

*T*he foremost exponent of the conceptualist position is Allen Carlson. In a series of stylish and forcefully argued articles over the last twenty years, Carlson has insistently grounded aesthetic regard of the natural world in the framework of understanding provided by natural science. The argument, which has never deviated in its essentials while contouring its borders in response to critics, is essentially this: Objects of our aesthetic attention in the natural world are not works of art; they are natural. Our appreciation of them must therefore be a way of thinking and responding that is fitted to the natural order. What we have come to know about nature objectively is cumulated in natural science. Therefore, natural science provides the only reasonable basis for appreciation of natural objects, corresponding in its own way to our developed standards of appreciation in the arts (knowledge of types, traditions, historical deviations, and so on). Relying on natural science, we can appreciate the chicory plant as an environmentally integral component in the wider natural order. Relying on natural science, we can see how this specimen is relevantly like and unlike others. This way of viewing the chicory plant affirms that this object is situated in a natural environment, and that affirmation is essential to our seeing it (aesthetically and otherwise) for what it is.[1]

The first problem with this argument is that it wrongly assumes that there is in the natural world a fact of the matter and that this fact is especially accessible to science. We should remember that it is the business of science to see what is similar as alike, and what happens as conforming to common rules of action. The artist may be struck with a feature of this particular chicory plant that leads her to take delight in it especially—say, the way that branch catches the light and brings it up against the shadow of the stalk. And so may we delight in it as admirers of the natural beauty of the plant apart from any artistic objective. But, science doesn't help us here. Science looks at the plant as chicory and sees it as an exemplar whose properties are tied to its type. To see the chicory plant as chicory is not to see it in the full range of its appearance. Categories are sometimes helpful in framing our experience of nature (or in inducing a conspectus of attention); but sometimes they aren't. A given object may fit in several categories, uncertainly in any category, or (especially in the case of objects of first impression) in no category at all.

The limiting condition on scientific knowledge is not some dim barrier of mystery, but simply its inapplicability to the unique. The sciences are bound to understand individual objects only as members of classes of things and to understand events as subject to generally applicable laws. The eye of the aesthetic observer, whether trained on artworks or on nature, is concerned to see unique aspects of things—how this odd clump of chicory catches the afternoon light, how this shattering icepack sounds, how this waterfall spray feels. Not *qua* chicory, *qua* icepack, *qua* waterfall; but simply *qua* this-here-and-now-object-of-regard. Brute, raw perception. To be managed later this way or that, but brute and raw at its inception.

Second, in our experience of nature, the object of contemplation is often not a thing that has a scientifically recognized type, but rather an indefinable constellation of features. Nature does not consist of a sum of natural kinds. Much of what we admire in nature is nameless, not because a category is missing in our repertory, but because it is a *combination* of looks, sounds, smells, glints, hues, swirls, and so on that simply have no names. These various features are drawn together into a conspectus of appreciation not by an organizing category, but by one or another (informal) framing device we call upon. We may for a while become aware of natural beauty in a protuberance of rock, moss, and varied plant life that looks composed into a unit of delectation just by its sunlit and shadowed contours and its relative isolation from its neighbors. We may take the graceful rhythm of wave action in a pond, its ever-changing patterns of lines and lights, as an aesthetic whole because just this much is marked out by the disturbance of wind. We may find, on a walk through the woods, that the fragrance of the conifers, the susurration of the leafy undergrowth, the feel of the soil underfoot, and the sudden aspect of a dead ground squirrel come together in an experience whose poignancy is organized by a general awareness of the cycle of life, death, and renewal. In each case, the framing at work is temporary and malleable; but, even as we move about in it and reposition the frame ("Now look at the lake from this side!"), we draw upon it to give us a something-here-and-now as the object of our aesthetic awareness.

More than anyone else, Ronald Hepburn has drawn attention to the importance of the aesthetic conspectus, as opposed to categories and subsumables, in imparting wholeness and focus to appreciation of nature. Hepburn insists that nature is frameless; but he denies that this means we cannot, by combining imagination with informed perspective, achieve a *rapprochement* with nature in which we "realize" what we observe. Realizing the natural object occurs when, for this reason or that, our perceptions find a place to dwell and linger.[2] As he points out, in our response to the flight of swifts, or the fall of an autumn leaf, or a wide expanse of sand and mud, the natural categories involved play at best a minor role in our appreciation.[3] I may care very little whether the birds whose graceful pattern I observe are swifts or larks, whether the leaf falls from a maple or an ash, and whether I am on a salt marsh or river estuary. My aesthetic attention is drawn to aspects of the natural spectacle that stand importantly apart from any category or concept. I am delighted by the peculiar way—there is no word for it—that the birds, twisting in their flight, catch the light just so, and then just so again. Natural objects are often, in this way, an immediate substance of my sensory awareness. They aren't just this or that, but the way this or that looks, feels, sounds, and so on. They are aspects, figurations, fragrances, and the like, the appreciation of which may have been cultivated by the contemplation of things of this or that type, but which are importantly free of the type itself.

Thirdly, there is an obvious way in which cognition can interfere with delectation. We may find that our experience of natural objects or natural settings is disturbed by what we have come to know about them. Our knowledge that a given object of our attention is *only* a chicory plant may detract from our awareness of its particular beauty in this light, under these circumstances, with this breeze, and so on. We have all been on walks through gardens when we didn't know the names of the flowers. It is hard to think that we would necessarily be in a better position to appreciate them aesthetically if we knew their names. Sometimes knowledge spoils experience. Knowing just what a thing is captures it in a category, and in that way makes it manageable or routine to us, whereas not knowing what a thing is and seeing it as just one more nameless splendor makes it unmanageable, exciting, and therefore, in its own way, important.

I don't want to make the clash of knowledge and appreciation seem simple and unproblematic. Nor do I mean to suggest that knowledge always (or even usually) gets in the way of our awareness of natural beauty. Sometimes what we know about a natural object or environment can help us to focus our awareness in fruitful ways, revealing features or aspects we would have otherwise missed. Sometimes we aren't even aware of a thing as an object of attention until we see it as a thing of a given sort, deploying our categorial recognition to pick it out of its background. In fact, the interplay between knowledge of various sorts and appreciative experience of various sorts is both very complex and very controversial. I take up this issue and the philosophical debate it has inspired in chapter 8. To make the point I am urging here, however, it will suffice to acknowledge that *some* forms of knowledge can, under *some* conditions, *sometimes* interfere with, rather than enhance, our aesthetic appreciation of natural objects. And I think this is a claim that is so obviously true that it is beyond reasonable debate.

To sum up, then, although natural science gives us lots of information about nature, it doesn't provide an account of the *nature* of nature needed to support the particular forms of appreciation we often bring to natural experience. By being indelibly committed to the cognitive, the categorial, and the regular, science provides no means of illuminating those aspects of our reflection on natural objects that are non-cognitive, particular, and anomalous.

NON-CONCEPTUALISM AND ITS PROBLEMS

Those who find the conceptualist position unacceptable may be inclined to agree with the view advanced by a host of non-conceptualists that aesthetic regard for natural objects is mainly a matter of imagination, or something like it, rather than understanding. The idea here is that certain aspects of our awareness *not* comprehended in any of our scientific categories are central to our genuine appreciation of aesthetic objects. Emily Brady emphasizes the role of imagination. Noël Carroll emphasizes the role of emotional arousal. Arnold Berleant emphasizes the role of personal engagement with the environment. Other theorists emphasize various other aspects of awareness. What binds them together is their common commitment to the view that the central features of natural aesthetic awareness are detached from concepts.

Kant, again, is the inspiration for those who want to take the appreciation of nature around the subjective turn. By urging us to see beauty judgments as cut off from information about their objects, he freed our sense of beauty from its intellectual entanglements. But Kant didn't think that, under his theory, just anything you please could be beautiful. And, similarly, non-conceptualists have to draw a line between what they think is a reasonable attribution of aesthetic value and what is not.

The problem here seems to lie with the notion of imagination (and allied non-cognitive vectors of appreciation). As some theorists see it, imagination is a free agency, penetrating its objects in any variety of ways. Brady identifies four ways: exploratory, projective, ampliative, and revelatory.[4] Carroll identifies a variety of ways in which we may be moved by nature, responding to objects and events with a range of appropriate emotions.[5] Berleant identifies the capacity we have for focusing on the wholeness and integrity of a situation in creating conditions for our engagement with it.[6] But the fundamental problem with these views and all other non-conceptualist approaches is the inherent limitlessness of non-conceptual *seeing-as*. If, faced with the choice between understanding and imagination, our appreciation of nature is committed to the unrestricted province of the latter, there can be no bounds on what we make of it. A river can be a bookmark and a star can be a good luck charm.[7]

A second problem with the non-conceptual approach has been pointed out by Allen Carlson. It is that the more nature is regarded as a realm free from the understanding-marshaling influence of science, the more it becomes a mystery—alien, aloof, distant, unknowable. It is a short step from declaring natural beauty ineffable to declaring it unintelligible. The more mysterious nature is made to appear, the more inaccessible it is to our inquiring intelligence. As Carlson puts the point,

> The mystery and aloofness of nature are a gulf, an emptiness, between us and nature; they are that by which we separate ourselves from nature. Thus, they cannot constitute a means by which we can attain any appreciation of nature whatsoever.[8]

The trick is to find a way to respect the intuitions that drive these views apart. I think this can easily be done: First, there is no denying that nature is something about which scientists know a lot. Second, knowledge clearly doesn't exhaust our reflection on natural objects. Third, imagination is an essential ingredient in our appreciative involvement with anything. It ought to be possible to build a perspective on the aesthetic value of natural objects that incorporates both natural science and imagination without giving pride of place to either. This is precisely what I aim to do.

SYNCRETIC AESTHETICS

What I argue for in the course of this book is both a way of addressing the cleft between rival views I have described and a way of re-integrating our thinking about art and nature. In this section I will draw upon the prior discussion to make five theoretical points that are fundamental elements in the argument developed in subsequent chapters. I conclude the section by pulling these points together to present a preliminary statement of the general conclusion that syncretic aesthetics aims to establish, viz., that there is a way of organizing the central insights of several competing theories into a single, comprehensive account of judgment concerning natural beauty that makes room for both science and imagination.[9]

My first point is this: If two things look alike (and are in all other sensible respects indistinguishable), then they are aesthetic twins. So, if the natural chicory and its synthetic counterpart are indistinguishable in the relevant respects, they are aesthetic twins. Now, if twins are to be separated in such a case, they will be separated as twins are in other instances. That is, features other than their origin will be taken into account. In the case of Warhol's *Brillo Boxes* and their look-alike counterparts the "is" of artistic identity does the trick.[10] But that artworld device works because a man-made institution provides a scheme of deeming (that, in Danto's example, makes it apt to say of a given patch of paint on a Breughel painting "that is Icarus") in relation to man-made works. Here the roles of convention and social consent are large. If there is an "is" of natural aesthetic identification, the roles of convention and consent are minimal. As Danto has repeatedly pointed out, it is, in a sense, theory that makes art possible. It isn't theory that makes the live chicory plant possible. But it *is* a certain, complicated interplay of personal and social perceptions that makes it possible to judge whether the chicory plant is beautiful. "Natureworld," if that is what we want to call this protracted process of interconnections, is—like Danto's artworld—a conceptual location in which those who have an informed stake in the non-artifactual world are appropriately situated to make natural beauty judgments. I present an ampler account of this theoretical notion in chapter 7.

The second point is that taking a natural object as natural is not simply a matter of regarding it as non-man-made. First, we should admit that, in our modern world, most of what we want to call "natural" is already, to some degree, man-made. We have carved out the areas we want to leave "unspoiled," and we have reserved other areas for limited access with the idea that those who see them will get a sense of what nature is really like. Sunsets often look the way they do because of pollution we create. When a great glacier calves, and tons of ice plummet into the sea, part of the job was done by gravity and part by the heat we've been injecting into the atmosphere. But, second, nature is not confined to what nature-seeking tourists come to see. The volvox colony in the microscope is nature. Orion's belt in the evening sky is nature. The bulge of my tulip in the spring earth is nature; my sneeze is nature. The fine wood grain in my coffee table is nature. When we speak about nature in general we are inclined to talk about the kind of experience folks have when they get out of their urban environments to see the unspoiled world beyond. But, there is no truly unspoiled world.[11] And there is a natural world right there in the place they left. Clouds come everywhere, as do bugs and weeds.

The third point is that the perspective of science is not the perspective most people bring to the experience of nature; and it is rarely the source of the delight we experience when we enjoy natural beauty. There are, to be sure, moments when we take pleasure in seeing this or that object as one of its type, a rocky promontory as an example of geologic upthrust, for example. But there are, equally, moments when our aesthetic pleasure consists in deliberate attention to nameless congeries of natural occurrences. One summer, on the Oregon coast, I knelt down to observe the ever-shifting patterns resulting from the intersection of multi-colored beach sand and streams running to the sea. There was a wonderful confluence of shapes and colors, fascinating in their sinuous interaction and disintegration. It was simply beautiful, so beautiful that dragging myself away from it was almost painful. But, there was no thought that it was beautiful as a *this* or *that*. In all of its aesthetic qualities, this call-it-what-you-will owed no debt to concepts. I discuss this example at some length in chapter 9.

The fourth point is that imagination is never unbridled. As Kant argued, when the imagination is stimulated, the understanding is too, in its way. And if we think we are, as non-ceptualists sometimes suggest, disposed to regard aesthetic objects as stimuli for any fantastic association we may call up (so that a raven might be a writing desk, say), then all aesthetic bets are off. Anything can be anything. But, if non-conceptualism restricts itself to the claim that things needn't be regarded as what they are *usually* taken to be, or what their standard classification makes them, then the point can bear the weight it needs to bear in the current controversy. Imagination works to see thises as thats. A cloud can be a bear, a disk of metal can be a dollar, and a sunset can be a display of colors and forms that stimulate delight, remind us of death, call up the palette of Turner, and so on. And in managing these transformations, imagination isn't running wild or going just anywhere it pleases. Instead, it is following out what seem like sensible and evocative associations. What makes these associations sensible and evocative belongs to the background culture in which they are made. I consider the contribution of elaborative imagination to natural beauty judgments in chapter 8, and the link between imagination and its background culture in chapters 9 and 10.

The fifth point is that there is nothing about either science or imagination that precludes both from cooperating in the intelligent appreciation of natural objects. As it happens, there is a pair of bald eagles nesting near my home. When I see one of them soaring over the neighborhood, I am delighted. I am aesthetically pleased. But my pleasure in the flight of this great bird doesn't depend very much on my recognition that, in the ornithological taxonomy, this is a bald eagle. Nor, for that matter, that it serves as a patriotic icon in our country. I see it swoop over the water, hover overhead, swinging its great white head this way and that, then sail up on a draft and disappear into the distance. I am certainly aware that it's a bird, that it's an eagle, and even that it is a rare bird, a bald eagle. I'm also aware that, in an urban environment, it is a rare and precious presence. I know that it needs certain things to eat, certain places to nest, certain climatic conditions to survive, and so on. So, I am at least minimally aware of ornithological lore that pertains to this creature as a being of its type. I just don't believe that that knowledge contributes very much to my sense of the eagle's beauty, or the beauty of its flight. If on some occasion I were to mistake a hawk for the eagle, but see its flight as beautiful—just as beautiful as the eagle flight—I would be making a serious mistake in science, but not in aesthetics.

Perhaps the most important single lesson that can be drawn from these five points, taken together, is that in thinking about the aesthetic qualities of a natural object, we can't confine our attention to class membership or to any one category of appearance. Rather, we have to regard the object as situated in a constellation of properties, some aesthetic, some scientific, some political, and so on. And, some of these properties attach to concepts and others don't. So, the best we can do in responding to them is to use those parts of our intelligent awareness that suits each. My awareness of background information about the eagle is not like the information about genre and type needed to locate a work of art in its niche and assess it, but more like information about the paint and canvas, or marble, or metal in the tuba, that are instrumental to the artistic production, yet not cognitive requisites for its appreciation. I don't want to deny that the more we know about something the better positioned we may be to appreciate it, in aesthetic or any other senses. But, at the same time, I suggest that some of what we know about a thing might help us to see it as a thing of its type without helping us to see whether, as a member of that type, it has aesthetic merit at all.

The key point science provides to the appreciation of natural beauty is the insistent vision that what is natural is more than non-man-made; it is a part of an order of being that has its own modes of growth and development, its own history, its own inter-relatedness. To see natural beauty as natural is necessarily to contextualize it in that way. But to say this is not to concede that all of the contents of nature are to be understood through any particular categories or concepts, including those of science. Rather, appreciating a chicory plant, an eagle's flight, a pattern of water in sand, are reactions that always, to some degree, leave concepts and categories behind. Paying respectful attention to the nameless ingredients that largely constitute these phenomena, we instinctively draw on a repertory of responses that we have cultivated in the course of our experiences as individuals and as members of responsive cultures.

This is where art comes back into the picture. The curved line that marks the edge of a leaf may call to mind the characteristic curvilinear treatment of human limbs in mannerist painters of the Northern Renaissance (in Cranach's work, for example). But, to see the leaf and the painted limb as alike need not be to see one as the reflection, or emblem, of the other. In drawing upon our familiarity with aesthetic characteristics in the arts as we contemplate nature we are drawing on a resource in which the sensibilities we apply to all manner of objects have been finely honed. If I have become aware of certain tonal modulations by listening to Handel flute sonatas, I am not turning the similar sounds I hear in the forest into ersatz flute sonatas. I am simply using the aesthetic skills I have to make the attention I pay to natural phenomena pay off—by discovering or discerning an instance of natural beauty.

Now, suppose, having steeped myself in the study of landscape paintings in all the great museums, I step out into a setting that a landscape painter would very likely have found a fit subject for portrayal. When I look at the natural scene, do I then necessarily see it as a scene—as scenic? Because my head is full of art, do I aestheticize nature in such a way as to make it artificial? I might, but I don't see why I must. No more than a summer on a farm would make me look at bucolic paintings as especially natural. The truth of the matter is that, as Eaton has pointed out,

> Human valuings are holistic; we rarely experience something purely aesthetically or purely ethically or purely religiously or purely scientifically. ... The task for all of us is to develop ways of using the delight that human beings

take in flights of imagination, connect it to solid cognitive
understanding of what makes for sustainable environments, and thus produce the kind of attitudes and preferences that will generate the kind of care we hope for.[12]

The curve of the leaf and the curve of the leg in the painting are both
aesthetically affecting because there is something about curves of a certain
kind that moves us. That something is not peculiar to nature, nor to art. It
pervades experience broadly, emerging first here then there with a cumulative
impact on the attentive observer.[13] When we pay attention to artistic beauty,
that attention prepares us to appreciate natural beauty—not as artistic, but as
one more area in which we find value. And likewise for the lessons of nature
for art.

In this chapter, I have suggested that appreciating nature aesthetically as
natural is more than a matter of recognizing its non-artifactuality; but neither
is it only the comprehension of natural objects under some particular concepts
and categories, nor again is it the reduction of nature to a plaything of unfettered
imagination and free association. Between the view of the conceptualists,
which overstates the influence of concepts and categories on appreciation, and
that of non-conceptualists, which understates their influence, there is a third
position, which I have called syncretism. There is a real difference between a
real flower and its glass look-alike. That difference begins with the recognition
that one is a product of nature. That entails seeing it as implicated in an order
whose historical course and direction is complex, interconnected, and largely
detached from human purposes. But this environmental recognition does not
require the invocation of science in framing aesthetic awareness of the contents
of nature. In reflecting on the richly various and largely nameless features
we find in natural settings, we rightly draw on associations, familiarities,
analogies, etc. that we have learned in other settings, most especially in art.
In drawing on these resources, we needn't impose the terms of one world on
the other. Rather, we make the most of our developed sensibilities to make the
most of nature and of the other worlds we occupy as well. And if it should turn
out that there are various harmonies, similarities, and affinities between them,
then all the better.

NOTES

1   See Allen Carlson, "Nature, Aesthetic Judgment and Objectivity," *Journal of Aesthetics and Art Criticism* 40 (1981), pp. 16-27; "Appreciation and the Natural Environment," *Journal of Aesthetics and Art Criticism* 37 (1979), pp. 267-76; "Interactions between Art and Nature: Environmental Art," in *The Reasons of Art: Artworks and the Transformations of Philosophy*, ed. Peter McCormick (Ottawa University Press, 1985), pp. 222-231; "Nature, Aesthetic Appreciation, and Knowledge," *Journal of Aesthetics and Art Criticism* 53 (1995), pp. 393-400; "Saito on the Correct Aesthetic Appreciation of Nature," *Journal of Aesthetic Education* 20 (1986), pp. 86-92; "Nature: Contemporary Thought," in vol. 3, *Encyclopedia of Aesthetics*, ed. Michael Kelly (Oxford University Press, 1998), pp. 346-49.

2   Hepburn, "Contemporary Aesthetics," p. 61.

3   The tide flat is considered *Ibid.*; the swift and leaf examples are taken up in Hepburn's "Trivial and Serious in Aesthetic Appreciation of Nature," in *Landscape, Natural Beauty, and the Arts*, ed. Salim Kemal and Ivan Gaskell (Cambridge: Cambridge University Press, 1993).

4   Emily Brady, "Imagination and the Aesthetic Appreciation of Nature," *Journal of Aesthetics and Art Criticism* 56 (1998), p. 143.

5   Noël Carroll, "On Being Moved by Nature: Between Religion and Natural History," in Kemel and Gaskell, *Landscape*, pp. 244-66.

6   Arnold Berleant, *The Aesthetics of Environment* (Philadelphia: Temple University Press, 1992), p. 37. Berleant develops the same ideas at greater length in *Living in the Landscape: Toward an Aesthetics of Environment* (University of Kansas Press, 1997).

7   Marcia Eaton presents powerful criticisms of Brady's version of non-cognitivism in "Fact and Fiction." She points out that the associations called up by imagination in response to natural objects are so various, so unrestricted that there is no way of knowing whether they are shallow or naïve, instructive or not, apt or delusional. I consider the dispute between Brady and Eaton at some length in chapter 8.

8   Carlson, "Nature: Contemporary Thought," p. 347.

9   The general thrust of the syncretic approach may be stated summarily as follows: Initial reactions to beauty are simply emphatic, positive sensory experiences, whether these are directed toward natural or artifactual objects. What makes natural beauty judgments distinctive is that they are directed at natural objects. Appreciating natural objects as natural entails giving appropriate recognition to the non-artifactuality of their

features. Appreciating natural objects as natural does *not* preclude drawing upon modes or styles of recognition and analysis that pertain to artifacts, where these suit the purpose of demonstrating or explaining beauty in these objects. A host of competing theories aim to explain ways in which initial reactions are to be interpreted and extended. If the several theories are right in some respects and wrong in others, it is reasonable to put together their acceptable aspects into a composite theory that rejects only what is wrong with them. Such a theory is neither a compromise nor a preferential recipe. It is, instead, what any sensible philosophical theory should be, a perspicuous effort to glean from all reasonable available sources the means to get a set of concepts right.

10 The "is of artistic identification" doesn't concern a thing's origin; it concerns its appropriate interpretation. Thus, a piece of driftwood, presented in a certain way, might be brought into the artworld by an informed determination that it *is* (in an interpretive sense) an abstract, expressive object quite apart independently of the fact that it was made by no one.

11 Pierce Lewis alleges that "nearly every square millimeter of the United States has been altered by humankind somehow, at some time." Pierce Lewis, "Axioms for Reading the Landscape: Some Guides to the American Scene," in *The Interpretation of Ordinary Landscapes*, ed. D.W. Meinig (Oxford University Press, 1979), p. 12. Malcolm Budd's powerful analysis of the aesthetic appreciation of natural objects begins with the concession that "much of our natural environment displays, for better or worse, the influence of humanity, having been shaped, to a greater or lesser extent, and in a variety of ways, by human purposes, so that little of the world's landscape is in a natural condition." Malcolm Budd, *The Aesthetic Appreciation of Nature* (Oxford University Press, 2002), p. 7.

12 Eaton, "Fact and Fiction," p. 155.

13 In a way, what I say here is reflective of Stan Godlovitch's defense of a perspective that refuses to impose one world's framework on another, but which nevertheless profits from the ability of the mind trained in both to respond richly, and differently, to both. See, for example, "Icebreakers: Environmentalism and Natural Aesthetics," *Journal of Applied Philosophy* 11 (1994), pp. 15-30.

CHAPTER 3

The Historical Roots of Syncretism: Early Developments

Syncretism, as I conceive it, is the Unitarianism of aesthetics. Unitarianism famously takes the theological position that a great many convictions are welcome and appropriate to the basis of faith without accepting the anarchic view that anything goes. Similarly, the position I defend here accepts a multiplicity of conceptions of natural beauty while it accepts a wide range of views as to the implications of these conceptions. But it doesn't condone conceptual anarchy. The fact that a good many ideas play into our current thinking about the way beauty is present in natural objects does not imply that any conception of beauty's connection to nature is as good as any other. In what follows, I present a gleaning of the historical record aimed at exposing the most durable and promising ideas from the past[1] as they bear upon questions raised in the previous chapter.

Present-day philosophers are quick to condemn the past. We often assume we have learned so much more than our forebears knew that we safely ignore what they had to say. But as T.S. Eliot nicely observed, even if we know more than they did, *they* are what we know.[2] Still, I should make it clear at the outset that I don't think all old ideas are good ones. The historical course of philosophical reflection reflects both gleaning and winnowing. While I hope to draw attention to those ideas that enjoy continuing theoretical leverage—if, often, in a refined and modernized form—I think it is important to recognize that many prominent ideas on these topics have not stood the test of time and are now properly regarded as moribund. As usual, the main (and often difficult) job in making sense of the legacy of the past is telling which is which.

A thread that runs through all of the questions posed at the end of the previous chapter is the connection between sense and intelligence in our appraisal of natural beauty. Conceptualists, I said, are wrong to regard judgments of natural beauty as invariably turning on natural types or categories when in fact they often turn on our awareness of combinations of features that are non-categorial. But they are right to insist that categorial knowledge (and more specifically, scientific knowledge) *can* be indispensible in framing and enjoying certain modes of the experience of nature. Conversely, non-conceptualists are, I alleged, wrong to suppose that imagination, by freeing appreciation from restrictive concepts, can *in and of itself* provide a means of forming the conspectus necessary to having coherent and intelligible experience of natural beauty. But they are right to give credit to the unique, the non-categorial, in that experience and to insist that imagination has a fundamental role in amplifying and enriching some modes of the experience of nature. Neither side wants to denigrate the roles played by both sense and intelligence in the aesthetic experience of nature. But what drives the two sides apart are perceived differences in the way sense and intelligence cooperate both in the production of the aesthetic experience of nature and in its appreciation. It is my view that these differences—as well as the most plausible basis for their resolution—are not recent developments. Instead they are rooted in the long philosophical history that organizes and informs present-day thought to a surprising extent. So it seems to me that the best way of beginning to settle the modern controversies is to explore their historical origins.

In this chapter I review the earliest trends of Western philosophical thinking on the respective roles of sense and intelligence in understanding the aesthetic qualities of natural phenomena. The account I present makes no pretense of providing a perspicuous representation of debate on this theme. Instead, I survey a limited number of historically prominent opinions with an eye to identifying rival principles, particularly as they add new ideas to the debate over conceptualism and non-conceptualism discussed in chapters 2 and 3. Nor is it my intention to identify a clear winner among the contenders. Rather, I hope to draw the most durable principles into a pluralistic account that gives each its proper place.

Any fair historical synopsis will make it plain that rival claims have emerged unsystematically, often not as answers to the same question, but as contributory elements in broader theories (metaphysical, theological, epistemological, etc.) aimed at different objectives. Nevertheless, it is possible to distill from this evolutionary process an inventory of principles reflecting differences in the attitudes their defenders take toward natural and man-made objects, differences in modes of delectation and appreciation developed toward these objects, and differences in these modes as they fit into general schemes of value in human life. The following survey is more than a brief chronicle of pertinent ideas. It is meant to show how various conceptions of nature, artifact, and natural beauty have fed into our present thinking, much as tributary streams feed into a river. Some of the ideas I discuss here no longer command much credence; but most continue to influence our thinking about these topics, affirming the sound conviction that the past is present in the present as well as in the future that the present invites.

ANCIENT VIEWS

To Plato, and to ancient Greek thinkers in general, the line we so instinctively draw between nature and artifact went largely unacknowledged. In the *Sophist*, Plato remarks that "things which are said to be made by nature are the work of divine art, and things which are made by man out of these are works of human art. And so there are two kinds of making and production, the one human and the other divine."[3] Similarly, in the *Republic*, he commends both artworks and natural beings for their grace and harmony in a way that suggests our appreciation of the one is pretty much on the same footing as our appreciation of the other. Both the embroidered robe and the rabbit are products whose aesthetic qualities are admirable to the degree to which production has succeeded in realizing their design.[4] The assumption here is that the design (i.e., the form) is perfect, while any rendering of it in the world of sensory experience will necessarily be imperfect to some degree, and that the merit of the object is a matter of the degree of match between it and its design.

It is well known that classical Greek philosophers showed very little interest in the representation of nature in art, even though natural forms were coming increasingly to replace abstract symbols in the art and architecture of their day. When these thinkers spoke of mimesis in connection with nature it was generally to make the point that artists imitated nature's methods rather than her products.[5] Moreover, the claim that natural things (i.e., all of the world except artifacts) are products of divine production does not entail that they are perfect, or perfectly beautiful. Indeed, in drawing his elaborate picture of the educational program for guardians, Socrates declares that "he who has received this true education of the inner being will most shrewdly perceive omissions or faults in art and nature."[6] This last remark is doubly revealing, in that it indicates both Plato's admission of natural imperfections and his commitment to a cognitive basis for aesthetic judgment.

Plato's view of nature and natural beauty is, of course, controlled by his idealistic metaphysics. In his famous theory of forms, moral, aesthetic, political, and spiritual values converge in the pure objects of knowledge separate from, and superior to, all objects of sensory experience. So if a knife, say, is good, useful, and beautiful, that will be because it conforms as well as a physical object can to the formal requirements of knife-ness that exist as perfect standards in an unchanging world accessible only to intelligence. Although many aspects of Platonic metaphysics have been decisively rejected—particularly its stubborn otherworldliness and denigration of the physical—there is a strand of thought in this account that has proven remarkably durable and persistent. It is a point about the use of standards in the recognition of aesthetic merit. We may not be willing to buy the "treasure chest" theory according to which the ideal form of a given item of experience is located in the heaven of concepts, or in sacred scripture, or in the informed taste of the wisest of men, or even in the canons of experts in a field. But there is a range of judgments for which most people would concede that degrees of quality (and deficiency) are properly measured by consulting a knowable norm.

If, for example, the question is whether this particular schnauzer is superior in schnauzer-ness to that one—which some would take to be a question equivalent to whether it is a more beautiful schnauzer—many dog-fanciers would insist that the matter be put to experts who make their judgments in accordance with standards recognized by the American Kennel Club, or some such official agency. These standards may change over time, but at any specific moment they are (pretty much) fixed and knowable. Moreover, they provide a cognitive basis for judgment that is largely independent of feeling. A competent dog show judge may, for many reasons, form a dislike for a given show dog and even feel—at some level of awareness—that the beast is unlovely, even ugly. But if, in applying the official canons of excellence to which she is committed as a judge, she finds that this dog conforms admirably to them, she will reach the judgment that it is a fine specimen of its kind, after all.[7] And to say that it is a fine specimen of schnauzerhood is, on one account of aesthetic judgment, to say in the same breath that it is beautifully schnauzeresque.[8]

Plato's predilection for turning aesthetic (and all other) value judgments into matters of measurement against a knowable ideal—a view we may call "cognitive idealism"—has proven remarkably durable. It was embraced and ramified by Plotinus and successive Neoplatonists, and through them became the dominant view of natural beauty among Christian philosophers in the Middle Ages. Aristotle, Plato's most famous student, accepted the main lines of his teacher's metaphysical position—agreeing that the merit of a thing hinged on the degree of approximation its qualities attained to an ideal—while reject-ing the bold distinction Plato had drawn between the world available to sen-sory experience and the world available only to intelligence. As Aristotle saw it, all natural beings are part of a grand teleological process in which nascent and immature entities strive toward their mature and fully-realized manifes-tations. The excellence (including the aesthetic merit) of a thing is predicated on its achievement in this world (rather than an ideal realm apart from it) of the conditions proper to the full nature of a being of its type. An acorn achieves its purpose, and at the same time the full complement of its value (including aesthetic value), in the attainment of its mature state in the well-developed, healthy oak tree. Likewise, a sculptor succeeds in his artistic objective, and creates beauty, only when he is able to bring out of the raw material of the stone a realized construct that manifests the nature (the "final cause") of its intended subject.

Aristotle began a deviation away from Platonic idealism in one respect by insisting that the relation between an object (natural or artistic) and its ideal is not one that divorces the worlds of sense and intelligence, but one that instead takes them to be parts of a common teleology.[9] Beyond this, however, Aristotle presented a line of response to the natural world that tied sense and intel-ligence together in a way that was altogether novel. While agreeing a thing had to conform to its type (its "formal cause") to be beautiful, he went on to assert that natural beauty is contextual:

> Beauty is a matter of size and order, and therefore impos-sible in either (1) a very minute creature, since our per-ception becomes indistinct as it approaches instantane-ity; or (2) in a creature of vast size—one, say, 1,000 miles long—as in that case, instead of the object being seen all at once, the unity and wholeness is lost to the beholder.[10]

Here we see the first hints at an account of beauty in nature that goes beyond conformity of a given thing to a standard and takes stock of the relation be-tween that thing and its surroundings and conditions of perception.

Moreover, while Aristotle's statement that "beauty is a matter of size and order" might be taken as endorsement of cognitive idealism as predicating value on matters of proportion and coherence proper to the formal qualities of an individual thing, it can also be taken as suggesting a wider standard of appreciation. Imagine, for instance, a perfectly formed oak tree, fully embody-ing all the virtues anticipated in its acorn progenitor, but so small that it would fit nicely into a thimble. Here, there is no question that the object can be seen, and seen all at once. But Aristotle seems to be saying that even in this instance, beauty can be denied by dimension. So, on this view, the world of our sensory awareness is a co-determiner of the aesthetic merit of natural objects. To be beautiful, the latter must be what their nature demands of them, but they also must stand in a certain relation to other things in their vicinity (an admittedly elastic notion) and to the conditions of perception. This is the beginning of what we might call "contextual idealism," the view that the requirement of conformity to a standard is mitigated by relations to conditions in the world of experience in determining the aesthetic merit of natural objects.

Still, Aristotle's account of beauty fastens on individual things as perceived in their context, rather than on combinations of contextual ingredients taken all together. This tendency of thought undoubtedly follows from the relative difficulty of applying the criteria of beauty—size, balance, and proportion—to perceptual complexes. Tatarkiewicz comments:

> He saw beauty in Nature, because there everything has suitable proportion and size, while man, the creator of art, may easily go astray. He spoke of the beauty of human bodies, never of the beauty of landscapes. This may be connected with the Greek conviction that beauty springs from proportion and accordance, both of which are harder to find in a landscape than in a single living creature, a statue, or a building. This was also the expression of a specific taste, while the Romantics preferred landscape arrangements, those of the classical period preferred isolated objects whose limit more clearly revealed their proportions, measure, and unity.[11]

Here, perhaps for the first time, we see the notion of *limit* at work in setting conditions favorable to aesthetic appraisal of natural objects. The Aristotelian notions of singularity and limitation provide an important foreshadowing of the modern notion of framing, an admittedly more elastic concept that works similarly to confine attention to what is comprehensible. As I see it, the operation of framing and the deployment of various framing devices are important elements in laying a foundation for the appreciation of natural beauty. I explore this theme at length in chapter 6.

Aristotle recognized lots of similarities between artworks and natural objects. In the *Physics*, for example, he points out that houses made by men are just as they would have been had they been made by nature and that, if trees had been made by men, they would appear just as they do, having been made by nature.[12] But, he also recognized that we enjoy art and nature in different ways. When we enjoy natural objects, he says, we simply enjoy the objects themselves (admiring the qualities of size, balance, and proportion that constitute their beauty). But, when we enjoy artworks, we enjoy them both for the objects they are and in appreciation of the skill of the artist in making them appear as they do. Thus, the two modes of appreciation yield pleasures that are different in kind, and not just in degree.[13] It is worth speculating whether, if Aristotle had been able to enjoy the fruits of post-Darwinian natural science, he would have thought of the two modes of appreciation as more nearly alike, appreciating art for the thing itself and the artist's skill in making it and appreciating natural objects for what they are as well as for the marvelous evolutionary process that brought them about.

MEDIEVAL AND RENAISSANCE VIEWS

The record of Medieval and Renaissance philosophical reflection on natural beauty is one of vacillation and contest between the cognitive and contextual versions of idealism. For the most part, Medieval thinkers adopted the former, while Renaissance thinkers gravitated toward the latter view. Plotinus, for example, insists that "both artworks and natural objects are imitations; both refer to the Reason-Principles from which Nature itself derives."[14] His metaphysics expresses its fidelity to Plato's idealism by compounding its complexity. Where Plato was content to separate reality and appearance, type and archetype, Plotinus piles archetype upon archetype upon archetype. He declares that "there is in the Nature-Principle itself an ideal archetype of the beauty that is found in material forms, and, of that archetype again, the still more beautiful archetype in Soul, source of that in Nature."[15] But, however compounded, this sort of analysis ultimately resolves itself into a cognitive idealistic account along the lines Plato proposed: If an agate, say, is beautiful, it is beautiful because it is what it should be, seen through however many archetypal layers may be necessary to come to the point.

It is hard to say who was the first Western philosopher to declare the superiority of beauty in art to beauty in nature, but Plotinus may be the man. Cicero and the Stoics had previously argued that nature is the greater artist, "possessed of a skill that no handiwork of artist or craftsman can rival or reproduce."[16] In the *Enneads*, however, Plotinus insists that beauty in art involves an expression of the ideal (Reason-Principle) that nature does not:

"Art," he says, "must itself be beautiful in a higher and purer degree since it is the seat and source of that beauty, indwelling in the art, which must naturally be more complete than any comeliness of the external."[17] Here the idea is that art requires a completeness that nature doesn't require. A painting should be composed and coherent, whatever its subject matter. But the subject matter of that painting is under no such constraints. It is what it is. If you value order, coherence, and harmony over randomness or anomaly, you may find yourself sympathetic to the view that art is "higher and purer" than nature. But otherwise you probably won't.

The prevailing Medieval view was that beauty, whether it be in art or in nature, is wedded to goodness and that goodness pervades the world. Taken as a whole, creation is beautiful, although some of its elements, taken in isolation, may seem ugly. But, as Augustine and others were to insist, even this apparent defect can be seen to be illusory once we take the properly capacious view of appearance. The beauty of a poem may become apparent only when we read it in its entirety, and likewise the beauty of creation can properly emerge only when we regard the whole of it. Tatarkiewicz speaks of this view as "aesthetic integralism," and he points out that it is an *a priori* metaphysical or religious position.[18] One modern version of this view is what Allen Carlson and others have taken to calling "positive aesthetics." It is the position that all of the natural world is beautiful, or at least positive in its aesthetic qualities, and that, accordingly, there is no such thing as natural ugliness.[19] The historical foundation for aesthetic integralism is perfectly evident. It was the generally accepted belief during the period of Christian hegemony that we and the world are all artifacts of divine creation and pieces of a grand design that we are (due to our fallen state) able to discern only imperfectly, "through a glass, darkly." Latter-day positive aesthetics, to the extent that it embraces the same general view, undertakes to free itself from this background metaphysics. Nevertheless, it generally buys into the background assumption that value in the particular is a function of value in the comprehended whole.

It is apparent in early Medieval writings that the beauty of nature is not to be thought of as a product of, or dependent on, the pleasure it brings to our senses. Rather, nature is beautiful because of the divine order and purpose it manifests. When the Church fathers compared art and nature, they were generally disposed to find similarities rather than differences. They thought of natural beauty as a manifestation of God's design, and artistic beauty a product of man's design. As human art is dependent on the divine as its model, it can never rise to the level of nature's perfection, for the very Platonic reason that copies can never be as good as their originals.[20]

This tendency of thought is abruptly terminated in the theory of beauty propounded by Thomas Aquinas, a view that, though it was pronounced in the fourteenth century, ushers in the humanistic perspective that was to take hold in the Renaissance. Thomas famously held that "those things are said to be beautiful which please when seen."[21] This conception of beauty moved it away from conformity to an ideal toward an empirically observable response (which was not entirely surprising, in that Thomas championed Aristotle's rather than Plato's style of idealism). Thomas's willingness to stake claims of beauty on pleasurable response is novel, but his approach to the relation of art to nature is not. He boldly insists that art must imitate nature, and offers in support of this claim the reason that artistic activity is based in cognition.

> [N]atural things can be imitated by art, because, by virtue of a certain intellectual principle, all nature is directed to its aim, so that a work of nature appears to be a work of intelligence, since it moves towards sure goals by definite means—and it is this that art imitates in its activity.[22]

Here Thomas is embracing the twin ideas that intelligence is at work both in nature and in art, and that art works, like nature, to link its goals to means in an intelligent way. This suggests a new way of wedding sense and intelligence. Nature and art produce their many effects in a great variety of ways. When their goals are linked intelligently to means appropriate to them there are successful results. When they aren't so linked the results fall by the wayside. What we take pleasure in perceiving is, for the most part, the display of successful outcomes of natural and artistic process. So, when we find things beautiful, we are always, in a way, confirming the successfulness of the means that led to the ends we appreciate, and in that way affirming our adoration of God's grand plan.

In general, Renaissance philosophers and artists were inclined to see the eye trained by attention to nature as the instructor to the artistic eye, and not the other way around. While both classical and Medieval thinkers were inclined to value order, coherence, and harmony over randomness or anomaly, Renaissance thinkers were more disposed to accord positive value to these latter qualities. They recognized human nature as part of nature-writ-large and, as careful observers of the latter, saw diversities where others had heretofore insisted on uniformity. When they said that art begins in nature they had in mind that it springs from human nature. And human nature, though it is in consonance with nature-writ-large, has its own complexity, internal tensions, and intricacy. Renaissance humanism was thus not simply one more chapter in the long-running story of the rivalry of art and nature for priority in the minds of their admirers. Instead, it ushered in a new way of thinking about the natural, one that reflected the conviction that, in one way or another, everything we experience is rooted in our own humanity—its capacities, its peculiarities, and its limits.

It was for this reason that Leon Battista Alberti insisted that the painter's education include not only training in empirical observation and draftsmanship, but also the liberal arts, including literature, logic, speech, geometry, and human affairs generally, as well as an introduction to "higher things."[23] The artist is no longer thought of as a rival of nature, but as working in concert with natural processes, producing out of the bounty of nature's exemplary materials and out of the inventiveness and sensibility natural to man products that please by satisfying human purposes in their natural context. In holding that it is human nature, rather than nature-at-large, from which art springs and to which it is ultimately responsible, Renaissance humanists did not preclude a deeper harmony between art and nature, based on a common mean or proportionality to be found in both. Indeed, it seems that Alberti and others thought that a common factor of this sort might be the reason for our pleasurable responsiveness to natural beauty.[24]

Leonardo da Vinci further refined Alberti's idea of the impact of nature and human nature on art. In the *Treatise on Painting*, he argues for the superiority of painting to poetry, observing that visible things derive from nature and painting derives directly from them, while words—the material of poetry—lack both directness and range in relation to nature's display. So, if there is a rapport that art may enjoy with nature (due to some principle of proportionality or harmony linking the two), painting is better positioned to display it than is poetry. Leonardo's point is far from obvious, but it is suggestive of another important truth about the relation of sense and intelligence in the apprehension of nature. David Summers explains Leonardo's claim as follows:

> Painting embraces all the forms of nature, but the poet
> has only words, which are not "universal" in the way that
> these forms are; "if you [poets] have the effects of dem-
> onstration we have the demonstration of effects." By this
> he seems to mean that, whereas the poet may set out his
> inventions as if by argument, the painter may simply show

that toward or away from which any number of arguments might move. Painting shows us at once the *infinity of the simply present, which is common, and universal.*[25]

As I see it, the key idea here is that the *repleteness* of natural phenomena is more readily presented in painting than in poetry because the former, and not the latter, is able to show what can't be said, namely the panorama of features and combinations of features for which there are no words. These things are "*simply present.*" And what they tell us is universal, not because they hook up with Platonic forms or any other metaphysical universals, but because they are available to everyone having intact senses, no matter what languages they may speak and how they formulate their thoughts within them. It is the commonality of these sensory presentations—their aesthetic presence—that provides a basis for shared aesthetic judgments with respect to natural objects.

Although Leonardo's invocation of natural repleteness served the limited objective of demonstrating the superiority of painting to poetry, it reveals a wider sense of aesthetic awareness in which Renaissance thinkers generally joined. Their never-ending controversy over the relative positions of art and nature in the cultural life of the educated citizen should not be allowed to obscure the humanists' profound affection for natural beauty and their sense that it bore importantly on human concerns. This affection is evident in many of the artworks of the period. It is there in the botanical profusion of Botticelli's *Primavera*, in the fascination with natural perspective that we see first in Brunelleschi and Masaccio, in the painstaking observational detail of Dürer's and Leonardo's studies of animals, plants, and anatomical features, as well as in many other works.

That an age so given to the magnification of human capacity and potentiality should manifest this continuing fascination with the non-artifactual elements of life is remarkable in itself. Even more remarkable, however, is its persistent conviction that attention to the natural would pay dividends in the development of complete human personality (or at least the personality of those to whom leadership should be entrusted). Part of this conviction, at least, was grounded in the lingering notion that nature bears divine lessons as God's instructive creation. But another part seems to derive from the growing conception of the human mind as richly absorbent and adaptive, informed not by pre-existing forms but by contact with empirical disarray—that is, with what later philosophers would call information. Renaissance thinkers were keenly aware of the endlessness of variety and detail in the world apart from our making. Exciting new scientific inventions—above all the telescope and microscope—made apparent how much of nature lay beyond our common sensory awareness. Rather than seeing the newly revealed vastness of nature as daunting or humbling, Renaissance philosophers and artists characteristically turned this awareness into another lesson in the grandeur of human responsiveness. If nature is vast, so is man's mind. If it transcends language's presentational capacity, so does man's mind. If it has depths and heights that may never be exposed and explored, so does man's mind.[26]

From even such a brief and superficial survey of classical, Medieval, and Renaissance sources as I have presented here it is possible to extract a number of important ideas about the roles of sense and intelligence in our reflection on natural beauty. First, the quarrel between cognitive and contextual idealism reveals a fundamental cleavage between two ways of grounding aesthetic value judgments as they apply to natural objects. One way, preferred by the cognitive idealists, looks to ideals or standards apart from any particular item or combination of items in experience. The other way, preferred by contextual idealists, makes some part of a thing's aesthetic merit turn on the relative success of the relation of its features or components to each other and the relation of the thing and its parts to the wider context in which we experience it. In the beginning, the gap between these two approaches was not wide. Plato and Aristotle agreed that the aesthetic value of particulars had to be measured against some standard beyond the particulars; but they differed over the relevance of empirical evidence in discrediting valuations made according to the standard. They differed over the pertinence of observable details to the qualification or disqualification of otherwise applicable ideal categories. In its historical setting, this wasn't a big difference. But it was a wedge that, once driven between rival approaches to natural beauty, never grew narrower.

The notion of limit that emerged in classical antiquity became prominent in every subsequent age. It is a key ingredient in any plausible theory of natural beauty. After all, nothing is apprehended as an object of potential aesthetic evaluation that is not already bounded in some way. The vast undifferentiated panorama of free experience is unintelligible, inexpressible, unaesthetic.[27] The notion of limit makes possible the idea of completeness. And it suggested the concept that order within a bounded context might satisfy our aesthetic interests just by the way in which ingredient elements are organized within the whole they constitute. The familiar—if always contested—notions of harmony, balance, integrity, tension-reconciliation, etc. are always posed in a conceptual framework within which ingredients are understood as parts of a whole, and moreover parts whose value depends on the way they contribute to the whole, and what the whole, taken aesthetically, makes of them. Aesthetically important concepts such as design, composition, and elegance are inevitably dependent on this primitive notion of ingredients and limits, as well as on the requirement that the relations among them must be satisfying.

A second prominent theme emerging from antiquity that retains considerable force today is the idea that nature is pervasively good. Many present-day thinkers who don't accept the theological foundation laid in Medieval times are nevertheless disposed to accept a view of all nature as positively valuable. This view entails that value concepts that apply in an importantly bipolar way in other normative domains (such as social relations) cannot apply in the same bipolar way to the world beyond human artifact. As I understand it, the idea draws what credibility it has from a view about the beauty *of* nature rather than beauty *in* nature. The beauty *of* nature is a concept that attaches to the claim that nature as a whole (by which is usually meant the entirety of terrestrial ecosystems) is worthy of aesthetic approval. This claim is, like the moral imperative to love all of mankind (based on the premise that humanity itself is loveable), open to the criticism that a normative attitude applied to the whole need not be applied to the part. Beauty *in* nature is a concept that applies to various parts (and constellations of parts) of the natural whole. Medieval philosophers didn't suppose that all of creation's parts were perfect just because creation itself was. After all, they all accepted the idea of man's fall and the attendant doctrine of sin. Similarly, even if one accepts the controversial premise that the natural order, taken as a whole, is beautiful, that provides little or no support for the claim that natural objects within that order are all beautiful.[28]

A third theme that emerges from antiquity is the idea (emerging first in the Renaissance) that, so far as it is available to us, nature must be seen through human nature. That is, the conditions through which we approach anything, made or unmade, are ultimately the conditions that show us this and that, but not the other, according to our human capacities. On the one hand, this notion is a confining one, indicating what can't be appreciated because it extends beyond human capacity; on the other hand, it is a liberating one, suggesting that whatever limits there may be to human access to the natural world and its intrinsic values are just the familiar limits of responsiveness. In the next chapter, we will see how philosophers came to conceive of the notion of human nature as a filter on the experience of natural phenomena. Although it was the eighteeenth century that showed us categoreal requirements of experience generally, the conviction that we are bound to experience whatever we do experience through the common conduit of human nature was established in antiquity. And this is an important development. Rather than thinking of a particular stone simply as a *that*, early thinkers came to think of it as a that-as-I-take-it, or at least as a that-in-relation-to-my-world. This way of thinking is the trailhead of a long tradition of reflection on connections between the perceiver and the perceived, seen as conditioned on what the perceiver may have at his or her disposal.

Finally, there is the important notion of repleteness. Leonardo thought that painting was superior to poetry for the reason that painting portrayed its objects completely, so that every part, nameable or unnameable, would appear in the artwork, whereas poetry could capture only what words could mention. This remark, in itself, might not be taken as having a direct bearing on aesthetic judgments regarding natural objects. But it does. If we accept that the reason painting is superior to poetry is that painting presents what is replete, we are acknowledging that there are innumerable details in lived experience that are important—and contribute to its value—though they can't be put in words. There is a disparity between thinking of the objects of experience (natural or artifactual) as chunks of reality carved up by thought, concepts, and categories into something knowable and thinking of them as ontologically dense expanses of features (and combinations of features) presenting a sensory world that transcends words. This disparity remains one of the key divisions between accounts of natural aesthetics down to the present day.

EARLY MODERN DEVELOPMENTS

The Renaissance produced an immense flourishing of artworks and ideas. And when it was over—a boundary question about which scholars quarrel endlessly—the foundation had been laid for what philosophers quaintly persist in calling Modern philosophy (beginning roughly at the end of the seventeenth century and running into the nineteenth). The Renaissance heritage confronted a world embroiled in rapid and intense political, economic, artistic, and intellectual transformation. Many earlier ideas were challenged and abandoned. But, as in all so-called post-revolutionary periods, a wealth of inherited ideas provided the resilient core of acceptable thought around which new theories were to be arranged. Early Modern philosophers, like their predecessors, were greatly concerned to reconcile the roles of sense and intelligence in relation to art and nature, and they undertook to do so in a rich diversity of ways. It would be pointless to attempt a comprehensive survey of their various theories here. For our purposes, it will suffice to derive from selected historical discussions certain key observations that were both potent reflections of general tendencies of thought in their time and successful in affecting subsequent aesthetic thought.

In the post-Renaissance age, an infectious empirical curiosity about nature and an enthusiasm for natural beauty spread across Europe. Three factors played prominently into this development. First, dramatic gains in methods of research and advances in technology laid the foundation of modern natural sciences. Second, a burgeoning middle class freed of feudal obligations was arising with the financial capacity, mobility, and recreational opportunity to enjoy nature's bounty as never before. And third, as ecclesiastical authority became less dominant over people's responses to the world of experience, a heady sense of individual taste and aesthetic liberation was emerging. A new passion for nature and natural beauty spread throughout society, emphatically manifesting itself in the painting, poetry, drama, and popular literature of the day. Philosophers responded by producing theoretical accounts of the aesthetic experiencing of natural objects that recast the component roles of sense and intelligence in the spirit of this new age. Three British thinkers stand out as particularly insightful—as well as influential—in the early stages of this new naturalism at the end of the seventeenth and the beginning of the eighteenth centuries: Anthony Ashley Cooper (the third Earl of Shaftesbury), Francis Hutcheson, and Archibald Alison.

In one sense, Shaftesbury was a traditionalist, a holdout for established views in a period of novelty and change. He was a Platonic (or neo-Platonic) cognitive idealist who subscribed to the view that the goodness to be found in nature and the goodness to be found in the human soul are both reflections of a divinely wrought greater good impressed upon all things. And he was a hidebound moralist in relation to the arts, insisting that our delectation of works of art be tied to moral sensibility and that aesthetic modes of response are valuable mainly as they contribute to good character, i.e., to a general disposition to contribute to the common good. Equally importantly, however, there is in his writings an evident relish in the physical encounter with natural phenomena rarely seen in earlier writers. His *Characteristics* is replete with fond descriptions of natural forms, "the shining grass or silvered moss, the flowery thyme," for example, enjoyed especially for their pristine appearance, "where neither art nor the conceit or caprice of man has spoiled their genuine order by breaking in upon that primitive state."[29] This delight is coupled with an evident disposition to inquire into the workings of the mind in its response to unspoiled natural beauty.

Shaftesbury's approach to this issue was novel. Rather than taking the delight we experience in nature as derivative from and dependent on an ulterior judgment—that we can find it pleasing *because* we enjoy God's handiwork, say, or as emblematic of a perfection transcending all experience—he supposed that we have been given an "inward eye," an intuitive sense of beauty that acknowledges its effects without the mediation of reasoning. Shaftesbury's foray in the direction of an inner standard of taste was tentative and ambivalent; but it was the initial thrust in a direction that gained momentum as time went on.[30] The main complaint about such a conception is, of course, that it threatens to collapse aesthetic judgment into limitless and anarchic subjectivity. If the determination that a given object is beautiful is final once one's internal sense has spoken, every person's judgment is just as valid as everyone else's and there is no basis for resolving interpersonal aesthetic controversy. Shaftesbury attempted to fend off this consequence by insisting that aesthetic judgments are ultimately objective in a roundabout way because the pleasure involved is not that of the individual alone. Instead it is one that we all should feel once we shed the distortive and sentimental differences separating our perceptions. This claim led him to launch a notion that has turned out to be one of the most potent and controversial of ideas in contemporary aesthetics. This is his view that, in one way or another, appreciation of an object's aesthetic qualities requires one to divest oneself of certain elements of consciousness peculiar to oneself as a sentient individual. As this view evolved, it became identified as the doctrine of "disinterestedness."

There is no shortage of evidence in Shaftesbury's writings that he thought of disinterestedness as implying some form of separation between aesthetic and practical judgments, a separation that at the very least disconnected our love of beauty from our love of possessions. In *Characteristics*, for example, he remarked that "[t]he bridegroom-Doge, who ... floats on the bosom of his Thetis, has less possession [of the ocean's beauty] than the poor shepherd, who from a hanging rock or point of some high promontory, stretched at his ease, forgets his feeding flocks, while he admires her beauty."[31] But it is clear that Shaftesbury's notion of disinterestedness didn't entail suspension of interests in the way—or to the extent—that was generally supposed by later thinkers. It was left to Hutcheson and Alison to amplify and clarify the concept and to ready it for its role as a central element in theories of aesthetic experience from Kant to Stolnitz.[32]

Francis Hutcheson did far more to advance the aesthetics of natural objects than simply refining his admired predecessor's idea of disinterested appreciation. It was he who made the case for a "sense of beauty" independent of cognition and reflection, one that produces pleasure merely upon the contemplation of certain perceived configurations of objects and qualities. As Hutcheson regarded this capacity, it was both more distinct (from other capacities) and more determinate (in the manner of its aesthetic reckoning) than

Shaftesbury's "inward eye." Its independence from the other senses and from cognitive powers is demonstrated by the fact that many people have excellent and intact senses and fine minds yet lack the additional ability to appreciate the beauty that abounds around them. Its capacity for producing beauty judgments is demonstrated by the (alleged) fact that in all contexts, natural and artifactual, it gravitates to one configuration of features—which he calls "uniformity amidst variety"—as productive of aesthetic satisfaction.[33] This notion of disinterestedness comes into play when Hutcheson distinguishes the sense of beauty from the prospect of obtaining the pleasures of beauty or its objects. Beauty as a form of pleasure is cut off altogether from desire, and made an intrinsic good to be savored for its own sake.[34] Similarly, beautiful objects (whether geometrical figures, animals, or facial expressions) can, he thinks, be taken to be beautiful only insofar as we enjoy them for their own sakes, and not for what we may know about them or what we may take to be the likely consequences of our interaction with them.[35]

There is in Hutcheson's formulation of the beauty sense something attractively general and egalitarian—certainly in comparison to Shaftesbury's restrictive and aristocratic notion. In Hutcheson's theory, the beauty sense is empirically grounded in receptive mechanisms through which humans are outfitted to perceive their world. Still, although this sense is taken to be a universal and innate capacity, it depends for its cultivation and refinement on instruction (Hutcheson was unusually sensitive to developmental differences between aesthetic capacities in children and in adults), and may (as do many other matters of taste) apply differently in varied contexts. Differences in beauty judgment between competent observers are thus to be chalked up to differences of perceptual contexts and to differing developments of the beauty sense. And those developments, in turn, depend on differences in education and perceptual history. All these may call up disparate associations of ideas. "The beauty of trees," he remarks, "their cool shades, and their aptness to conceal from observation has made groves and woods the usual retreat to those who love solitude, especially to the religious, the pensive, the melancholy, and the amorous."[36] This shows us his willingness to connect the aesthetic qualities in natural objects to a variety of other qualities, including both the moral and the religious. As he sees it, beauty judgments require disinterestedness, and may vary from person to person according to the degree this requirement has been met.

As Dabney Townsend has pointed out, Hutcheson's approach to the analysis of beauty judgments is important not only for its amendments and refinements of prior accounts, but for a major shift in thinking that it brought about. After Hutcheson, it becomes much more difficult—and eventually it becomes impossible—to take beauty to be some substantial relation built into the structure of the cosmos. First, Hutcheson argues that beauty is a feeling raised in us, and one that is traceable, at least as our senses are constructed, to certain uniformities in our perception of objects. Second, he insists that the combination of uniformity and variety is instrumental in producing the response of beauty by means of an internal sense, and that this fact is amenable to empirical observation.[37] By putting empirical observation on the pedestal formerly reserved for *a priori* hypotheses, Hutcheson closed the door on one chapter in the history of reflection on natural beauty and opened the door on another.

The first man through this door was Archibald Alison, whose *Essays on the Nature and Principles of Taste* (1790) picked up the line of thought Shaftesbury and Hutcheson had begun and drove it to novel and—as present-day commentators have come increasingly to see—prescient conclusions. To begin with, Alison took the notion of disinterestedness beyond where Shaftesbury and Hutcheson had left it and gave it what Allen Carlson calls "its full theoretical development."[38] This amounted to claiming that the disconnection between aesthetic appreciation of an object and any other form of mental regard is absolute. So Alison wasn't merely a non-conceptualist; he was the first *absolute* non-conceptualist. As he saw it, attention turned upon, say, a glistening pond must, to fathom its beauty fully and appropriately, divorce itself from any cognitive interference. It must take in what the senses present—the play of light, the shifting colors, the air movement, etc.—without allowing other, extraneous ideas to shape and interpret the experience. The result, says Alison, is an emotion, isolated and purified, that can in turn set into motion an operation of the imagination by which it is ramified into a "train of ideas of emotion."[39] It is important to see that the initial perception of the pond is not just a trigger to a series of free associations or idle reveries. Rather, the emotion it engages calls up images and "affective qualities" that make sense in connection with it, fit it, show us more of what we can perceive in it, and amplify its presence in relation to other things in our lives. If we can't achieve the level of disinterestedness needed to detach our practical concerns and interpretive ideas from the beautiful experience, we are bound to stultify the process by which imagination productively builds upon it.

This view might be seen simply as the inevitable outcome of the crude associationist psychology that dominated the epistemology of the day. But it might also, and more appropriately, be seen as an initial bold gesture toward the empowerment of imagination in beauty judgments. Beauty, as he saw it, is not a matter of simply seeing the glistening pond and savoring it with a vacant mind. It is a matter of putting oneself in a position to have a responsive emotion (which might require preparation, not only of one's senses, but of one's emotive capacities), then enjoying the variety of images and associations that come to mind as unified with, and importantly analogical to, that emotion and its object.

The worry that such a position inevitably invokes is its potential for inducing disarray in associative emotion. Once a train of association starts down the tracks, who is to say where it goes? And, equally importantly, who is to say, when it goes this way rather than that, whether it commits us to an aesthetic mistake? Alison was well aware of this line of objection, and indicated a number of constraints on trains of ideas of emotion that he deemed sufficient to insure their overall coherence. The first is the commitment of all ideas in the train to the refinement and articulation of the initial aesthetic experience. If the pond's luster calls up the sheen of the moonlit cornfield, fine. If it calls up Pond's cold cream or the unpleasant time you had trying to find a parking place at Fresh Pond Shopping Center, we need to go back to the original experience of the pond's luster and start again. The second constraint is the empirically observable regularity of certain patterns of association. Over time, an object of a given type may come to be linked with socially determined affective associations. Thus, for example, white lilies have come in some parts of modern society to be associated with mourning and grief. They might, of course, just as well have been associated with victory and delight; but a steadily evolving social habit or convention has left us with the line of association we have, rather than that alternative. Third, there are certain linkages of thought that are fixed by the human constitution itself—for example, the link between fetid odor and repulsion (and the ideas of death and decay), which later thinkers would explain as indebted to the survival instinct bred into our animal nature. And finally there is the requirement of overall consistency. It will not do, Alison insists, to think of each link in the chain as independent once attached, allowing a chaotic, idiosyncratic forking of thought at every point. Rather, the chain as a whole must carry out a single "principle of connection."[40] Alison was convinced that these constraints were adequate to insure that the abundance of possible associations would not render incoherent the aesthetic emotion they were meant to enhance. His contemporary critics and latter-day commentators have been less convinced of this.

One more thinker from the heyday of early British natural philosophy deserves mention here. Edmund Burke added a piece to the theory of natural beauty that was in the air but had not been fully incorporated into the empiricist account of aesthetic effects. This was the distinction between beauty and sublimity. Burke's general position on the basis of our appreciation of aesthetic qualities is neither remarkable nor plausible. He held that, despite all apparent differences, people everywhere are generally in agreement in their beauty judgments, and that these judgments derive from our common instinct of self-preservation.[41] But, he distinguished these judgments, which are born of positive pleasure, from others, in which we enjoy the sense of danger or pain without actually being in dangerous or painful circumstances (for example, our delight in the vastness of the ocean). The latter—which he thought involved the strongest emotion of which we are capable—he called the sublime. It too, as he saw it, springs from our interest in self-preservation, but in a cautionary or defensive way, rather than merely by satisfying our interest in what is pleasing and comfortable. Beyond introducing the notion of sublimity into the philosophical conversation and remarking at length on the kinds of features in things (both natural and artificial) that contribute to its effects on us (greatness of dimension, difficulty, magnificence, and so on), Burke did little to clarify the notion itself or to articulate the connections that might obtain between it and beauty in our appreciation of their objects. This project was left to later thinkers, and in particular to Kant.

There are, I believe, at least five important new ideas about natural beauty and its appreciation we can extract from the work of the seventeenth- and eighteenth-century English nature philosophers I have mentioned. First there is the powerful notion of inwardness. All of the empirically-inclined thinkers of this period looked to the response of the individual rather than to features in the beautiful object to which he or she responded to understand the nature of beauty in general, and natural beauty in particular. We can discard the exotic metaphysical claim of an inner sense of beauty comparable to the other senses without discounting the idea that beauty judgments are fundamentally personal, rooted in individual experience in a way that judgments about most aspects of the same things are not. David Hume is responsible for the idea that moral judgments cannot leave us cold. His point was that our admission that certain persons or events have moral quality already commits us to a disposition to approve or disapprove them and to act accordingly.[42] For the most part, the English natural philosophers were making the same point in relation to beauty judgments. There is something in us, they said, that responds to things and aspects of things we find beautiful, something that moves us. We may wish to quarrel about the ways in which natural beauty moves us, but we cannot reasonably claim both that we deem a natural object beautiful and that it doesn't move us at all, doesn't dispose us in any way to act in regard to it, to want to protect it, applaud it, and so on.

The inwardness involved here might be thought of as the reflection of a determination that individual experience not be regarded as simply a matter of rule-and-case subsumption. You look at the bright display of contrasting colors on the maple leaf at your feet on a cold October morning and, without thinking of the matter, you say, "How beautiful!" The quality of that judgment is not adequately captured if we think of it as one of bringing a particular—this particular maple leaf—under its appropriate general classification, whether that be the class of beautiful maple leaves, the wider class of beautiful leaves, that of beautiful botanical things, or even that of beautiful things. Theorists of this period thought that the recognition of the maple leaf's beauty was not, or not merely, a matter of seeing that it fit an established standard, but of seeing that it affected its observer in a certain way. The claim that this capacity was located in a separate and identifiable part of the mind is neither easily defended nor of any great moment in later aesthetic debate over the issues involved. The important and enduring point is that the judgment involved in deeming this particular leaf beautiful is both personal and immediate. It affects the person who perceives the object, and it is not derivative from a prior standard. Whatever qualification we may wish to attach to the subjectivity of this approach in our final analysis, it makes a point about the intimacy of the connection between beauty judgments and the emotional and dispositional capacities of those who make such judgments that cannot be ignored.

The second point has to do with the notion of disinterestedness that threads its way among all these theories. As originally considered, disinterestedness entailed the suspension of a limited range of mental elements. As the concept later evolved, the range of these elements expanded. But, the fundamental point established in this period was that some sort of leave-taking—a reflective awareness divorced from routine awareness—takes place when we make competent judgments about natural beauty. As I have stated it, this may seem to be a very small point, a recognition of a quite modest difference between two familiar states of mind. Still, it is a difference that makes a difference. I see the maple leaf as I rush to class, but don't take it in as an aesthetic object. I'm too hurried to pay attention. Yet I could, before I rush off, stop to pay attention to it, to savor its characteristics and, in doing so, break into the course of my personal concerns to see features of this leaf that are disconnected from all of my other interests and yet command attention in their own right. This in-its-own-right aspect of the response to aesthetic qualities of objects we value is a pivot on which a lot of later theory turns.

The third point has to do with the notion of "unity in the midst of variety" that Hutcheson promoted, a notion that owes its continuing appeal to the fact that it is at once inviting and worrisome. It is easy to think of constellations of objects—in art or nature—which owe their attraction to the fact that, despite their differences, they have been drawn into an attractive order. Naturalists often feel that something like this is what they find aesthetically appealing in their fondness for ecosystems. It is also what so-called formalists have taken as a standard of excellence in assessing works of art. Design coherence is obviously one of the primary objectives in all of the arts. But it is a condition constantly exposed to attack by the novel and unconventional. There is in the modern mind (at least) an undeniable fondness for features of experience that disrupt prior unities, that cut across the established bases within which components get organized into systemic wholes. We like some disarray as much as we like some regularity.

The point I want to extract from this historical theme, however, goes deeper. It is that the concepts of "unity" and "variety" are powerful currents underlying our aesthetic regard for natural objects generally. My deeming the maple leaf beautiful is likely to turn on a complex comprehension that these colored elements and those other colored elements are just right (or at least right enough to be moving), given the shape and surface qualities of its exposure. There is something in us that organizes the components of a multifarious perceptual surface into appreciable order. And the orderliness of the result is, or can be, an important component of our appreciation of that surface.

The fourth point draws upon the importance these theorists gave to imagination in regarding natural beauty. It is a prominent feature of Alison's approach that an idea should generate another idea, and that another, and so on, as our response to a beautiful object evolves. The notion that aesthetic reaction entails a train of ideas is at once inviting and dangerous. The notion that one idea leads to another is, in itself, an axiom of education. Yet the notion that one idea leads to another without substantial direction is a recipe for intellectual chaos, even madness. To get between these extremes and to get at what is going on between them in this context, we need to clarify the notion of imagination that separates them. Education may go one way and associative instinct another. In some people's thinking, imagination is just a part of mind that kicks in when we are not interested in facts, or tired of them. We turn to elements of our awareness (unconscious or subconscious, perhaps) that embroider on the actual to provide a new liveliness or lilt to experience. In other people's thinking, however, imagination is not a non-conceptual maverick, stimulating us to think any way we please about an experience, but an important cognitive contributor to what that experience is. Mary Warnock is not alone in insisting that "the imaginative emotion ... is not a pleasure just attached arbitrarily to certain limited experiences. It is part of the actual creation of the experience."[43]

The fifth and final point we have inherited from the English nature philosophers has to do with sublimity. Later philosophers would do much more with the notion. But even in its initial historical appearance, sublimity opens up an important divide in theory. Not all our positive appreciations of natural objects need to be clustered under the rubric of beauty. If sublime objects strike us positively but not beautifully, how many more categories of aesthetic response might be needed to accommodate the full range of our appreciation of natural objects? Burke's analysis doesn't help us much here. Kant's later analysis may not seem to address the proliferation of response categories in a satisfactory manner, either. But it does at least aim at drawing together all of our aesthetic responses to natural objects—beauty, sublimity, and all the rest—into a comprehensive account. It may be that the articulation of categories of response proper to the range of natural objects under our regard will remain a problem for every generation of aestheticians. Yet the divide that opened in the heyday of Modern philosophy between beauty and sublimity inspired an important twofold recognition: First, that there are important contrasts in the felt quality of our aesthetic responses to natural objects and, second, that the differences that create these contrasts may be complementary elements in a properly capacious theory of aesthetic experience.

NOTES

1   The sweep of my attention is limited to Western philosophical history. I do not deny that important, and different, strands of thought on these issues have been pursued in other traditions; but I have neither the space nor the competence to discuss them here.

2   T.S. Eliot, *The Sacred Wood: Essays on Poetry and Criticism*, 3rd ed. (London: Methuen, 1932), p. 52.

3   Plato, *Sophist*, sec. 265 in *The Collected Dialogues of Plato*, ed. Edith Hamilton and Huntington Cairns (Princeton University Press, 1961), pp. 1012-13.

4   Plato, *Republic*, Book 3, sec. 400 in Ibid. p. 645.

5   Wladyslaw Tatarkiewicz. *History of Aesthetics*, vol. 1, ed. J. Harrell (The Hague: Mouton, 1970), p. 333. Tatarkiewicz points out that this line of thought has very early origins. Plutarch reports that Democritus comments on human imitation of birds' activities. Later, Lucretius was to claim that music's origins lay in windsong and poetry's origins lay in birdsong.

6   Plato, *Republic*, sec. 401.

7 In this way, judgments of merit regarding natural kinds (or types within kinds) are very much like judicial pronouncements controlled by received legal rules. U.S. Supreme Court Justice Harlan Fiske Stone once famously remarked that "we sometimes have to make decisions that make us gag." This remark underscores the conceptual distance between standards authoritatively applied and the sometimes contrary feelings of those who apply them.

8 In chapter 7, I return to this issue to offer a critical appraisal of the role of typal assessment in natural beauty judgments.

9 In *Parts of Animals*, 639b, Aristotle goes so far as to say that the relation between the ideal (the final cause) and its material is closer ("more dominant") in nature than in art. Here we see one of the earliest clear indications of philosophical awareness of parallels and differences between the grounds of artistic and natural excellence. Aristotle, *Basic Works*, ed. Richard McKeon (New York: Random House, 1941).

10 Aristotle, *Poetics*, 1450b-51a.

11 Tatarkiewicz, *History*, pp. 152-53.

12 Aristotle, *Physics*, II 8, 199a.

13 Aristotle, *Parts of Animals*, I, 5.

14 Plotinus, *The Enneads*, V, viii, 1,2, 2d ed., trans. Stephen MacKenna (London: Faber& Faber, 1956), pp. 422-23.

15 Ibid., 3, pp. 424-25.

16 Cicero, *De Natura Deorum*, Book II, quoted in Tatarkiewicz, *History*, p. 210. Cicero held that "works of art, being produced by men, cannot be as excellent as the works of nature; but they can be gradually improved by selecting the beauties of nature." Ibid., p. 204.

17 Plotinus, *Enneads*, V, viii, l., p. 422.

18 Wladyslaw Tatarkiewicz, *History*, vol. 2, p. 287. Among those who subscribed to this view were Basil, Alcuin, and Erigina. The point on which they agree seems to be that though not all aspects of the world apparent to us seem beautiful, the world is as a whole the manifestation of divine beauty.

19 Carlson discusses this topic at length in chapter 6 of *Aesthetics and the Environment: The Appreciation of Nature, Art, and Architecture* (London: Routledge, 2000).

20 This was, after all, the main thrust of Plato's argument for the exclusion of artists in the perfectly just state in *Republic*, Book X.

21 Thomas Aquinas, *Summa Theologiae*, Question 5, article 4, in *Basic Writings of Saint Thomas Aquinas*, vol. 1, ed. Anton C. Pegis (New York: Random House, 1944), p. 47.

22 Thomas Aquinas, reported in Tatarkiewicz, *History*, vol. 2, at p. 262.

23 Leon Battista Alberti, *Della Pittura*, in *Opere Volgari* vol. 2, ed. C. Grayson (Bari: G. Laterza), 1973, p. 92, reported in David Summers, *The Judgment of Sense: Renaissance Naturalism and the Rise of Aesthetics* (Cambridge University Press, 1987), pp. 9-10.

24 Summers, *Judgment of Sense*, p. 134.

25 Ibid., p. 139. (emphasis added).

26 It is a characteristic feature of Renaissance thought that artistic excellence is less indebted to divine inspiration than to innate talent and training. Beardsley points out that Dürer's famous analogy of the artist to a mirror could not offer any explanation of aesthetic creativity. (*Aesthetics from Classical Greece to the Present: A Short History* (New York: Macmillan, 1966), p. 130.) But the idea that nature's inexhaustibility itself provides the basis for human innovation insofar as it requires departure from standard conceptual bounds does not run up against this problem.

27 This is a theme taken up in chapter 6.

28 Allen Carlson discusses various lines of support for positive aesthetics in his *Aesthetics and the Environment*, chapter 6. All of the arguments derive the positive aesthetic qualities of particular natural objects from a position taken on the positive qualities (aesthetic or otherwise) of nature as a whole. It is very difficult, if not impossible, to support the view that all of the natural world is beautiful if we set aside evaluative claims about nature in general and begin with our aesthetic responses to particular objects. If, as I will argue, the beauty of a natural object is a function of an aesthetic experience had by an observer, it becomes even more difficult to defend the positive aesthetic thesis. If an informed observer reacts to the broken, blackened remains of a forest fire in much the same way that she reacts to an ugly artwork (a dark period Goya, say), it is hard to see why she (and we) shouldn't say that it is ugly, too.

29 Anthony, Earl of Shaftesbury, *Characteristics of Men, Manners, Opinions, Times* (1711), ed. John M. Robertson (Indianapolis: Bobbs-Merrill, 1964), vol. 2, pp. 125, 142.

30 The most meticulous account of Shaftesbury's views in this direction, as well as their implications for later thought, is Dabney Townsend, "Shaftesbury's Aesthetic Theory," *Journal of Aesthetics and Art Criticism* 41 (1982), pp. 205-13.

31 Shaftesbury, *Characteristics*, p. 127.

32 Jerome Stolnitz provides an excellent account of the evolution of this concept in "Of the Origins of Aesthetic Disinterestedness," *Journal of Aesthetics and Art Criticism* 20 (1960), pp. 131-33.

33 Francis Hutcheson, *Treatise I: An Inquiry Concerning Beauty, Order, Harmony, Design*, in *Philosophical Writings*, ed. R.S. Downie (London: Everyman, 1994), p. 15. Hutcheson insists that the principle governing beauty judgments is the same in artifactual and natural realms: "The same foundation we have for our sense of beauty in the work of nature. In every part of the world which we call beautiful there is a surprising uniformity amidst an almost infinite variety." Ibid., p. 16.

34 Ibid., pp. 12-13.

35 Hutcheson's aesthetic views are far more subtle, both in detail and in texture, than I am able to convey in this brief characterization. The best guide to this subject is Peter Kivy's study, *The Seventh Sense: A Study of Francis Hutcheson's Aesthetics and Its Influence in Eighteenth-Century Britain* (New York: B. Franklin, 1976).

36 Hutcheson, *Treatise I*, pp. 36-37.

37 Dabney Townsend, "Francis Hutcheson," in *The Encyclopedia of Aesthetics*, vol. 2 (Oxford University Press, 1998), p. 441.

38 Allen Carlson, *Aesthetics and the Environment: The Appreciation of Nature, Art, and Architecture* (New York: Routledge, 2000), p. 24.

39 Archibald Alison, *Essays on the Nature and Principles of Taste*, 6th ed. (Edinburgh: A. Constable & Co., 1825), as reported in Beardsley, *Aesthetics from Classical Greece*, p. 203. Alison refers to these sequences of thought variously ("trains of taste," etc.); the important thing is that, though the initial emotion is the untrammeled motive influence on the whole sequence, it is as a result of the process enlarged and clarified.

40 Ibid.

41 In *A Philosophical Enquiry into the Origin of Our Idea of the Sublime and Beautiful*, Burke takes the complacent position that agreement in taste is pretty nearly universal: "I never remember that any thing beautiful, whether a man, a beast, a bird, or a plant, was ever shewn, though, that it were to an hundred people, that they did not all immediately agree that it was beautiful, though some might have thought it fell short of their expectation, or that other things were finer. I believe that no man thinks a goose to be more beautiful than a swan, or imagines what they call a Friezland hen excels a peacock." (London: J. Dodsley, 1770), cited in *Contextualizing Aesthetics from Plato to Lyotard*, H. Gene Blocker and Jennifer M. Jeffers eds. (Belmont: Wadsworth, 1999), p. 68.

42 I discuss Hume's views on aesthetic judgment in chapter 7.

43 Mary Warnock, *Imagination* (University of California Press, 1976), p. 206.

CHAPTER 4

The Historical Roots of Syncretism: Modern Developments

*I*t is a commonplace in philosophical literature to refer to Immanuel Kant as having made the "subjective turn" into modern times. As we have seen, however, some of his most important ideas were anticipated earlier. And, as is evident to anyone paying historical attention, subjective turns and reversals of those turns have been made throughout Western philosophical history. Nevertheless, Kant deserves recognition as the thinker who drew a bold line between existence and experience that hadn't been drawn before, and who elaborated this distinction in a way that contributed several important ideas to our thinking about the experience of natural objects. In the late modern period beginning with Kant, scores of philosophers joined the ongoing conversation over natural beauty and its proper analysis. Here again, it is not my objective to present a survey of these intellectual developments but to extract from them a set of ideas that form a direct line to the philosophical analysis of natural beauty today. Accordingly, I will pay attention to only three developments in modern subjectivist aesthetics: Kant's grand initial transcendental project; Schopenhauer's elaboration of this project into a distinctive conception of aesthetic experience; and the latter-day refinement of this conception in the hands of the so-called aesthetic attitude theorists.

The subjectivist thrust of these developments should not be understood as implying a license for free-associative or ineffably personal criteria of natural beauty. Instead, the philosophers I consider generally endorse the idea of placing personal responses within an aesthetic community where the expression and transmission of aesthetic claims are vital and no individual judgment is decisive. When someone smells the fragrance of a lilac, that sensory moment is undeniably individual. But it is also something that calls upon an established pattern of responsiveness cultivated in that person's aesthetic community. Its communication to others, and thus its location within a social context of judgment, depends upon the general recognition and intelligibility of such patterns of responsiveness. There is a constant demand within this body of theory to sustain the integrity of the sensory moment and its immediate impression against countervailing impersonal effects while, at the same time, defending the interpersonality of judgments founded on that moment.

KANT AND THE SUBJECTIVE TURN

Immanuel Kant's most important contribution to aesthetics in general was his attempt to explain the internal, mental effects of aesthetic judgments in a general account of human capacities and their interrelation. He undertook to show how beauty judgments inevitably turn on features native to us as human beings, and thus ultimately accessible to everyone. Kant's aesthetics is tied up with his metaphysics and epistemology, so that what he actually says in the *Critique of Judgment*—the great treatise that gives attention to aesthetic issues—is reliant on the account of human nature presented in two previous works, the *Critique of Pure Reason*, and the *Critique of Practical Reason*. Consequently, the way in which Kant frames aesthetic response to various objects is encumbered by the formalities and arcane terminology developed in his earlier work. It is nevertheless possible to prize Kant's aesthetic insights apart from the formidable conceptual architecture of his earlier account of human thought without losing sight of his point. One of the remarkable things about Kant's aesthetic treatise is that it pays far more attention to beauty and sublimity in nature than to these qualities as they are to be found in works of art. Several passages in the *Critique of Judgment* seem to indicate Kant's conviction that natural beauty is superior to artifactual beauty.[1] Modern commentators have pointed out reasons for discounting this apparent value ranking.[2] But it is clear, simply from the attention he paid to examples of experience Kant drew from nature rather than from art, that he was especially interested in understanding our aesthetic relations to natural beauty. Indeed, it is hard to resist the inference that he regarded the aesthetic qualities of art as generally emergent from, if not parasitic upon, those of nature.

At least three of Kant's important contributions to our understanding of natural beauty can be sufficiently detached from their theoretical background to stand on their own feet. The first is his idea that judgments of beauty, whether in nature or in artifact, ultimately inform us as much about ourselves as they do about their objects. Beauty, as Kant sees it, is a judgment that is reached only when certain conditions prevail. The observing subject must approach the object with disinterest (meaning lack of concern regarding the object's existence or ownership). Once the senses make the object present to the mind's reflective awareness, a certain indirection is established. Rather than being referred to the cognitive center for identification (This is a rose; that is a sea urchin, etc.), it is referred first to the faculty of imagination, where it is associated wordlessly and non-conceptually with other sense presentations. Then the notion in question (the rose or sea urchin) goes on to stimulate the understanding (i.e., the cognitive center), but not by conceding classification membership. Rather, it acts on understanding much in the way that certain keys struck on a piano make strings vibrate other than those struck. Kant calls this "free play," (*Freispiel*), meaning that the relation between imagination and understanding is not fixed, or determined: "The cognitive powers brought into play by this representation are here engaged in a free play, since no definite concept restricts them to a particular rule of cognition."[3]

Now, there are many ways of interpreting Kant on this important and controversial point.[4] But, in its simplest construal, it suggests that some of our responsive capacities (those of the imagination) are concerned with taking stock of and registering the sensory appearances presented to us in the world of phenomena, whereas others (those of the understanding) are concerned with rendering these phenomena intelligible by finding the appropriate fit between them and the array of cognitive means (concepts, terms, relations, etc.) at our disposal. Kant insists that in beauty judgments it is the imagination (i.e., the non-cognitive faculty) that is directly stimulated and the understanding (the cognitive faculty) that is only indirectly and subsequently stimulated. The free play that occurs between these faculties is pleasant and extends over time.[5] Both the pleasure and the temporal extension are important. It cannot be that the pleasure felt is simply a response to the stimulus of the beautiful object itself. Rather, Kant says it is a satisfaction we feel in the harmonious *interplay* of the faculties this stimulus brings about. Part, at least, of the delight we experience when we enjoy a beautiful sunset is the pleasure we can take in the way our response to that sunset makes us aware of our own distinctively human mode of response to things. The fact that the interplay of faculties takes place over time suggests that beauty experience is not momentary, but progressive, involving a *development* of mental activity. Here again Kant is saying that what pleases us in moments of beauty perception is in part an appreciation of the growth and expansion of our capacities. I look at the sunset and delight in it, not in the way the dog beside me does, and not just in the way I did when I first began to see it, but rather in a way that grows and deepens with the play of my powers of appreciation.

Kant holds that if we put the claim that these powers I recognize in myself are the common stock of mankind together with the condition that beauty judgments are necessarily disinterested (thus eliminating the potential differentiating quality of any one person's stake in an object's actual existence), we can conclude that beauty judgments, though subjective, are at the same time potentially universal. That is, if we discount the effects of incidental distraction, distortion, and sensory imperfection, all human beauty judgments regarding a given object ought to be convergent because they call into play the same mental apparatus in all observers. I agree with the consensus of scholars who deny that Kant's conclusion that beauty judgments are subjectively universal can actually be deduced from the twin premises of disinterestedness and the interplay of common human faculties. But Kant's failure of logic shouldn't preclude approval of the *thrust* of his position. In coming to the determination that the sunset is beautiful, he is saying, we are not just marking a pleasant response—the delight we feel, for example, when we encounter a warm current in a cold ocean swim. We are instead taking up sensory phenomena in a way that makes us aware of both the thing we see and our seeing of it, a way that grows in us as we allow the various parts of our responsive capacities (call them what you will) to interact with each other. And, without going all the way with Kant to suppose everyone similarly situated would experience the beauty of this particular sunset just as I do, we can certainly admit that there is something to be said for the claim that our judgment that the sunset is beautiful imputes to others a basis for similar responses. That is to say, one need not agree with Kant about the features we share with all other human beings to agree that a beauty judgment makes us aware both that there is something important going on in ourselves and that that something is probably not exclusive to us.

The second of Kant's novel contributions has to do with his account of sublimity. As we have seen, the aesthetic response to sublimity had been explored earlier by the British natural philosophers. But in Kant's hands it took on a cast and range of implications it previously lacked. First, Kant located sublimity firmly inside the mind of the percipient, rather than in the object perceived.[6] Second, he recognized the capacity of judgments of sublimity to enlarge our self-awareness by inducing us to "measure ourselves against the apparent almightiness of nature."[7] Third, and most importantly, he suggested that judgments of natural sublimity are connected to *moral* awareness in a way never before supposed.[8] When, standing on the shore, I am struck by the immensity and vast power of the ocean whose waves break incessantly before me, I may find that my ability to comprehend what I perceive is overwhelmed by the phenomenon itself. I may feel cognitively swamped or defeated in this moment. But, in the next, I recover and am uplifted by the thought that I am capable of thinking of all of this. I am able to contemplate the limitless and yet not be conquered by it. Kant maintained that this two-stage experience of sublimity contains an intimation of moral value in that it impresses upon us the reality of "human dignity," by which he meant the capacity unique to humans to reason freely in relation to laws governing either the universe or our behavior. However much of this ambitious account we may wish to reject as speculative and romantic, it calls to our attention an undeniable rift in thought that often accompanies our experience of natural grandeur, a tension between two aspects of ourselves in which we feel alternatively humbled and magnified. The claim that there is, in such experiences, a tinge of moral awareness may also ring true to us if we are of a mind to think of moral and aesthetic values as being often intertwined, as several contemporary aesthetic theorists have maintained.[9] Nor did Kant limit the connection of moral and aesthetic value in natural objects to our experience of the sublime. In one particularly striking passage, he asserts that

> to take an immediate interest in the beauty of nature ... is always a mark of a good soul; and that, where this interest is habitual, it is at least indicative of a temper of mind favorable to the moral feeling that it should readily associate itself with the contemplation of nature.[10]

The important point here is not that our experience of natural beauty and sublimity reveals a secret metaphysical nexus between the aesthetic and the moral, but that reflection on certain of our encounters with natural objects forces us to broaden the range of value we take to be entailed in them, very likely in ways that make the line between recognized sorts of value less distinct.

Kant's third important contribution to the modern aesthetics of natural objects is what we might call the "thesis of reciprocation." It is the idea, running throughout the *Third Critique*, that lessons learned from nature are informative in the realm of art and vice versa. As we have seen, earlier thinkers were inclined to see nature as our teacher as we learn to appreciate art, or art as our teacher as we learn how to appreciate nature. Rarely did they see the two as sharing instructional authority. But, despite various passages in which he seems to tip this way or that, Kant's final position on the relation between the two seems to be best understood as purely and equally reciprocating. "Nature," he says, "proved beautiful when it wore the appearance of art; and art can only be termed beautiful, where we are conscious of its being art, while it yet has the appearance of nature."[11]

Part of the motivation for the reciprocation thesis is Kant's conviction that our appreciation of natural beauty involves the delight we take in the experience of purposiveness-without-a-purpose—a sense that the object or objects in question seem pre-adapted to our powers of appreciation. This is not the same thing as a claim that the natural world is to be regarded as beautiful only insofar as it satisfies some sense of design we discover in it. Rather, it is a nod in the direction of an ineffable sense of accord between mind and its objects that we find equally pleasurable whether we experience it in nature or in art. Natural beauty arouses in us the notion that nature is not alien to our powers of cognition, and artistic beauty arouses in us the very similar idea that the order presented in the artwork reflects this same harmony. "Thus," as Donald Crawford puts the point, "somewhat paradoxically, natural beauty pleases us ultimately because it is like art—it seems designed for our contemplation of it; and artistic beauty pleases us ultimately because it is like nature—it presents a formal purposiveness akin to the organic unity in nature...."[12]

As I indicated at the outset, I heartily endorse the view that our judgments of beauty, sublimity, etc. in the natural and artifactual worlds inform and reinforce each other as we try to understand our experiences in both realms. The reciprocation thesis embodies a bold doctrine of mutual effect in aesthetic learning as well as appreciation. It is important to recognize that our capacity for aesthetic appreciation isn't an innate skill. It requires development, nurturing, and training.[13] We go to nature to understand artistic beauty just as we go to art to *enhance* and *refine* our understanding of natural beauty. The important Kantian point is that when aesthetic attention can be turned on experience in general its characteristics and virtues distribute themselves across the whole field. There is ample opportunity for mutual reinforcement in the interplay of features in one part of the field with features in another. If Turners can help us see the beauty of sunsets, sunsets can help us see the beauty of Turners. And why should we think of one or the other as the dominant teacher?

SCHOPENHAUER AND THE AESTHETIC ATTITUDE

By insisting that beauty has as much to do ultimately with the pleasurable interplay of human faculties as with the features in things that stimulate this interplay, Kant gave aesthetics a subjective turn. Following this lead, his successors propounded a wide variety of theories of aesthetic subjectivity, most of them highly speculative, many obscure, and a few simply preposterous. Some of these theorists undertook to explore the *phenomenology* of beauty perception, considering in greater detail than Kant had the various elements of consciousness at work in the formation of aesthetic responses to things. Others (particularly the transcendental idealists) chose to reconnect the subjective qualities central to Kant's account with objects of perception themselves. So, for example, Schelling declared: "The ideal world of art and the real world of objects are ... products of one and the same [aesthetic] activity.... The objective world is only the primitive, as yet unconscious, poetry of the spirit."[14] Hegel went even farther, incorporating the experience of nature into a vast and complicated system of conceptual evolution through which the human spirit discovers and manifests itself. In this system, natural beauty sometimes occupies an important role as the exemplar of truth.[15] But it is more typically treated as a mere stepping stone on the long path of the progress of spirit toward its ultimate realization. As an inadequate manifestation of the Absolute Idea, the beauty of nature is just one more stage through which spirit passes on its way upward, toward art and beyond. Because transcendental idealism relegated natural beauty to this subservient role in intellectual and aesthetic development, its natural aesthetics came to be regarded by many later philosophers as a theoretical aberration attributable to a form of metaphysical myopia.[16]

There was, however, one strand of Kant's theory of natural beauty that not only took hold among the romantic theorists, but was refined and advanced by them into what has become a prominent theme in modern-day nature aesthetics. This is the idea that a certain reflective state of mind is required for aesthetic awareness—a state of mind demanding disinterestedness and, as the romantics saw it, something more. Arthur Schopenhauer is generally credited with being the first expositor of the extended notion of disinterested awareness that came later to be called the "aesthetic attitude" theory. Schopenhauer's exposition of this approach no less cluttered and obscured by his idiosyncratic metaphysics than Kant's was by his. But again it is possible to peel the important aesthetic ideas away from their theoretical background and get a reasonably clear picture of their enduring pertinence.

Where Kant had insisted that aesthetic appreciation of natural beauty required an approach that was disinterested in that it took no stock of an object's existence or ownership, Schopenhauer insisted that it should also involve a form of regard in which perceiving subjects lose themselves in contemplation of the object, forgetting themselves to the point of becoming unaware of the difference between subject and object. In *The World as Will and Idea*, he puts the point as follows:

> If ... a man relinquishes the common way of looking at
> things, gives up tracing ... their relations to each other,...
> if he thus ceases to consider the where, the when, the why,
> and the whither of things, and looks simply and solely at
> the what; if, further, he does not allow abstract thought,
> the concepts of the reason, to take possession of his con-
> sciousness, but instead sinks himself entirely in this, and
> lets his whole consciousness be filled with the quiet con-
> templation of the natural object actually present, whether
> a landscape, a tree, a mountain, a building, or whatever
> it may be; inasmuch as he *loses* himself in this object ...
> *i.e.*, forgets even his individuality, his will, and continues
> to exist only as the pure subject, ... and he can no longer
> separate the perceiver from the perception,... then,... in
> such contemplation the particular thing becomes at once
> the *Idea* of its species, and the perceiving individual be-
> comes *pure subject of knowledge.*[17]

The first part of this famous passage (the antecedent) can easily be read as the characterization of a posture of mind deemed requisite for the encounter with beauty, a certain abnegation of self and absorption in the experience itself. The second part (the consequent) is more obscure, although it too underscores the deep subjectivity of aesthetic regard. As Jerrold Levinson has pointed out, Scho-penhauer demands that the appreciation of natural beauty depends on the con-templation of Ideas—"visible essences of willing"—so that what the observer gains from this experience is a satisfaction that comes about from perceiving in a given object a manifestation of the Will that runs through all of creation.[18] I sup-pose we could, in a conceptually generous spirit, take this to be an extension of the idea imbedded in Kant's notion of conceptual interplay that every observed thing amplifies our notion of the class in which it belongs. If I see a landscape, I not only see what is before me but also see what I understand as "landscape" be-ing informed and altered by this perception. But this business of informing and altering becomes, in Schopenhauer's hands, a complicated and arcane undertak-ing—one that is ultimately separable from the issue of what quality of beauty the landscape may have. For this reason, the part of Schopenhauer's analysis that seems most pertinent to modern readers is his insistence that—in some way or other—subjects must lose themselves in their objects to be party to their beauty. The idea that self-loss of this kind can be informative, pleasurable, perhaps even ennobling, became a hallmark of later romantic aesthetics.

The second theme of Kantian natural aesthetics on which Schopenhauer use-fully embroidered was the notion of sublimity. Kant had, as I have mentioned, taken sublimity to be a two-stage recognition of (first) the limits and (second) the powers of human responsiveness in relation to the overwhelming. In a way, Kant presents sublimity as a passive phenomenon, something that happens *to* one in certain powerfully affecting natural (or intellectual) circumstances.[19] Scho-penhauer presents sublimity as a more active phenomenon, turning the business of tension-and-resolution into a challenge to the willing aesthetic subject. He presents the overcoming of initial rebuff to our powers as an ordeal, one in which the pleasurable result is won only by working to get to the point where apparently alien forces are seen as part of the general force of will in the universe:

> Nature convulsed by a storm; the sky darkened by black threatening thunder-clouds; stupendous, naked, over-hanging cliffs, completely shutting out the view; rushing, foaming torrents; absolute desert; the wail of the wind sweeping through the clefts of the rocks. Our dependence, our strife with hostile nature, our will broken in the con-flict, now appears visibly before our eyes. Yet, so long as the personal pressure does not gain the upper hand, but we continue in aesthetic contemplation, the pure subject of knowing gazes unshaken and unconcerned through that strife of nature, through that picture of the broken will, and quietly comprehends the Ideas even of those objects which are threatening and terrible to the will. In this con-trast lies the sense of the sublime.[20]

The important new idea here is that the effacement of self required by adoption of an aesthetic attitude appropriate to contemplation of natural phenomena is compatible with a bold assertion of self—an assertion required to overcome discordant and terrible aspects of those same phenomena.

Once it had been raised by Schopenhauer, the question that plagued suc-cessive generations of aestheticians was this: How can self-loss be a gain? On the one hand, it seems obvious to anyone who gets caught up in an experience of intense aesthetic appreciation—whether it be in the concert hall, on the sea shore, or at the microscope—that an important part of what goes on is the negation of some ordinary aspects of awareness in favor of others connected to the thing observed. On the other hand, it seems that any true loss of self is likely to be a loss of capacities to respond to the experience in a serious and intelligible way. For these capacities are closely allied to, if not partially constitutive of, the self. The tension between these two aspects of appreciative awareness was to become a central theme of debate between later aesthetic attitude theorists and their opponents.

RECENT AESTHETIC EXPERIENCE THEORY

Of the many strands of natural aesthetic theory that descend from the nineteenth century to our own, I will trace just one. Although the theoretic strand I trace is not generally regarded as the brightest and boldest path to current theory, it is, I believe, the one that best synthesizes historical themes of importance I have identified so far and the one that eventuates in the most plausible approach to present-day analysis of the issues these themes touch. The dominant idea in this strand of thought is the notion that the value of natural beauty (and likewise the value of natural sublimity and other similar values) is rooted in a distinctive kind of positive experience—one we can set ourselves up to have, can cultivate, develop, and refine. This experience is usually described as pleasurable, but not as a mere matter of superficial delight. It is detached, as involving a certain disconnection of thought from some of its usual modes. It is complex, as involving interaction of a variety of mental capacities. And it is instructive, as teaching us something about ourselves even as it teaches us about modes in which the natural world may be perceived. As I have already intimated, this notion has ancient antecedents, but was given its primary impetus in the works of Kant and Schopenhauer, the chief expositors of what I have described as the "subjective turn." Latter-day advocates of this subjectivist position have sought to improve it in two ways. They have attempted to demystify it, divesting it of background metaphysical and epistemological assumptions with which it had become entangled. And they have undertaken to demonstrate links between value in the experience of natural beauty, value in the experience of artifactual beauty, and value in the experience of other kinds of appraisal.

The first important move in this direction was made in Edward Bullough's landmark essay, "'Psychical Distance' as a Factor in Art and as an Aesthetic Principle," published in 1912.[21] Bullough sought in this piece to explain the transformative effect of a suspension, or truncation, of the usual patterns of experience in bringing out otherwise unnoticed, unappreciated aspects of the perceived world. He meant the notion of "psychical distance"—as he called this mode of putting the phenomenon "out of gear with our practical, actual self"—to be a factor in aesthetic experience generally and thus equally relevant to art and to natural phenomena. However, the key example on which his argument turns is drawn from the experience of nature, and the force of this example has seemed to many of his readers to apply most pertinently to that sphere. The example is one of dread and delight in a setting very familiar to the substantial ocean-going public of the period:

> Imagine a fog at sea: for most people it is an experience of acute unpleasantness. Apart from the physical annoyance and remoter forms of discomfort such as delays, it is apt to produce feelings of peculiar anxiety, fears of invisible dangers, strains of watching and listening for distant and unlocalised signals. The listless movements of the ship and her warning calls soon tell upon the nerves of the passengers; and that special, expectant, tacit anxiety and nervousness, always associated with this experience, make a fog the dreaded terror of the sea (all the more terrifying because of its very silence and gentleness) for the expert seafarer no less than for the ignorant.
>
> Nevertheless, a fog at sea can be a source of intense relish and enjoyment. Abstract from the experience of the sea, for the moment, its danger and practical unpleasantness; … direct the attention to the features 'objectively' constituting the phenomenon—the veil surrounding you with an opaqueness as of transparent milk, blurring the outline of things and distorting their shapes into weird grotesqueness; observe the carrying-power of the air,… note the curious creamy smoothness of the water, … and above all, the strange solitude and remoteness from the world,… and the experience may acquire, in its uncanny mingling of repose and terror, a flavour of such concentrated poignancy and delight as to contrast sharply with the blind and distempered anxiety of its other aspects.[22]

The important idea here is that a number of pleasurable and revelatory aesthetic qualities are apparent to the observer only on the condition that a certain frame of mind, an aesthetic attitude, is maintained. This frame of mind is a departure from the normal or instinctive one. The observer must *subtract* from the experience some of what he initially feels and he must direct his attention to the phenomenon's *objective* aspects. This operation interposes "psychical distance" between the self that was first caught up in practical anxieties and the self that ends up experiencing the poignant aesthetic qualities.[23] As Bullough presents it, this (admittedly metaphorical) concept of distance denotes a *scalar* mode of regard. It is possible to "overdistance" things or to "underdistance" them, and in either case, their distinctive aesthetic qualities are lost.[24] This quality of scale—the notion that distance has its fit proportions—is a new idea, and something that sets Bullough's account of the disconnectedness involved in aesthetic appreciation apart from earlier ideas of disinterestedness.

Also new is the concomitant notion that what is desirable in the appreciation of aesthetic aspects of experience is the practiced achievement of a mean state of regard. As Beardsley summarized his point, "what [Bullough deemed] most desirable is the utmost decrease of distance without its disappearance."[25] This is an evocative idea, but one that Bullough left largely unexplicated, just as he did the idea that the psychic distance has a positive, elaborative aspect complementing its negative, inhibitory aspect. Later defenders of the "aesthetic attitude theory" sought to repair these deficiencies. Its critics attacked the theory as psychologistic (as making the validity of aesthetic claims turn on the existence of a psychological state in the observer rather than the presence of determinable value-contributing features in the observed), as hopelessly incomplete, or as requiring conceptual gymnastics irrelevant to sound aesthetic judgment.

By far the most durable element in Bullough's approach is the suggestion that aesthetic qualities emerge in an experience only through a *change* in mode of attention and not simply through the intensification or refinement of an ongoing mode. This is far from being a novel idea, but it was now given the prominence and elaboration it had previously lacked. On Bullough's account, one must stop perceiving things one way and start perceiving them in an altogether different way if one is to appreciate the full complement of their aesthetic qualities. This stoppage-and-rearrangement is a price that needs to be paid to win access to beauty, at least in some, if not most, circumstances, as he saw it. Bullough's claim was that the change in attitudinal awareness is, when conditions are right, followed by a change in affective awareness, and that it is in this way that aesthetic experience transcends mere pleasantness to be transformative.

Bullough's novel and evocative idea was subequently pursued by a number of aestheticians loosely aligned under the banner of "aesthetic attitude theory."[26] Jerome Stolnitz is a leading representative of this group. He defines the aesthetic attitude as "disinterested and sympathetic attention to and contemplation of any object of awareness whatever, for its own sake alone,"[27] and considers that it conduces to intrinsically valuable aesthetic experience in which "we are absorbed and find satisfaction in the very act of awareness."[28]

Stolnitz argues that, in our usual modes of awareness, we are responsive only to those aspects of things that promote or hinder our purposes. We therefore see but limited and fragmentary features of our perceptual environment. Yet we can prepare ourselves for, and deliberately take on, a different mode of awareness in which we "sympathetically" give the object the lead, as it were, in showing how it can be interesting in ways independent of our purposes.

Attention of this sort will, he says, exclude not only the (Kantian) interest in owning or having an object at hand, but also the cognitive interest in gaining knowledge about an object and judgmental interest in evaluating, or ranking that object in relation to other objects. Stolnitz regards this restraint as a feature of aesthetic experience that puts the aesthetic value of nature on a par with that of art. If, in crossing my lawn, I regard the odd dandelion not as an obnoxious weed and eyesore, but as what it is on its own terms (it might, for example, be seen as a dazzling array of brilliantly colored rays supported on a slender stem) I may see what I otherwise would miss, and find in it a measure of splendor. Similarly, if I refrain from thinking of a famous painting as an object which critics have variously hailed and derided and for which a museum paid a huge sum but, rather, take it on its own terms, I may find my experience of it enhanced. These are, at a fundamental level, kindred experiences, and, as Stolnitz sees it, potentially reinforcing. Thus, the aesthetic attitude theory, as he sees it, is entirely congenial to the thesis of reciprocation:

> We can learn from art to be more perceptive in the appreciation of nature and vice versa.... Aesthetic attention can light on any object, man-made or not, and the development of discrimination which results from the encounter with any one object can increase the enjoyment of any other.[29]

For Stolnitz and many other aesthetic attitude theorists, there is no aesthetic attention without a preconditioning attitude of disinterested, sympathetic awareness. But once that precondition is met, the resulting attention is relatively unrestrained.

Schopenhauer had supposed that the aesthetic attitude could be turned on and off at will, aestheticizing everything (and even, as he sometimes said, making everything beautiful). Bullough, Stolnitz, and later aesthetic attitude theorists adopted the more moderate position that the aesthetic attitude is a necessary, but not a sufficient, condition for experiencing beauty and other aesthetic properties in things. It is a matter of some dispute within this camp as to whether the aesthetic attitude is something that one can entertain just by deciding to entertain it. Some proponents (e.g., Langfeld) hold that the capacity to entertain this attitude is something one must cultivate and practice if one is to make proper use of it, and that only when it is so developed can it become our "dominant adjustment."[30] Others hold that it is more instinctive.

Those theorists who don't insist that an aesthetic attitude is a necessary condition of aesthetic experience but who do insist that there is a real divide between ordinary and aesthetic experience form a larger and more heterogeneous camp. It is perhaps not quite fair to say that John Dewey insisted on this divide when he famously declared that the combination of factors that informs our experience generally and lends it value are common to science, art, politics, and many other human enterprises. But Dewey's analysis of these various enterprises revealed that his core conception of experience was aesthetically charged. He famously and fundamentally distinguished between having experience (which is inevitable and continuous in our lives) and having *an* experience, which occurs only when there is a wholeness, or unity, to the elements in a portion of experience such that "the material runs its course to fulfillment."[31]

Admittedly, this wholeness which Dewey takes to be the key feature of aesthetic experience is an endlessly contentious and mysterious notion. Various constellations of objects and features can be regarded as a whole at one level, or for one purpose, and as parts of different wholes at other levels and for other purposes. Attention is forever framing and reframing the ingredients of awareness, and there doesn't seem to be any fixed or certain way of determining whether any particular set of ingredients constitutes a whole, in the relevant sense. As Dewey presents it, however, wholeness is meant to be clarified by its relation to other elements of aesthetic experience. Aesthetic experience involves, he says, a wholeness that has continuity. It involves the smooth flow of each part of experience into the next. It has rhythm. It involves the punctuation of that flow, articulating its internal order. It has contour. It is organized by a dominant mode of patterning. And, most importantly, it has a certain "consummatory" quality. It resolves concentrated energy in a way that lends completion to past events as they catch up the present.[32]

Dewey insisted that the stale and humdrum phases of our lives are substantially different from and inferior to those phases of our experience in which we attend to them as wholes with beginnings, middles, and ends. As Dewey saw it, we grow into our abilities to have experiences gradually throughout life, and the ability to find expressive meanings in things works itself equally into the world of nature and the world of art.[33] His famous commitment to early education can be seen as a manifestation of his devotion to encouraging the expansion of awareness as it penetrates the various worlds we inhabit—science, commerce, art, and all other spheres of human attention. Dewey's defense of aesthetic experience as an identifiable sphere within this larger field of awareness was embraced and developed by a substantial number of later philosophers.[34]

The most vigorous recent defense of a more-or-less Deweyan notion of aesthetic experience as a detachable ingredient of general experience was mounted by Monroe Beardsley. Beardsley was a proponent of a form of analytic aesthetic theory generally unsympathetic to Dewey's style of philosophy but nevertheless congenial to his view of experience. He found much of what Dewey said in describing and defending his notion of *aesthetic* experience to be vague, cryptic, and unsusceptible to empirical demonstration. Nevertheless, he thought that Dewey's notion that experience gets carved into *experiences* in its submission to various (generally aesthetic) strictures was a fruitful way of looking at the distinctive ways art and nature may affect us. The problem, as Beardsley saw it, was to accept this intuition while realizing at the same time that there are so many different ways in which aesthetic awareness gets distributed that the notion of a common core of aesthetic experience will always be suspect. His response was to try to build a defensible concept of aesthetic experience out of generalizations that arise from recognizable social practices and common usage. If, he reasoned, there are points on which pretty much everyone agrees, they must be respected in a theory that aims to make sense of experience generally.

There are, Beardsley proposed, four points on which nearly everyone will agree. First, we take it to be a distinguishing mark of an aesthetic experience that it involves attention trained on interrelated elements of a phenomenal field (e.g., visual and auditory patterns, literary plots, or designs of movement in dance). Second, an aesthetic experience is commonly taken to be one of a certain degree of intensity. It involves a bonding of emotion to its object in a way that makes the experience seem concentrated. Third, the experience must hang together, or be coherent, to a high degree. This is a coherence that withstands interruptions, as when we lay down a novel to water the lawn. Fourth, and finally, the experience must be complete in itself. That is, it must have its own internal structure, but it must be also responsive to elements that are alien to it, elements that could make it a greater whole. Beardsley held that what memory preserves as aesthetic experience is cut off from the ordinary run of experience by these factors.[35]

Quite a number of philosophers joined Beardsley in advocating the view that aesthetic experience is distinguishable from the rest of experience and is independently important. Some placed special stress on the complex activity of observation, including seeing things to be first one thing then something else (aspection).[36] Others argued for a requirement of "rapt attention" that fixes on an object and doesn't drift off into either irrelevant associations or self-consciousness.[37] Still others insisted on the inclusion of empathy involving the fusion of the observer's perceptive activities with the qualities observed.[38] There is no common thread running among all these accounts. Instead, what binds them together, if anything does, is the fundamental Wittgensteinian-Beardsleyan notion that aesthetic experience is a "cluster concept," an idea lacking necessary and sufficient conditions, but which constitutes nevertheless a recognizable body of conceptions united by family resemblance. And it is, at the end of the day, a family we can recognize.

Aesthetic experience is obviously contingent in many ways on social and cultural contexts. And yet it remains anchored to individual response. In a given community, people come to look at, think about, and speak of the world in a multitude of ways. They come to be familiar with, and come to value, received modes of appreciation and their implied judgments. But in these same settings people are usually expected to contribute their own appreciative vision to the established appreciative base. It is only in this way that a culture's aesthetic identity can thrive and evolve. In this respect, our appreciation of natural aesthetic qualities mirrors our appreciation of artifactual aesthetic qualities. Poetry, for example, depends upon our appreciating both where language has been and where it might go now. Nothing about the poetic enterprise compels writer and readers to understand "sanctuary" in a way that implies its historical origin. Instead, it invites them to take that term, bearing its multitudinous accretions, into new corners of experience in which it may have resonance. The same can be said for aesthetic judgments as they apply to natural objects. What is established in our historical, culturally-conditioned awareness of natural things supplies a base. Reflective natural beauty judgment entails appropriate appreciation of this base coupled with an expectation that each new contribution of aesthetic attention alters the base.

CRITICAL RESPONSES TO THIS THEORY

From this position two lines of thought diverge. One takes the view that a lack of clear conceptual boundaries condemns the aesthetic experience view to incoherence and uselessness. The other takes the view that the flexibility and context-dependency such a position offers is an asset, not a liability. Critics who have taken the first track have generally insisted that the familiar notion of aesthetic experience fails to mark out any real domain of awareness. In *Principles of Literary Criticism*, for instance, I.A. Richards declares that there simply is no such thing as aesthetic experience, and that what we experience in looking at a painting on a museum wall is not substantially different in kind from what we experience in getting up, dressing, and making our way to the museum.[39] Francis Sparshott argues that "the concept of experience is a mass of question-begging confusions," and that adding the qualifier "aesthetic" does nothing but introduce "ambiguities and muddles indigenous to the context."[40]

Others have attacked the ingredient notion of disinterestedness. Noël Carroll, for one, insists that there is no such thing as disinterested attention because disinterestedness alludes to motivation, or causal factors that may prompt certain acts of attention, but not to the attention itself: "There is only attention and inattention, not some rarefied animal called "disinterested attention."[41] And others have rejected the standard account of aesthetic emotion as falsely supposing that there is a special emotion, distinct from all others, present in our encounter with all (and only) aesthetic objects. Nelson Goodman, for example, derides this idea as a question-begging invocation of "aesthetic phlogiston" that "explains everything and nothing."[42] But the strongest and most persistent attacks on the notion of aesthetic experience have focused on the claim that it depends on one's having and maintaining a certain state of mind, the aesthetic attitude. Sparshott rejects this notion as hopelessly obscure and irrelevant to aesthetic theory;[43] Goodman rejects it because it wrongly presents the mind engaged in aesthetic response as passive, rather than active.[44]

Perhaps the most telling blows against attitude-based accounts of aesthetic experience are those struck by George Dickie in a series of articles beginning in 1961. Dickie argues that the aesthetic attitude is nothing more than an outworn myth, one that remains dangerous due to its propensity to mislead aesthetic theory.[45] Dickie insists that it is a mistake to think that compatibility of an object with disinterested attention of a certain kind could be a criterion of aesthetic relevance. Moreover, as he sees it, the aesthetic attitude theory wrongly supposes a kind of surrender on the part of the spectator, one that requires that judgment and appreciation cannot happen at the same time. But, as Dickie sees it, this claim flies in the face of common experience:

> Is there ... any evidence that acts of distancing and states
> of being distanced ever actually occur in connection with
> our experience of art and nature? When the curtain goes
> up, when we walk up to a painting, or when we look at a
> sunset, do we ever commit acts of distancing and are we ever

81

induced into a state of being distanced? I cannot recall com-
mitting any action that suspends practical activities or being
in a psychological state that prevents practical activity.[46]

Dickie doesn't think that the issue needs to be decided on introspective evidence
alone. As he sees it, nineteenth-century aesthetic attitude theorists put theory
on the wrong track by failing to distinguish individual from institutional and
culturally-bounded aesthetic powers and activities. His fundamental point is
that our attention to aesthetic objects, whether in the world of art or in the
world of nature, need not be thought of as anything separate from or significantly different from our ordinary, usual mode of attention. There is attention,
motivated and directed in various ways. There is misattention, in which attention is focused, but on the wrong object. And there is inattention, in which
attention is insufficiently focused to capture the appropriate qualities of a given
object.[47] But to suppose that there is some *additional* mode of aesthetically colored awareness is neither supported by experience nor required by theory.

More specifically, Dickie attacks Beardsley's account of aesthetic experience as endorsing spurious notions of unity and coherence. There are, after all,
lots of ways in which we respond positively to artworks, ways that crucially involve an appreciation of contrast and conflict rather than some unifying motif.
And part of what we delight in with regard to some works is their incoherence,
their ability to stretch and extend our experience in hitherto unimagined directions. Dickie concludes that there is no clear sense in which some special
contingency, called aesthetic experience, is required for, or fundamental to,
our appreciation of what is going on in the artworld.

Recently, a number of philosophers have sought to resuscitate aesthetic
experience (and at least some of its historically prominent ingredients) in the
aftermath of these attacks. Beardsley himself began the counterattack with a
defense and refinement of his original theory in an essay aptly named "Aesthetic
Experience Regained."[48] I discuss Beardsley's revised position in the next
chapter. Noël Carroll has developed what he calls a "deflationary account" of
aesthetic experience that, by restricting itself to "design appreciation," seeks
to avoid the pitfalls encountered by previous accounts.[49] Similar efforts have
been launched by Ralph Smith[50] and Marcia Eaton,[51] among others.

The general line of counterattack has been this: Although it may have been
presumptuous and unrealistic to assert, as early defenders of the notion sometimes did, that there is some one special state of mind, utterly divorced from
other states of mind, into which appreciators of natural and artistic beauty
plunge when they appropriately train elements of consciousness on their ob-

jects, there is nevertheless a real difference between states of awareness tied to everyday concerns and other states of awareness in which practical concerns are submerged by an interest in the sensible properties of objects themselves. There is, the proponents of this view argue, something that people have in mind when they say of an encounter with a natural object that it was an aesthetic experience beyond the obvious claim that they were attending to sense-available qualities in that object. In the next chapter, I take up modern-day efforts at resuscitating the concept of aesthetic experience.

WHERE THIS LEAVES US

In drawing to a conclusion this brief and partial review of the evolution of the aesthetics of natural aesthetics from Kant to the present, I want to identify four important ideas that, emerging in this period, lead to key elements in the syncretic theory of natural beauty I defend in subsequent chapters.

First, there is the refrain running through theories I have surveyed in the previous sections that aesthetic value judgment necessarily entails subjective responses of certain sorts. To say of the fragrance of the honeysuckle that it is beautiful is not, or not merely, to declare that it meets a certain aromatic standard, or that it is enough like other fragrances already declared beautiful that it deserves the title as well. Rather, it is, or is also, to acknowledge a distinctive positive reaction in the standard (i.e., unimpaired) olfactory observer. Now, one can quarrel with any particular account of the required reaction without denying that there *is* a reaction, or a range of reactions that characteristically come into play when we make natural beauty judgments (and judgments of sublimity, ugliness, majesty, etc.). It seems to me that the positive response to natural beauty typically involves both pleasure and a dispositive element, an element that inclines us to act with respect to the object of attention in one way or another. As Hume pointed out, it is an essential feature of moral judgments that they do not leave us cold. We cannot make them without expressing a disposition of approval—one that, other things being equal, commits us to a positive response (e.g., defense, promotion, or abetting of the thing or action deemed good) regarding it.[52] The historical trend I have identified as "the subjective turn" points inevitably in the direction of an aesthetic counterpart to this claim. To deem something beautiful is not just to register a certain psychological effect, but to be moved in a certain way by it and to be disposed (conditions being suitable and other things being equal) to act in its favor (e.g., by protecting, preserving, fostering, promoting it). To deem something ugly is likewise not simply to state a fact about one's mind, but to be disposed to act in a way that rejects, repels, avoids, or otherwise negatively disposes of it. And this entails a disposition to act in one way rather than another.

This leads to the second point. As Kant pointed out, beauty judgments, in the course of registering our assessment of certain aspects of experience, also tell us about ourselves. The pleasure we feel in responding to the beautiful nightingale song is not a simple enjoyment akin to the relief that comes from scratching a mosquito bite. It is instead a complex awareness in which the sound pleases us for what it is and also for what it calls up in our reaction to it. Part of the pleasure we feel is the sense of the enlargement or deepening of our repository of aural delights. We are pleased by the song itself, pleased in our enjoyment of it, and pleased to feel ourselves affirmatively disposed toward the prospect of its future enjoyment by others.

This is a point about which we must be careful. It would be easy to think of the internal aspect of beauty judgments I have described as leading to an obnoxious self-consciousness in episodes of aesthetic awareness. There is something deeply offensive in the posture of an aesthete who relishes every encounter with beauty for the joy it brings him in becoming more familiar with his own capacity for appreciating beauty. But self-indulgent self-awareness of this sort is completely alien to the kind of enlarging effect I think aesthetic experience normally has on us. I will say more on this point in chapter 7.

The third idea is, in a way, a counterpoint to the second in that, at least in many instances of the appreciation of natural objects, one must lose oneself—or block out some parts of quotidian awareness—in order to enter fully into the experience of the beauty at hand. Although philosophers have quarreled endlessly about whether it makes sense to say that any such loss is entailed in aesthetic experience generally, and also about what aspects of awareness are and are not to be suspended in such moments, it is hard to deny that detachment from some aspects of some quotidian concerns is sometimes conducive to bringing objects of natural beauty fully into focus. In standing outside in an autumn evening, it is important not to notice how cold it is while appreciating the aurora borealis.

Let me make it clear that I do not suppose that any, let alone every, experience of natural beauty should absorb attention in such a way that it transfixes and thus obliterates other reflections in the observer. Aesthetic experiences of natural beauty should not be thought of as a kind of blind rapture. There is a profound difference between exotic transport (as when it is alleged that alien beings transform our thoughts) and the experience of natural beauty that takes us away from where we were before. When naturally beautiful objects absorb our attention, they do so in ways that go beyond our present attention, but not in ways that obliterate continuing connections to our communities and cultures. When certain experiences strike us as powerful and worth remembering, they do so because they tie in with other elements in our consciousness that are important in our lives or because they show us a persuasive way of departing from these same elements. If, in experiencing the radical transformation from blind fear to delectation by one's experience of the sea fog, one has disengaged one part of one's awareness in favor of another, one has also opened oneself up to a range of perceptions to which one may otherwise have been blinded. Although these perceptions are, in some way or another, grounded in the cultural matrix from which one begins to make aesthetic judgments, they are fresh, original, and personal.

The fourth idea is that, as we find it in natural objects, aesthetic value is often inextricably tangled with other values, including moral values. This point is hardly new. It was the prevailing thought in ancient aesthetics, as we have seen. But this idea was given a fresh and individualistic footing by Kant and his successors. To Plato, the acorn, if beautiful, was at the same time good because all things of this world were meritorious to the degree their material manifestations mirror the forms. To Kant, the towering mountain, if sublime, is at the same time good because it provides us with a recognition that we can enjoy, in its presence, the moral dignity of a being who appreciates the eclipsing of mortal powers of comprehension and rises above this defeat. A good number of other philosophers have followed this lead. The idea that aesthetic and other values are importantly connected is no longer regarded as eccentric and outré.

The syncretic theory I defend builds on the foundation laid down by philosophic proponents of the distinctiveness of aesthetic experience. But it stops short of insisting that *every* aesthetically appropriate encounter with natural beauty requires detachment, distance, rapt awareness of the thing for its own sake, and so on, let alone disconnection from all other normative values. Instead, it admits that while some aesthetic encounters with natural beauty involve an apparent "loss of self," other encounters sustain important continuities between appreciation and practical awareness. Some of our experience with natural objects presents us with aesthetic value alone. Some mixes this value with other values.

The capaciousness of this approach may seem an invitation to conceptual anarchy. But it isn't. Instead, I think, it confirms commonsense belief and widespread evidence. As I see it, the long history of reflection on these issues has taught us three valuable lessons: First, that every judgment is *contextual*. It is focused and made intelligible within a community of discussion and reflection upon the kinds of things available and important to that community's attention. Second, that every judgment is *processive*. Just as ideas grow and are refined in the course of social histories, our aesthetic judgments grow and are refined in the course of our lives. And third, that there is *progress* over time in aesthetics, so that any plausible theory constructed today must be mindful of, and responsive to, both triumphs and failures of theory in the past.

My point in surveying prominent Western philosophical reflections on the aesthetic experience of nature was to show how where we are now emerges from and reflects where we have been. If it teaches us nothing else, history teaches us that nothing is altogether new. While the view that I am advancing is novel, and in some ways at odds with prevailing theoretic tendencies, it is firmly rooted in and supported by the tradition of thought I have traced.

NOTES

1   For example, Kant says:

> The superiority which natural beauty has over that of art ... accords with the refined and well-grounded habits of thought of all men who have cultivated their moral feeling. If a man with taste enough to judge of works of fine art with the greatest correctness and refinement readily quits the room in which he meets with those beauties that minister to vanity ... and betakes himself to the beautiful in nature, so that he may there find as it were a feast for his soul in a train of thought which he can never completely evolve, we will regard this his choice even with veneration, and give him credit for a beautiful soul, to which no connoisseur or art collector can lay claim on the score of the interest which his objects have for him. *Critique of Judgment*, tr. J.C. Meredith (Oxford: Oxford University Press, 1952), pp. 158-59. Passages like this led Beardsley among others to conclude that "Kant ... gives natural beauty the commanding place in this theory." *Aesthetics from Classical Greece*, p. 238.

2   Theodore Gracyk makes a particularly forceful case in his entry "Kant on Nature and Art," in the *Encyclopedia of Aesthetics*, vol. 3, pp. 41-44. He points out that, as Kant uses the term, "*Natur*" sometimes denotes (in reference to pure judgments of taste) the totality of objects experienced, including both art and nature, so that there can be no opposition between them.

3   Immanuel Kant, *The Critique of Judgment*, trans. J.C. Meredith (Oxford University Press, 1952), p. 58.

4   Detailed and thorough studies of this issue are presented in Paul Guyer's *Kant and the Claims of Taste* (Cambridge University Press, 1997), pp. 60-105, and in Donald Crawford, *Kant's Aesthetic Theory* (University of Wisconsin Press, 1974), pp. 78-91.

5   The importance of the temporal extensiveness of this response has been highlighted by Paul Guyer in *Kant*, pp. 83-85. The centrality of the experience of pleasure in the response is highlighted by Malcolm Budd in *Aesthetic Appreciation of Nature*, pp. 29-34.

6   Kant, *Critique*, trans. Meredith, p. 104: "[T]rue sublimity must be sought only in the mind of the [subject] and not in the object of nature that occasions this attitude by the estimate found of it."

7   Ibid., p. 101.

8   Budd presents particularly insightful analyses of both Kant's notion of sublimity and his claim that there is a connection between morality and our interest in natural beauty in *Aesthetic Appreciation*, pp. 55-61 and 66-81.

9   The leading proponent of this view is Marcia Eaton (see her *Merit, Aesthetic and Ethical*); others include Charles Altieri, Arnold Berleant, Mark Johnson, and Martha Nussbaum.

10 Kant, *Critique*, trans. Meredith, p 157.

11 Ibid., p. 167.

12 Crawford, *Kant's Aesthetic Theory*, p. 134-35.

13 I discuss this "growing up" process in chapter 9.

14 Friedrich Wilhelm Joseph von Schelling, *System of Transcendental Idealism* (1800), trans. A. Hofstadter, in *Philosophies of Art and Beauty*, ed. Albert Hofstadter and Richard Kuhns (University of Chicago Press, 1964), p. 355.

15 Georg Friedrich Wilhelm Hegel, *Aesthetics: Lectures on Fine Art*, trans. T.M. Knox , vol. 1 (Oxford University Press, 1975), p. 123: "Now as the physically objective Idea, life in nature is beautiful because truth, the Idea in its earliest natural form as life, is immediately present there in individual and adequate beauty."

16 Theodor Adorno, for example, remarked that "Hegel was patently insensitive to the fact that the genuine appreciation of art is impossible without that elusive dimension called the beautiful in nature." *Aesthetic Theory* (Boston: Routledge & Kegan Paul, 1983), p. 93. Adorno blamed Hegel and later idealism in general for suppressing aesthetic interest in natural beauty in deference to aesthetic attention to those features of experience that present the effects of autonomy and dignity as manifestations of the human consciousness, or spirit.

17 Arthur Schopenhauer, *The Works of Schopenhauer*, abr., ed. Will Durant (New York: Ungar, 1928), pp. 98-99.

18 Levinson's article on Schopenhauer in the *Encyclopedia of Aesthetics*, vol. 4, pp. 245-50 is a masterpiece of lucid and succinct exposition. Even Levinson, however, is unable to dispel the obscurity of Schopenhauer's

theory that the particular becomes the Idea of its species in the act of disinterested contemplation. The fault is Schopenhauer's, not his.

19 It should not be forgotten that Kant recognized that sublimity attached to mental concepts such as mathematical infinity just as much as it attached to natural phenomena.

20 Schopenhauer, *Works*, p. 127.

21 Edward Bullough, "'Psychical Distance' as a Factor in Art and as an Aesthetic Principle," *British Journal of Psychology* 5 (1912), pp. 87-98. The influence of this essay on the subsequent course of aesthetic theory is remarkable in that the author was principally a linguist rather than an aesthetician, and in that (as his publication choice indicates) he thought of his contribution as chiefly psychological rather than philosophical.

22 Ibid., pp. 88-89.

23 Beardsley points out that Bullough's account of aesthetic distance entails a conception of framing: "Distance is a matter of degree, depending upon both subjective and objective factors. Among the objective factors are those that 'frame' it—the silence before and after the music, the stage, the pedestal." In *Aesthetics: Problems in the Philosophy of Criticism* (New York: Harcourt, Brace & World, 1958), p. 553.

24 The urban vacationer out for a sail underdistances the fog phenomena if he is prevented by fear of disaster from breaking away from his practical concerns. For the blasé theatre-goer, stage emotions may have become so familiar and stale that off-stage experiences may become overdistanced, and all the world may come to seem a play. See Ibid., at pp. 325-26.

25 Ibid., p. 324.

26 The idea that there is an important divide between aesthetic experience— however it is to be analyzed—and quotidian experience became an important theme in the work of a much wider range of thinkers (among them John Dewey, Vernon Lee, Elisio Vivas, and Monroe Beardsley), whom we may marshal under the banner of "aesthetic experience theory."

27 Jerome Stolnitz, *Aesthetics and Philosophy of Art Criticism: A Critical Introduction* (Boston: Houghton Mifflin, 1960), p. 35.

28 Ibid., p. 42.

29 Ibid., p. 52.

30 Herbert Sidney Langfeld, *The Aesthetic Attitude* (New York: Harcourt, Brace & Company, 1920), pp. 23-24. Langfeld describes a scene in which two men are tramping through an oak copse under a darkling sky, one of them familiar with the setting and supplying from his imagination features he might have seen were the objects more clearly visible and the

other unfamiliar with the scene but possessed of an artistic temperament, who sees irregular brown masses and clouds of dust. The former sees only the path through the woods, the latter a scene tinged with atmosphere and mystery. "Indeed," he notes, "it seems hardly necessary to add that the study of the appreciation of natural beauty is necessary if we are to understand the first stage of artistic creation. It is in such contemplation that the artist and appreciator are one" (Ibid., pp. 22-23).

31 John Dewey, *Art As Experience* (New York: Capricorn, 1958), p. 35.

32 Important contributions in this direction include Jay Appleton, *The Experience of Landscape*, rev. ed. (London: Wiley, 1996); Evelyn Dissanayeke, *Homo Aestheticus* (NY: Free Press, 1992); Grant Hildebrand, *The Origins of Architectural Pleasure* (University of California Press, 1999); Stephen Kaplan and Rachel Kaplan, *The Experience of Nature: A Psychological Perspective* (Cambridge University Press, 1989); Gordon Orians and Judith Heerwagen, "Evolved Responses to Landscape," in *The Adapted Mind*, ed. J. Barkow, L. Sosmides, and J. Toobey (Oxford University Press, 1992); and Carl Sagan and Ann Druyan, *Shadows of Forgotten Ancestors* (New York: Ballantine, 1992).

33 John Dewey, *Experience and Nature* (New York: Dover), 1958.

34 This line of development is well documented in T.M. Alexander, *John Dewey's Theory of Art, Experience, and Nature: The Horizons of Feeling* (SUNY Press, 1987).

35 Monroe Beardsley, *Aesthetics: Problems in the Philosophy of Criticism* (New York: Harcourt, Brace & World, 1958), pp. 527-28.

36 Virgil Aldrich, *Philosophy of Art* (Englewood Cliffs: Prentice-Hall, 1963), p. 20.

37 Eliseo Vivas, *Creation and Discovery: Essays in Criticism and Aesthetics* (Chicago: Gateway, 1955), pp. 146-47.

38 Vernon Lee (Violet Paget), *The Beautiful* (Cambridge University Press, 1913).

39 I. A. Richards, *Principles of Literary Criticism* (London: Routledge & Kegan Paul, 1925), pp. 15-17. Beardsley points out that Richards's denial of aesthetic experience is "so hedged about with concessions that all its force is removed. He agrees that aesthetic experiences 'can be distinguished,' though 'they are only a further development, a finer organization of ordinary experiences, and not in the least a new and different kind of thing.'" And this, says Beardsley, is all that the Aesthetic Experience theory (at least in its Instrumentalist incarnation) requires. Monroe Beardsley, *Aesthetics*, p. 552.

40 Francis Sparshott, *The Theory of the Arts* (Princeton University Press, 1982), p. 473.

41 Noël Carroll, *Philosophy of Art: A Contemporary Introduction* (London: Routledge, 1999), p. 187.

42 Nelson Goodman, *Languages of Art: An Approach to a Theory of Symbols* (Indianapolis: Hackett, 1976), p. 247.

43 Sparshott, *Theory of the Arts*, pp. 469-71.

44 Goodman, *Languages of Art*, pp. 241-42.

45 George Dickie, "Bullough and the Concept of Psychical Distance," *Philosophy and Phenomenological Research* 22 (1961), pp. 233-38; "The Myth of the Aesthetic Attitude," *American Philosophical Quarterly* 1 (1964), pp. 56-65; "Attitude and Object: Aldrich on the Aesthetic," *Journal of Aesthetics and Art Criticism* 25 (1966), pp. 89-91; "Stolnitz' Attitude: Taste and Perception," *Journal of Aesthetics and Art Criticism* 43 (1984), pp. 195-203. The main lines of the criticism presented in these articles also appear in Dickie's book *Art and the Aesthetic: An Institutional Analysis* (Cornell University Press, 1974).

46 Dickie, *Art and the Aesthetic*, p. 99.

47 To defenders of the aesthetic attitude theory, it may seem that there is a close relation between these last two states and what Bullough had in mind in speaking of "overdistancing" and "underdistancing."

48 Monroe Beardsley, "Aesthetic Experience Regained," *Journal of Aesthetics and Art Criticism* 28 (1969), pp. 3-11. (The article is reprinted in his *Aesthetic Point of View*.)

49 Carroll, *Beyond Aesthetics*, pp. 41-62.

50 Ralph Smith, "Philosophy and Theory of Aesthetic Education," in *Aesthetics and Arts Education*, ed. Ralph Smith and Alan Simpson (University of Illinois Press, 1991); Albert William Levi and Ralph Smith, *Art Education: A Critical Necessity* (University of Illinois Press, 1991), pp. 146-50.

51 Marcia Eaton, "A Characterization of 'the Aesthetic,'" in her *Aesthetics and the Good Life* (Fairleigh Dickinson University Press, 1989); Marcia Eaton and Ronald Moore, "Aesthetic Experience: Its Revival and Its Relevance to Aesthetic Education," *Journal of Aesthetic Education* 36 (2002), pp. 9–37.

52 It should not be thought that the position I am sketching here entails that one must be positively moved on every occasion in which one acknowledges beauty in an object. One can truthfully insist that Bach's *Art of the Fugue* and the song of the meadowlark are beautiful even upon occasions when a headache prevents one from being positively moved at all. In such instances, one is simply *reporting* what one would, under normal aesthetic conditions, be prepared to *express*.

CHAPTER 5

Aesthetic Experience Revisited

*I*t is a common perception that among the encounters we have with natural objects that we are inclined to speak of as aesthetic experiences there is a certain quality of *sameness*. Or, at least that there seems to be enough alike in them to call these experiences by the same name. Yet it is apparent that there is no set of common characteristics—in the things or in the states of affairs observed or in mental states resulting from the observation—in virtue of which all and only the various encounters so identified can be qualified as aesthetic experiences. As I have mentioned, this lack of a common thread running through the category has led critics to be skeptical of the claim that "aesthetic experience" picks out anything at all or serves as more than a vague gesture toward pleasure or approval. Skeptics argue that even if people *say* that they have, or enjoy, aesthetic experience, there is no way of making out what they *really mean*, let alone whether their claims are true, because the concept they are invoking is itself amorphous. Or, if it isn't exactly amorphous, it certainly doesn't admit of anything like precision.

If the skeptics are right, the only sensible strategy is one of retreat. If we can't be sure we are talking about the same thing, or if we are destined to keep missing each other's points altogether, we should simply give up and talk about something else. But skepticism of this sort is unwarranted. At the very least, it ignores what people want to declare about themselves and their relation to natural objects when they identify some of these objects as beautiful. Typically people want to claim that, in deeming natural objects beautiful, they are responding to strong positive aesthetic experiences they have had with respect to these objects, experiences they would want to have in the future, and experiences they would recommend that others have. There is a prominent personal dimension to this response in that only an individual can be moved by natural objects in the way that creates the distinctive experience that qualifies as beautiful. But there is at the same time a prominent social dimension to the response in that it is only in the context of an aesthetically responsive community that interpersonal notions of natural beauty can arise. And it is only in the context of potential communication of what is personally encountered that aesthetic judgments of any kind can come to make sense. These contexts are not locked in the present. Instead, they reflect past traditions of sensory awareness, currently evolving cultural views, and aspirations for the trajectory of values toward future generations. In this chapter, I address the aesthetic intuition supporting this set of responses.

COLD PLUMS

In a well-known poem, "This is Just to Say," William Carlos Williams compacts gustatory and verbal delight. This is the poem in its entirety:

> This is Just to Say
> I have eaten
> The plums
> That were in
> The icebox
> And which
> You were probably
> Saving for breakfast
>
> Forgive me
> They were delicious
> So sweet
> and so cold [1]

Among the many reasons this poem works, two stand out: First, we enjoy its evocation of the larcenous speaker, whose confession so nicely combines apology and delight. Second, we vicariously savor the plums themselves, relishing their sharp tang and chill, just as did the departed speaker. The hurried, casual rhythm of the lines invites us to linger on final words, reporting the taste of the fruit … "so sweet … and so cold." There is something real, something natural, in the way those lines fall together. Something that clicks into the responsive rhythms of our everyday sensory lives. No matter how dutifully they have been trudging through an American poetry anthology, most readers stop and smile when they read these lines. Stop, smile, and salivate.

To many people, the act of the purloined plum eating is quintessentially an aesthetic experience, while the reading of the poem is not. The gustatory pleasure is pure and detached from any ulterior objective. Appreciation of the poem, by contrast, is heady, culture-mediated, and perhaps even theory-laden. Its aesthetic component—our vicarious delight in the taste of the plums—gets lost in our thinking of the lines as craft, as poetry, not delectation. When we think about the poem as a poem, our experience may be impressive and delightful, but in quite a different way. It isn't simply a matter of *aesthetic* experience any more; it is a matter of *literary* experience, or critical appreciation, or something else more closely tied to understanding rather than sensory response.

Other folks will see it just the other way around. To them, the plum eating doesn't rise to the level of aesthetic experience. Like Kant's rendition of Canary wine tasting, it is mere sensory pleasure, lacking the reactive complexity or cognitive component that makes aesthetic experiences (in the artworld, say) delightful in their own special way. It is the poem that gives us what the plums can't—a human artifact redolent with artistic tradition, a topic with rich and multi-layered content, ripe for interpretation. Proponents of this latter view will argue that, within the endless variety of human experiences, we designate as aesthetic just those that unite sense and intelligence in the way this poem does. The poem shows us what we are as humans, responsive to lived events and responsible to each other in relation to them.

There are, of course, lots of other theoretical postures available. Conceptually generous theorists (like me) insist that both the plum tasting and the poem tasting are aesthetic experiences. To extravagantly generous theorists, *everything* that hits us in a certain way should qualify, gustatory or intellectual, direct or indirect, raw or cooked. Others will disallow that *either* experience should count as aesthetic because they think the whole concept of aesthetic experience is so contorted and confused by now that it has lost all descriptive capacity and should be abandoned.

What is really at issue here? Even though modern-day philosophers are committed generally to making sense in theory of what people actually think and do, we often pump up our theories to make them prescriptions for practice. This tendency is exacerbated by the professional imperative to mark out bold and uncompromising stands (making claims for x-isms against all y-isms) and then to show that all such stands are untenable. The idea of aesthetic experience may have once been the private property of philosophers, but it no longer is. Today, at least in the United States, it has remarkably widespread currency. Aesthetic experience is an idea that most students pick up in elementary school classes. It is part of continuing public dialogue over zoning laws, landscape design, parks, wilderness preservation, and so on. It is something artists—rappers no less than watercolor painters—say they want to stimulate. It is something that lots of people think about—or at least say that they think about—a lot. The having of aesthetic experience is, in most modern cultures, something deemed worthwhile and important. It is certainly deemed important by pre-college educators. And it is reasonable to infer that they (and the parents of the students they teach) deem it important because they are convinced that it will conduce to improvement in some form or other in later education as well as in life beyond. It must be discouraging to these people to discover that many philosophers—the very persons who might be presumed to be most informed about aesthetic experience—have pretty much given up on it.

As I have already mentioned, however, not all present-day philosophers have given up. A number of counterattacks have been mounted by philosophers who have sought to restore respectability to the concept of aesthetic experience. To begin with, they point out, the by now standard complaint that the concept is too vague or ambiguous to be useful is easily blunted. If it has no entirely clear boundaries, in this respect it is like a lot of other important concepts we continue to deploy usefully. After all, even if Morris Weitz's celebrated anti-essentialist attack on the concept of art[2] were taken to be successful, it would provide no good reason to foreclose paying attention to some things as artworks and others as not, let alone to homogenize our responses to both sorts of thing. The same point applies in the aesthetic domain outside of art. If efforts to define the concept of aesthetic experience remain controversial, and even if the concept is held (perhaps for Weitzian reasons) to be indefinable, this would not preclude its sound and intelligible use in connection with natural beauty. As Wittgenstein himself pointed out, the fact that a country's borders are contested doesn't mean that one can't sometimes be sure that one is in this country rather than that, let alone that the countries on either side of the border are blurred into one.

The most prominent champion of the effort to restore respectability to the idea of aesthetic experience in the wake of early anti-essentialist attacks on its coherence was, of course, Monroe Beardsley. Beardsley's approach centered on identifying features of aesthetic experience by virtue of which we find it *gratifying*, rather than worrying endlessly over whether the features we have identified are jointly necessary and sufficient. As I mentioned above, his view was that a person has an aesthetic experience just when the greater part of his or her mental activity during a particular stretch of time is "united and made pleasurable by being tied to the form and qualities of a sensuously presented or imaginatively intended object" on which it is trained.[3] Beardsley was well aware that the focal notion of unification invoked in this analysis is coarse-grained and imprecise. But that, he thought, doesn't mean that it is unclear or unworkable. The features to be drawn together in the course of aesthetic experience are endlessly various, as are the unities they compose. Although a baseball game, a sonnet, and a daffodil have altogether different features, and these features are unified in altogether different ways, we have no difficulty in experiencing each as a pleasurable unity. Coarse-grained and imprecise as the notion of unification may be, it is, Beardsley insists, an idea deeply rooted in social reality. It is part of our aesthetic culture, part of what we do to enjoy beauty in our world, to draw together the sensible features of various objects into delectable wholes and enjoy their wholeness.

Suppose I eat that cold, delicious plum. I savor the experience. I relish the tang and the temperature. And, during the time that I am doing these things, I am concentrating my awareness on this plum in such a way that its several sensible qualities (its purple skin, its just-right softness to the touch, its moist, pale interior, its sharp fragrance upon being opened, its fibrous succulence, and so on) are drawn together into a focal object of attention. This plum—this particular manifold of sensible characteristics—is relished for what it is, cut off for the time being from other elements in my world and drawn together by the pleasurable interplay of its features. If, when I conclude my attentive contact with it, I judge that the plum was delicious, I am expressing a determination that a) the experience of this sensory manifold, this awareness, was satisfying and worthwhile, and that b) it was satisfying and worthwhile in the way that our aesthetic culture denominates "delicious." Was it not only delicious, but *beautiful*? This is not a question that can be readily answered at this point. To be sure, there are contexts in which someone will express the same aesthetic judgment by saying either "delicious" or "beautiful," treating the terms as functional synonyms. Perhaps the plum-tasting example is one of these. But equally, there are contexts in which people want to insist that something (say, Canary wine, to take Kant's example) is delicious without being beautiful. Just what more (or other) might be required to warrant the latter judgment is a matter I take up in chapter 7, below.

If it is fair to say that Beardsley would, for the reasons I have given, regard the episode of plum eating delight as a fine example of an aesthetic experience, it is just as fair to say that he would regard the reading of Williams's poem (under the right conditions of response) as an aesthetic experience, too. This is partly because the semantic and rhythmic qualities I have mentioned conduce to a unified delectation of the requisite kind. There is undeniably a sensory component in speaking or hearing poetry that can be highly pleasing. There is also a cognitive component in which what we think about what we hear in the poem imparts another aspect of pleasurable unity to it. Our cognitive enjoyment of the vicarious experience the poem portrays can be focused and intensified by appreciation of culture-born allusions. We may, for instance, enjoy the normative coloration given to "delicious" by its subtle suggestion of the wrongness of "delict." But another part of our pleasure in *this* kind of poem is invitation to participate vicariously in the whole gustatory-cum-larcenous experience portrayed. Here there is no question that the natural and artifactual experiences are interdependent. Enjoying the poem entails imagining the experiences it portrays. Enjoying the plums, the anonymous narrator not only savors them, but savors them in a distinctive, guilty-yet-not-so-guilty way, knowing that he or she will leave the note that we read as the poem.

Promising and important in its time as it was, however, Beardsley's formulation of aesthetic experience did not wear well. Practically no element of his account has gone unchallenged. Are all aesthetic experiences pleasurable? Must the state of mind reached in aesthetic experience be unified? If so, how much unity is required, and what kind? Aren't there lots of experiences in which sensory elements are united and sensorily attended to (e.g., the medical examination of urine specimens) that we would be reluctant to call aesthetic experiences? It was because these questions proved hard, if not impossible, to answer that Beardsley's account of aesthetic experience lost favor in the philosophic community. Once that landmark account came to be generally regarded as inadequate, it dragged down other similar efforts in its wake, so that, for some time, little effort was made by philosophers to resuscitate the concept. Lacking defensible criteria of application, the concept languished. Philosophers chose to describe the business of sensible engagement with art and nature in other terms. Noël Carroll has described this situation as a "moratorium on discussing aesthetic experience in the humanities." It is, he thinks, a moratorium that needs to be lifted. I agree.

HUNKERED-DOWN AESTHETIC EXPERIENCE

In *Beyond Aesthetics*[4] Carroll makes a fresh case for reviving the concept of aesthetic experience. After reviewing and dismissing three historically preferred versions he argues for the superiority of a fourth conception, which he calls "the deflationary account."[5] This account is deflationary in the sense that it avowedly resists the tendency to over-generalize that plagued earlier accounts and also in the sense that it doesn't try to make aesthetic experience the sole or uniquely important appropriate response to aesthetic objects. There are many appealing features in Carroll's conception of aesthetic experience. By being less ambitious than its predecessors it avoids the vulnerability that attaches to their extraneous claims. By concentrating attention on the content of aesthetic experiences, rather than on their phenomenology or psychological preconditions, it circumvents some of the problems that plagued the aesthetic attitude theory and kindred forms of aestheticism. And, by limiting its criterial claims to features of what Carroll calls "design appreciation" and "quality detection," it confines itself to the least controversial themes in the historical debate over aesthetic response.

Nevertheless, I don't think the concept Carroll leaves us with will do the job that aesthetic experience has historically been understood to perform and needs to perform. The very virtues that make Carroll's claim proof against standard criticism—its self-proclaimed conceptual modesty, its narrow focus on experiential content, etc.—are restrictions that make the one he defends look quite unlike the concept of aesthetic experience earlier philosophers had been interested in defending. It seems to me that Carroll has purchased conceptual security at too high a price, namely, the price of conceptual relevance. I would like to suggest a different way of salvaging aesthetic experience—one more closely connected to its common contemporary uses.

Carroll's strategy is one of paring down the concept to the point where false claims of necessary conditions fall away, and a defensible residue is left. My strategy is, in a way, the opposite. I begin with unopposed standard examples (the plum-tasting, for example), and add features that may well be neither necessary nor sufficient qualifiers, but which cumulatively warrant status ascription in a cultural context. Carroll faults what he calls the "traditional account" (e.g. Clive Bell's formalism) for having wrongly coupled the notion of disinterestedness to the concept of aesthetic experience. He points out that agents can surely appreciate the form or expressiveness of aesthetic objects while regarding them as instrumentally valuable.[6] This doesn't seem to me to be an adequate ground for dismissing the "traditional account." The point the much-abused art-for-art's-sake crowd *really* wanted to make was that our engagement with aesthetic objects, artifactual or natural, ought to take us away in one manner or other from the plans, preoccupations, and obsessions of our otherwise recognizably non-aesthetic lives. An admission that not every aesthetic experience requires the bold and entire detachment usually recommended by the mainline aesthetic attitude theorists (Bullough, Stolnitz, et al.) need not undermine the important value of *some* manner of detachment in most, if not all, aesthetic experiences. There is detachment and there is detachment.

Carroll also argues that the psychological basis of the traditional account is faulty because we can't be sure whether, in a particular instance, an experience's value is really intrinsic or not. It might, without the experiencer's knowing it, turn out to be instrumentally valuable. So it won't do to insist on intrinsic value as a necessary condition of aesthetic experience, as the traditional account is said to do. But, again, it hardly matters whether the plum taster's sense that he is savoring the plums for no extrinsic reason is right or not if the quality in question *counts towards* the experience's being qualified as aesthetic without being a necessary condition of its being so. Jane, a friend who delights in inconsequential pranks, might find the succulence of the plums intensified by her knowledge that it was naughty of her to take them. James, a plum merchant, might delight in the sweet, cold tang of the plum for evaluative reasons beyond their aesthetic immediacy. In neither case does the taster's predilection nullify an enjoyed quality the rest of us could enjoy as well.

When Carroll turns to what he calls the "pragmatic account" he commends the part of the approach that centers the notion of "having an experience" on content rather than affect, but he rejects the idea that this Deweyan notion (or its close relatives) could supply sufficient conditions for identifying experiences as the relevant experiences. If, as Carroll suggests, the contemporary artworld experience of dispersion rather than unity-in-diversity is a respectable norm, then the coherence ideal Dewey thought of as central to aesthetic experience must be abandoned. But, as I see it, there is no reason to reject this ideal. Instead, there is a very good reason to incorporate it, or some similar view of organic harmony, into a wider conception of aesthetic experience. The plum taster and the poem fancier both make something of the experiences they have by separating them from the undifferentiated experiential panorama against which they emerge. In taking them to be recognizable against their background they regard them as distinct foci of appreciation, and hence, to that extent, unitary. Again, it counts towards an experience's qualifying as aesthetic that it be articulated and unified in the way the pragmatic account supposes. The alleged failure of the pragmatic account turns on our willingness to assume that it requires an ampler kind of articulation and unity. But it is far from clear that it does.

The "Allegorical Account," the third account Carroll considers, is a view adumbrated, but never fully developed, in the works of Theodor Adorno, Herbert Marcuse, and other likeminded folks. Their idea (as he portrays it) was that the idea of aesthetic experience should be regarded as a stimulus, a goad, to change the way we live. The experience is an emotive incentive to make us criticize what is and aspire to what isn't yet. This account fails, as Carroll sees it, because it trades on only preferred allegories and because it implicitly accepts some antique concepts (e.g., Kantian disinterestedness) in a way that leaves opposing allegorical options open. Here again, I don't see why the notions of an incentive to conceptual liberation and of freedom from certain interests (or even, more narrowly, the Kantian concepts of disinterestedness and free play of the faculties) need condemn the account we are considering unless they are construed as necessary or sufficient conditions of aesthetic experience. But they needn't be; and there is no evidence that their advocates took them to be.

Carroll's preferred concept of aesthetic experience, the one he thinks stands a chance of saving the concept from its historical critics, restricts itself to two features: design appreciation and quality detection. He says that these features are disjunctively sufficient conditions for aesthetic experience.[7] In fairness, I should point out that Carroll limits his analysis to the appreciation of artworks rather than aesthetic objects more broadly. But even so, it seems to me that the line of attack he mounts against the other three concepts can be turned against his broader position. Imagine that an elementary school English teacher requires her charges to undertake both of these missions—design appreciation and quality detection—with respect to Williams's poem, "This is Just to Say." Some students may find that, in the course of answering these directives, they enjoy an experience that is worthwhile and important; others may not. The question is: Are the notions of design appreciation and quality detection at work here so thin and affect-free that any moderately competent job of doing them will qualify as aesthetic experience? If so, it seems that Carroll's concept is at odds with standard usage. The English teacher whose lackluster charges barely accomplish the twofold assignment, but without any spark, any fresh insight, any enthusiasm for their subject, would hardly be likely to conclude that the students had aesthetic experiences in doing their work.[8]

GRAINS OF SAND

There is, fortunately, a way of avoiding this outcome, a way of retaining some of the content customarily associated with the concept of aesthetic experience while keeping it both elastic and coherent. To begin with, two key points need to be made: First, aesthetic experience is, along with the emotional elements it comprehends, a culture-bound concept.[9] It is dependent on language and community for recognition in and by the individual. One should not expect that the conceptual cluster it composes will be tidily resolvable into any simple explanatory formula for all cultures and all times. And second, as it is usually confronted within a variety of cultural contexts, the aesthetic experience issue is what historians of philosophy sometimes call a *sorites* problem. If you put a grain of sand on the table and ask observers whether it is a pile, they will surely say no. If you add a second grain, they will say the same thing. And so on for the third and fourth and fifth, and on and on and on. Yet at a certain point, they will agree that there is a pile of sand on the table. When? There's simply no way of knowing. It's a matter of cumulation without any decisive line of qualification. Aesthetic experience is a sorites phenomenon in that it comes into being when a number of contributory elements add up in such a way that an indeterminate, but nevertheless recognizable, line is crossed. All of the elements in the survey of theories I have mentioned in the preceding chapters might count as contributors. And many others too.

Although this view doesn't make for conceptual tidiness, it needn't result in conceptual disarray. In fact, the approach I am proposing is already a practiced and proven method in ethics. What makes anyone a good person? Not this or that feature alone, surely. Rather, we think of people who are good as folks who are kind, caring, reciprocating, dutiful, tolerant, and so on, and so on. No *one* of the traits we mention will be decisive. Yet, we do make confident judgments about the goodness of people based on the way in which their various good-making characteristics add up. Not everyone who has some of these traits (even in good measure) and not others is a good person. In ethical evaluation, we regularly demand a cumulation of variously-weighted pertinent moral traits in estimating that they have crossed a qualifying line—one that reflects general and social norms, but one we may be unable to delineate exactly. A good person is not one who has met some tidy criterion of goodness by having all and only moral traits a, b, and c, but one who has accumulated moral weight from traits a through z in a way that warrants our acquiescence in the claim that the goodness line has been crossed.

There is an advantage to looking at aesthetic experience in just this way. We needn't worry so much about the attainment of a conceptual threshold that we can't be pleased at partial results. A person who hasn't attained full moral goodness can still take some credit for having acquired one or more good-making characteristics. Similarly, some natural object may have a constellation of features that are beauty-conducive without their inducing a beauty response in their overall effect. In a given cultural community—the art-critically savvy world of twenty-first-century American connoisseurs, say—Carroll's preferred criteria of design appreciation and quality detection may well prove to be disjunctively sufficient conditions for aesthetic experience. But to another community they may seem only contributors—by themselves insufficient—to the attainment of that experience. Romantics who deem emotive affect vital to aesthetic experience would very likely take Carroll's criteria to be altogether too spare, too cool. They would insist that experience doesn't count as aesthetic unless it stirs the blood in a certain way, disposing us favorably toward its objects. Others might insist that the disinterestedness that Carroll so easily dismisses is, after all, an important contributor. Still others might insist that aesthetic experience involves mirroring, a recognition of one's experiential involvement during its very course. And so on. Each of these qualities, and countless others, might, in various cultural contexts, be regarded as contributing to aesthetic experience while qualifying as neither a necessary nor a sufficient condition. Yet once enough of them are present, the community judgment might be that the accumulation has crossed a threshold and we are warranted in deeming the experience aesthetic.[10]

In his last book, *The Aesthetic Point of View*,[11] Monroe Beardsley returned to the issue of aesthetic experience, admitting that his previous formulations of the notion had proven less than fully successful (although he continued to think the basic idea behind them remained sound) and seeking to amplify his account in such a way as to bring out its full range of value. He declared that, in the midst of all the mystery and uncertainty in this area, there were two things about which he was sure: First, that there *is* such a thing as aesthetic value. Second, that it cannot be defined except in terms of aesthetic experience. The key, he thought, is to make clear what makes an experience aesthetic. In his final exposition—meant both to take stock of criticisms he accepted and to incorporate ideas he had come to find congenial—he identifies five criteria to be applied as a (Wittgensteinian) family,[12] with the proviso that an experience must have the first and at least three of the rest to count as aesthetic. The criteria are: 1) Object directedness; i.e., the willingly accepted guidance of one's mental states by properties on which attention is fixed with a feeling that "things are working themselves out fittingly." 2) Felt freedom; i.e., a sense of release from concerns about past and future, a sense of harmony with what is presented as if freely chosen. 3) Detached affect; i.e., a sense that objects of interest are set apart from us at some emotional distance, permitting us to rise above even dark and disturbing things. 4) Active discovery; i.e., a sense of the mind's exercising active constructive powers to make things cohere, a sense of intelligibility. 5) Wholeness; i.e., a sense of personal integration, a contentment involving both self-acceptance and self-expansion.[13]

The formulation Beardsley presents here is instructive in many ways, but two ways deserve special attention. First, it shows that Beardsley himself had come to what verges on a sorites solution to the problem he posed. Although he identified five features that an experience might have in order to be aesthetic, he held that it is aesthetic if it has the first feature and at least three of the others. The idea is that the quality of being aesthetic attaches to experience not by virtue of its having any one quality alone, nor of its having any particular set of qualities, but by virtue of its having some suitable *combination* of qualities from an identified set. "[I]f we do not insist a priori that the aesthetic character must be a single and simple one, but look instead for a set of central criteria, we may find that we can accommodate and reconcile insights and discoveries from several quarters."[14] Second, Beardsley came to see that the way to defend aesthetic experience from its persistent critics was to broaden the field of analysis, pointing out the ways those experiences we are inclined to call aesthetic connect with, and complement, other facets of life we normally deem valuable in other ways.

The importance of recognizing aesthetic experience as an identifiable and valuable part of life is implicated in these other valuable parts of life. On this point, Beardsley's final position anticipates integrationist (anti-separation thesis) views of Marcia Eaton, Martha Nussbaum, Richard Wollheim, and others I have mentioned earlier. As Eaton has pointed out, the multiplicity of reasons real people give for their aesthetic preferences within their cultural contexts is a stubborn and fundamental fact about the social phenomenon of appreciation.[15] It is pointless to try to reduce these various reasons to some simple calculus of value. The same point holds for the aesthetic experience in which these preferences are determining features.

It may well seem that this way of looking at things makes the determination that a given experience is an aesthetic experience analogous to the determination that a given putative artwork is an artwork in recent versions of the institutional theory of art.[16] Just as the institutional theory is now understood to imply that the art-status of an artifact is achieved, rather than conferred, and achieved in light of the artworld's evolving and fluctuating criteria of recognition, so the view I am presenting takes aesthetic experience to require acknowledgment by the community of those who have a stake in aesthetic experience that enough contributing elements are present to warrant the conclusion that this or that experience is aesthetic. If the institutional theory is right, there is nothing a priori about artwork status. And if the view I am advancing here is right, there is equally nothing a priori about the status of aesthetic experience. Both ultimately depend on people in a given community deciding that enough qualifying features are present for the status in question to be acknowledgeable. But both contemplate the possibility of creative dissent, so that individual experience contrary to the community norms can contribute to the modification of those norms.

To return, finally, to the plums and the poem: How should we judge whether either the depicted plum eater or the poem reader contemplating the depiction truly has an aesthetic experience? Exceptions to any formulaic answer we propose won't be hard to find. Carroll proposed what amounts to an answer, but, as I have suggested, the kind of attack Carroll mounts against earlier views can easily be mounted against his own. I think we should be guided, instead, by the objectives people generally have in mind as they deploy the language of aesthetic experience. People here and there, in all walks of life.

The art teacher who is trying to get her young students to respond intelligently and well to beauty in the world about them will be pleased to see these students begin to put aside their habitual distractions and preoccupations when they get caught up in the prospect of fish scales and mud flats. She may recognize that some of what they experience has aesthetic dimensions. Her students may discover ways in which these things have content that is made whole and intelligible by invoking some coordinating principles. They may come to see these things as rare, or wonderful, or provocative, and so on, and so on. No one of these experiential factors may be enough to make the teacher altogether confident that she is warranted in speaking of what her charges have enjoyed as an aesthetic experience. But it seems to me that, if enough of these factors are observably present in a sufficient degree, then, within a given cultural context, the teacher would be warranted in making that claim. And if the pile of sand gets high enough, it would be preposterous for her to think the claim unwarranted.

NOTES

1   William Carlos Williams, "This is Just to Say," in *Collected Poems 1909-1939*, vol. 1 (New York: New Directions, 1938).

2   Morris Weitz, "The Role of Theory in Aesthetics," *Journal of Aesthetics and Art Criticism* 15 (1956), pp. 27-35.

3   Beardsley, "Aesthetic Experience Regained," p. 5.

4. Carroll was once, as it happens, Monroe C. Beardsley Professor of Philosophy at the University of Wisconsin.

5   Noël Carroll, *Beyond Aesthetics: Philosophical Essays* (Cambridge University Press, 2001), pp. 41-62.

6   Ibid., p. 47.

7   Ibid., p. 60.

8   Carroll has amplified his position more recently in "Aesthetic Experience: A Question of Content," in *Aesthetics and the Philosophy of Art*, ed. Matthew Kieran (Malden, MA: Blackwell, 2006), pp. 69-97. However, the newer statement adds no new strength to the earlier stated position; nor does it provide any new substantial basis for rejecting rival views.

9   This point is argued at length in Part I of Marcia Eaton, *Merit: Aesthetic and Ethical* (Oxford University Press, 2001). I will spell out the way in which I think the culture-bound and subjectively individual elements of aesthetic experience play out in natural beauty judgments in chapter 7.

10 It might seem that this way of putting things is just a roundabout expression of the claim that the various contributory elements I have mentioned amount to a disjunctive set of conditions that are jointly sufficient to establish the claim that a given experience is an aesthetic experience. But it isn't. Normally, we regard a set of conditions as jointly sufficient to establish a claim if these conditions are present *to any degree*. It is the nature of sorites phenomena that the several contributory conditions accumulate in various amounts, establishing the claim only when they, taken together, add up in such a way that we regard the relevant threshold line as having been passed.

11 Monroe Beardsley, *The Aesthetic Point of View: Selected Essays*, ed. Michael Wreen and Donald Callen (Cornell University Press, 1982).

12 Wittgenstein presented the idea of "family resemblances" in *Philosophical Investigations*. After comparing a wide variety of quite different things we call "games" (card games, Olympic games, chess, etc.) he says "I can think of no better expression to characterize these similarities than 'family resemblances'; for the various resemblances between members of a family: build, features, colour of eyes, gait, temperament, etc., etc. overlap and criss-cross in the same way." Ludwig Wittgenstein, *Philosophical Investigations*, 3d ed., ed. and trans. Elizabeth Anscombe (New York: Macmillan, 1953), p. 31.

13 Beardsley, *The Aesthetic Point of View*, pp. 288-89.

14 Ibid., p. 286.

15 Eaton, *Merit*, pp. 26-27.

16 The revised standard version of this theory is to be found in George Dickie, *The Art Circle* (New York: Haven, 1984).

CHAPTER 6

The Framing Paradox

A standard feature of most artworks that contributes importantly to our aesthetic experience of them is the *frame*. A traditional easel painting is bounded by a frame that sets limits on our range of visual attention and makes it possible to see the contents within it as intelligibly organized. Even unframed paintings are bounded by their canvas edges. Similarly, dramas, operas, dances, and various other performances are framed by the confines of their theatrical context (the proscenium arch, the amphitheater setting, the architectural backdrop of the Baths of Caracalla, etc.). Analogously, works of literature may be seen as framed by their covers, works of music by the temporal limits on their performance, sculptures by the dimensions of their material form, and so on. By contrast with all of these, however, nature can seem strikingly and importantly *unframed*. When I admire the display of stars in a desert night sky, for example, there is no boundary that guides or limits my perception except the extreme boundary of the visual horizon (and that turns out to be no boundary at all, provided I am willing to travel far enough). When I wander through a forest, finding this or that of its myriad features beautiful, I am not conscious of any frame that organizes them. Even if, for a moment, I notice the way the path opens upon a lovely mountain vista, caught between dense shrubbery and overhanging limbs, in the next moment I am free to walk through this apparent frame into a never-ending sequence of changing scenes. The same limitlessness of objective and malleability of perception characterize our aesthetic experience of nature from the microscopic to the telescopic scale, and from the wilderness setting to the urban setting. Art is framed, and nature is not.

But is this really so? The claim that nature—or our experience of nature— is importantly and distinctively unframed is an entrenched dogma among leading environmental aestheticians. Just about every recent philosopher discussing natural beauty has touched on the point. Ronald Hepburn, one of the first and foremost of environmental philosophers, recently returned to the issue in an essay devoted to de-trivializing the aesthetic appreciation of nature. Here he advanced the notion of nature's inherent unframed-ness as an affirmation of some of our basic and powerful aesthetic intuitions:

> Although analogies with art suggest themselves often enough about how to 'frame' the objects of our aesthetic interest, where to establish the momentary bounds of our attention, on other occasions the objects we attend to seem to repudiate any such bounding—to present themselves as essentially illimitable, unframable, or to be in a way surrogates for the unbounded.[1]

While it may be true that both nature-as-a-whole and certain appreciable natural objects (such as those Kant singled out as sublime) are essentially divorced from any possible framing devices, I do not think that we should conclude from this that the notion of framing is always (or even generally) inapplicable to the aesthetic experience of natural beauty. In this chapter, I consider some of the prominent arguments in favor of the Nature Unframed position. I then consider various ways in which we may be said properly, and even inevitably, to frame, bound, or confine our attention in respect to natural objects in our aesthetic regard—the Nature Framed position. Facing these positions off against each other produces what I will call "The Framing Paradox." I conclude the chapter by indicating the most plausible path to a solution of this paradox and its contribution to the theory of natural aesthetic experience whose rudiments I laid out in the previous chapter.

NATURE UNFRAMED

Modern arguments against the idea that the proper aesthetic regard of nature is, like that of art, reliant on frames of one kind or another to organize its contents have divided into two strands. The first emphasizes the role frames assume in separating the framed contents from their background environment, and takes them to be inapplicable to natural experience because of the detachment such a separation entails. The second emphasizes the essentially static character of frames, pointing out that firmness of location frustrates their potential capacity for rendering intelligible the essentially dynamic aesthetic experiences of natural objects.

The leading advocate of the first strand of anti-framism is Hepburn. In a seminal essay titled "Contemporary Aesthetics and the Neglect of Natural Beauty," he makes the important point that our posture with regard to nature is quite different from our posture with regard to art: "We are in nature and a part of nature; we do not stand over against it as over against a painting on a wall."[2] The distinction between the viewpoints of the insider and the outsider is, on this account, all-important in relation to the issue of framing. As he sees it, the principal functions of frames in relation to artworks are a) the detachment of the work from its background or aesthetic matrix and b) the affirmation of the completeness of the work as presented:

> Though by no means all art-objects have frames or pedestals, they share a common character in being set apart from their environment, and set apart in a distinctive way. We might use the words "frame" and "framed" in an extended sense to cover not only the physical boundaries of pictures but all the various devices employed in the different arts to prevent the art-object from being mistaken for a natural object or for an artifact without aesthetic interest.... Such devices are best thought of as aids to the recognition of the formal completeness of the art-objects themselves, their ability to sustain aesthetic interest, an interest that is not crucially dependent upon the relationships between the object and its general environment.[3]

On this view then, we look at, say, Constable's *Water-meadows near Salisbury* (1829) in one way and we enter into aesthetic engagement with the actual objects Constable portrayed (a bank of willows reflected in a pond set against a cloudy sky) in quite another way. The first way confines the attention to *just this*, exclusive of anything else beyond it. It moves toward thinking of the ingredients in the painting as "altogether right" (or not) in relation to each other and to the space given them. The second way extends attention, savors the incidental complications brought on by going beyond what was given. Hepburn points out that the chance train whistle cannot be integrated into the music of a string-quartet. Nor can it be brought into our experience of *Water-meadows near Salisbury*. But, in the unframed natural experience, this sound is simply one more sound in the aesthetic environment, and one that may, as he puts it, "challenge us to integrate it in our overall experience, to modify that experience so as to make room for it."[4] Hepburn doesn't deny that the frames art uses to its compositional advantage are beneficial in their own domain. His point is that the alienation of what lies beyond the frame is the price art pays for composition. It simply can't extend its reach beyond its grasp.

Completeness is the second element. Hepburn argues that the framing of objects makes it possible for us to see what is confined by the frame as complete, while it is important for us to see natural objects as incomplete, limitless in their perspectives, immensely rich with possibilities. "If," he says, "the absence of 'frame' precludes full determinateness and stability in the natural aesthetic object, it at least offers in return … unpredictable perceptual surprises."[5] The possibility of these surprises is taken to impart a sense of openness and adventure to the experience of nature. It would seem that any framing of natural objects must violate this sense of openness and adventure.

Both of these claims, however, are open to criticism. To begin with, Hepburn's claim that we are *in* nature but not in art fails to recognize the full impact of artifactuality in aesthetic awareness. The whole business of in-ness is controversial. To many people, it seems that they are no less in art than in nature. In-ness is a function of culture, language, historical background, and so on. It is true that I can't be in a landscape painting in the way that I can be in a landscape, but my aesthetic take on the two might be very similar. Not because I take the landscape to be a proto-painting, but because the aesthetic features I find in each affect me similarly. Entrance into an artwork (a novel, a drama, a painting, an opera) may be easier for some than entrance into a natural environment. And, once one is in the artwork, one may become aware of worlds of experience that transcend the bounds of the artwork. In fact, one expects to do so. Few spectators attend Shakespeare's plays to envelop themselves in the world of late sixteenth- and early seventeenth-century England. They expect that the drama they see will present themes that, framed well and cogently, transcend their frame to make points today. Just as the incidental train whistle may penetrate, alter, and possibly enhance one's appreciation of the streamside environment, so a momentary flash of attention that calls up something from Tom Stoppard's *Rosencrantz and Guildenstern are Dead* may penetrate, alter, and possibly enhance one's appreciation of Shakespeare's *Hamlet, Prince of Denmark*. Both incidental awarenesses are, in a sense, alien to their aesthetic environments. Yet each can contribute positively and productively to the aesthetic experience at hand.

Hepburn's claim that frames importantly detach their contents from their surroundings is true enough, but it doesn't necessarily entail the anti-framist conclusion to which it is taken. Every act of discernment detaches content from background. Every sensory conspectus gathers a collection of impressions into some kind of whole. There is nothing special about the frame that requires a distinctive act of aesthetic discrimination. A sculpture is set apart from its background as something worth contemplating for its own set of reasons. But a rock crystal is equally set apart as an object worth contemplating, for its own very different set of reasons. Detachment is a socially determined and infinitely malleable condition. If frames do the job in one aesthetic context, it is perfectly acceptable that something *equivalent* to frames does the job in another. The obvious fact that there are no frames (in the familiar sense) in nature doesn't imply that human intelligence approaching nature doesn't inevitably do something like framing. And doing so need not always be a bad thing.

Secondly, Hepburn's claim that frames affirm the completeness of a work (in a way that violates natural incompleteness) can be squared with the familiar practice of taking this or that conspectus of natural objects as complete-for-relevant-purposes. It is important to remember that aesthetic regard is not the only, and not always the most important, view we take on natural objects. The indentations on my thumb that make up a fingerprint are natural. They are what they are, bounded and confined by my thumb, and ready for recording by people who demand an entirely personal reference to myself. I would argue that natural framing by conventional reference to fingerprints as configurations of finger skin contours can lead us to as much completeness as the frame around, say, Velásquez' *Las Meninas*. It all depends upon what purposes we have in mind when we think of this or that thing as importantly complete or incomplete.

Las Meninas is, in fact, the perfect illustration of my point. This is a painting about frames. It shows us frames upon frames—frames around paintings, a doorway, an easel, a mirror, and, of course, around itself. But no one who looks at this painting intelligently fails to feel implicated in the framing process the painting portrays. We are, it reminds us, all caught up in the boundaries and borders that make us what we are. Here Velásquez, who portrays himself in the work, looking out at potential viewers while painting on a huge easel whose surface we cannot see, seems to be saying (among many other things), "If you, the viewer, think you are outside the picture—and hence outside the frame—you are mistaken." Hepburn wasn't wrong to say that frames make us especially aware of their content as opposed to what is cut off from that content. But it is a mistake to think that the awareness that happens because of the frame is confined to what lies wholly within the frame. We always and inevitably think beyond the borders that confine our attention. And we realize as we do so that our thinking this way is facilitated by the focus the borders provide.

Are natural objects properly to be regarded aesthetically as complete or incomplete? Hepburn's view is that our perspective on these objects should always be tentative and provisional, just because it is in our interest to think of natural things as opening themselves up to imaginative play, thus as remaining essentially incomplete. But, again, it seems to me that completeness and incompleteness here are elastic and context-relative terms. Just as no one seriously contemplating a framed artwork takes the aesthetic experience it evokes to be strictly bounded by its frame, no one seriously encountering natural beauty in an unframed context should take it to be strictly unbounded.

The most prominent exponent of the second strand of anti-framism is Allen Carlson. Carlson opposes the idea that the aesthetic experience of natural objects requires framing (or its equivalent) because the business of framing is one of imposing static conditions, whereas the business of appreciating natural objects is necessarily dynamic, requiring an evolving and ever-changing appreciation of objects through interaction with them. He calls the distinction between art as framed and nature as unframed "an obvious but important" difference, reflecting the fact that, when traditional artworks are framed, "formal qualities are in large part determined by the frame."[6]

I think what he has in mind is this. Certain qualities in artworks depend upon the organizing force of the frame in that they come into being only through the design that takes place once the frame encloses its contents and thus presents them as a display of this-and-no-more. A painting, for example, becomes a composition only through its dimensional limits, limits that make it possible for the various patches of color laid on the canvas to form a composition in their relation to each other and to these limits. A symphony is heard as formally constrained by its conventional organization within movements adding up to an aesthetic whole. Formal qualities are those features of enjoyable arrangement that come into existence in this way. It is, Carlson says, because the frame is static and the aesthetic object is appreciated within the frame that formal qualities become "an important determinate aspect of the work," and can be "easily appreciated and evaluated," as they must be if the work is to be fully and correctly evaluated.[7] But in the natural environment, he says, the notion of a static frame is both inapt and distortive. And for this reason it is inappropriate to a proper appreciation of natural beauty.

As Carlson sees it, the natural environment can appear to have formal qualities only when a viewer *imposes* a frame on it. This is an imposition bound to be partial and incomplete in that "for any part of the environment there are a near infinity of possible frames and positions that would in turn produce a near infinity of different formal qualities in a near infinity of different ways."[8]

It is because the perspective one takes toward aesthetic qualities in the environment is properly dynamic rather than static that the problem of infinities piled upon infinities occurs. One doesn't just stand there looking at nature as one might look at Constable's *"Water-meadows near Salisbury."* One goes into it, or through it, or around it, and in so doing renders both the notion of framing and its attendant formal qualities otiose. I take it that Carlson thinks this result is inevitable because an ever-shifting or constantly revised frame is really no frame at all, and because contents composed by an endless series of frames are not really composed. He sums up his argument as follows:

> [O]ne cannot both be in the environment that one appreciates and frame that environment; if one appreciates the environment by being in it, it is not a framed environment that one appreciates. Consequently, framing itself must be seen as an inappropriate way of attempting to aesthetically appreciate and evaluate the natural environment.[9]

Seen as an argument against conceptions of natural aesthetic experience that treat the natural environment as "scenery," or a sequence of "views" taken up for serial delectation, this observation is certainly true. But it carries no weight against a conception of natural aesthetic experience that treats natural objects—whether singular or in groups—simply as things we become aware of as the objects are corralled in various ways by concepts, categories, and a wealth of more informal devices.

For one thing, the static/dynamic distinction incorporated in this view is inherently suspect. Our regard for framed artworks is not made static by the fact that they are framed. Nor is our regard for natural objects made dynamic just because they are unframed. The frame around *Las Meninas* confines and organizes its ingredients. It doesn't circumscribe our sense of what that painting is or what it tells us today. Undisclosed elements are part of most artworks, and awareness of them may be essential to their appreciation, and at least enhances our appreciation of them. The devices of allusion, parody, mythic embodiment, political satire, and so on, depend upon them. Our sense of a work's place in the give-and-take of artistic statement depends upon them. Our sense of what the work means to us as an interpretive audience depends upon them. This is not to deny that the frame does important and irreplaceable work. It is only to say that it doesn't do all the work of making the artwork what it is for us. Similarly, the apparent unboundedness of natural aesthetic experience shouldn't be thought to nullify the interpretive influence of focusing and organizing elements in our attention that serve to limit, and thus make cognizable and appreciable, parts of the natural panorama.

It is important to remember that appreciation of the beauty of an environment is quite a different thing from the aesthetic regard directed to its ingredients. When we are thinking of a wilderness, an ecosystem, or a stream, the absence of limiting conditions, or frames, may be essential to our valuing the thing as a continuous, organically integrated whole. As Carlson puts it, "the natural environment … has a certain openness and indeterminateness that makes it an unlikely place to find formal qualities."[10] This stance may be particularly valuable if we are concerned with the integration of aesthetic and other values in preserving and protecting what is valuable in our natural environment. Carlson's assault on frames in regard to the *environment at large* doesn't seem to carry as much force against natural *objects*—my fingerprint, the pattern of dust on last summer's picnic table, the sparkling cave of crystal in a geode, or fingers of lightning against a night sky—that seem discretely appreciable.

To the charge that things within nature are discretely appreciable, Carlson's response is that cutting nature up into pieces for delectation is tantamount to turning it into scenes, or scenery. It is an enterprise that is as false and foolish as the eighteenth- and nineteenth-century fascination with looking at nature through a "Claude-glass," or the twentieth-century tourist gimmick of admiring coastal scenery through a camera obscura.[11] But articulating the world we didn't make into elements whose beauty we can appreciate in a way that is independent of our admiration for the whole need be no concession to the scenery cult. Suppose I train my attention on a dandelion in my front yard. Here is a perfectly natural thing, something I didn't plan for, let alone welcome. But I can nevertheless enjoy its wonderful symmetrical petal display, its intense color, its elevation on a slender stalk. Not everyone will concede that dandelions are beautiful, but the judgment is possible. And it is possible quite independently of any overall judgment about the natural environment, the dandelion's place in it, or in my lawn. It would be just as absurd to think that anyone who takes the humble dandelion to be beautiful *must* see its beauty as deriving from its meritorious aesthetic place in a larger environment as it would be to regard it as just one more attractive element in the ambient scenery.

Carlson's invocation of the Claude-glass as a false frame obscures the operation of many framing devices we conventionally and constantly employ in our engagement with natural objects. Suppose at the end of a long and enjoyable trek, a hiker discovers in her jacket pocket a thistle head that had fallen into it somewhere along the way. As she turns it over in her hand, she takes stock of the fabulous intertwining of its parts, the subtle gradations of its colors, the contrasting solidity of its core and delicacy of its tendrils, its feel, and its faint scent. There is a perfectly familiar and secure sense in which her judgment that the thistle head is beautiful can be taken to be valid without resort to the aesthetic context out of which it was extracted. It is beautiful, she thinks, and the "it" that controls her judgment is simply the physical borders of the object itself. In this respect, her judgment is framed in the way a similar judgment about the aesthetic value of a particular sculpture might be framed. Just as, in one sense, the thistle can be understood ultimately only in its biological setting, so can the sculpture be understood only in its artistic and cultural setting. But just as, in another sense, the thistle can be appreciated simply for what it is—what it presents to the senses—so the sculpture can be enjoyed for its distinctive sensible presence. For that matter, just as the thistle's aesthetically admirable qualities are the effects of its evolution, so are the sculpture's.

The lesson to be drawn from these observations is that part and whole are not so easily articulated as anti-framists of our second kind suppose. We certainly have one sort of aesthetic experience in exploring natural environments with all of our senses. But, we must not think that that experience (which is never of "the whole," but can at most be "a whole") should obliterate or denigrate the experience of natural elements that are its parts. The fact that there is no frame for the whole doesn't entail the non-existence of framing devices that make its parts appreciable.

NATURE FRAMED

There are countless ways in which we habitually frame natural objects for aesthetic delectation. Carlson's attack on formal qualities in the appreciation of the natural environment need not be taken as a blanket indictment of formal qualities in the appreciation of its parts. Many beautiful natural objects are more-or-less self-framed.[12] This seems to have been the case in the example of the thistle head, offered above. How could anyone look at a dandelion, or a rock, or a thumbprint, as anything other than a thing framed by its physical limits? How could anyone think that someone uninformed about the grand interdependence of everything in the natural environment couldn't still make a safe call about the beauty of a rabbit that has wandered into her backyard?

Say that our specimen observer finds this rabbit beautiful and, asked to tell us why, points out the appealing interplay of its colors, the sheen of its fur, the delicacy and poise of its movements, and so on, and so forth. And if asked why all of this made her think the rabbit beautiful, she says that in overall appearance it reminded her of Dürer's famous rabbit drawing, and in its movements it reminded her of Thumper, the cartoon rabbit in the Disney movie *Bambi*. Should it be an indictment of this aesthetic judgment that it turns to artifacts for its references, rather than taking stock of the wider environment in which the rabbit is involved? Pro-framists think not. The rabbit isn't just a rabbit. Even as it is observed in the backyard, it can be contemplated within at least two artistic traditions, engraving and film. It is recognized not just for what it is but for what it suggests about the notion of rabbithood we carry forward in our culture. Many of us may not agree with the way our specimen observer sees the rabbit. But we cannot deny that the way she sees the rabbit is thoughtful, responsive to sensory qualities that normally count in beauty judgments, and yet fully aware that the rabbit in question is a natural object.

Carlson denigrates the aesthetic value of scenes. But scenes are simply evaluative takes on natural settings. Often they are pleasing for the very reasons that those natural settings are pleasing. One needn't see them as epitomes of postcard picturesqueness to appreciate them. A scene may be made a scene by its natural borders. A view out of a cave, if beautiful, is controlled by the walls of the cave that help to make it a beautiful view. A walk on the beach may be made whole and aesthetically appreciable by its having a recognizable beginning, middle, and end. A microscopic natural object might be rendered beautiful not just by its sensible contents but by their relation to the visual field within which it is framed. A medium-sized natural object (e.g., an elk) might be considered to be framed by its own physical dimensions, and appreciated for its beauty in those terms. We constantly and habitually organize parts and wholes in our experience, whether we are dealing with natural objects or artifacts.[13] We don't live life as a vast undifferentiated panorama of experience. We frame what we experience as we go along.

My point is that framing in the aesthetic sense is a lot different from framing in the physical sense. Frames around pictures are simply emblems of the wider business of framing that we engage in all the time. If I see the thistle head as a thistle head rather than as a miscellaneous weed or as a piece of trash, that will be because I can call up a category, or frame, within which I can regard it. The categories Kendall Walton identified as importantly determinative of our aesthetic judgments about art are examples of the carving-up process that is involved in all aesthetic experience.[14] But they are not the most prevalent examples. Many of the ways we isolate natural objects for aesthetic regard are inarticulate. Some natural objects we deem beautiful are bounded by their names. This, for example, is a beautiful gladiolus. And it is beautiful *as* a gladiolus. It isn't a lily, and might not be beautiful as a lily.[15] In many circumstances, the very classification into which the object falls sometimes puts us in a position to decide what features count toward its being correctly deemed beautiful. But many other natural objects of aesthetic attention are not bounded by names or categories. The gentle pit-a-pat of water dripping from dozens of springlets into a narrow gorge. The odd soft-hard feel of tiny zeolite crystals in the fissure of a sea ledge. The way silhouetted forms interplay and overlap in a forested horizon at twilight. Odd catches of sea-marsh fragrance. The taste left by a weed stem one has been idly chewing on. And so on and on. Even if we should agree that it is an aesthetic mistake and a denigration of nature to think of environmental beauty as nothing other than a series of scenes, framed and composed for our enjoyment as quasi-artworks, we needn't deny that we often gather together the elements of our experience of nature into wholes as a way of focusing attention on them, experiencing *them* against their background. Sometimes this does amount to looking at nature in the way we look at art. Sometimes it doesn't. The occasional act of seeing a mountain setting as the very thing that might make for a great landscape painting is no more injurious to our sense of the beauty of the natural environment than the occasional act of thinking how much a certain birdsong is like one of the recorder parts in a Telemann quartet.

Jerome Stolnitz is a leading pro-framist in regard to natural aesthetics. In *Aesthetics and the Philosophy of Art Criticism*, he argues that

> [a]lthough nature lacks a frame when it simply exists, apart from human perception, this is not true when it is apprehended aesthetically. Then the spectator himself imposes a frame on the spectacle of nature. He selects what he is going to attend to aesthetically and himself sets boundaries to it. We all do so at one time or another.[16]

The business of setting boundaries Stolnitz mentions can be accomplished in a great many ways. The most obvious, of course, is the way the landscape painter employs when she holds up an empty frame, or her hands, determining that just this much and no more will be the range of her aesthetic attention. This is a familiar means of converting the experience of unorganized natural phenomena into scenery, or a scene. But, we are also selecting a range of objects for aesthetic attention and setting boundaries when we simply decide that this cloud mass and not that, this tree and not that, this section of the pond surface and not that is what we want to have as the focus of our experience. When we do this, scene and scenery may be the last things in our minds. We want to take aesthetic stock of the natural objects that capture our attention, and nothing more.

How do we do it? We draw upon memory, imagination, and our culturally acquired capacity to direct attention in such a way as to put some things in the foreground of awareness and others in the background. A fern frond can be made to stand out from a crowd of similar fronds on a cliff face just by deciding to pay close attention to it and not the others. One could equally decide to pay attention to a cluster of five fronds, or only to their stalks, or to the way they are swaying in the breeze, or the intensity of the color in their veins. In deliberate acts of selective attention, we informally frame and reframe natural objects of sensory awareness all the time. Not every informal act of framing, of course, will produce an aesthetic experience. The frame is only a precondition of the processes of reflection and delectation that can take place within it.

Stolnitz quotes with favor a famous remark of Santayana's: "A landscape to be seen has to be composed."[17] The subtle truth behind this gnomic statement is that *some* measure of bounding and interpretation is needed if the observer is to turn the restless, endless sensory field into appreciable wholes. Here we may wish to recall that Aristotle, who never spoke of the beauty of landscapes, insisted that the possibility of beauty turns on the concept of limitation. Limit, as he saw it, is what makes it possible to take natural objects as wholes, so that their parts may be regarded as composed, or not. If well composed, according to the canons of suitability specific to it, a natural object might be beautiful, and otherwise not. Drawing on this thought, we can generalize the point Santayana was making: To be seen as beautiful, a natural object has to be composed. And to be composed, it must be bounded, so that its parts can be parts of a whole.

Carlson's attack on what he calls the "scenery cult" portrays its proponents as busy converting raw environmental beauty into framed scenes that charm in the way picture postcards charm, by articulating what is essentially limitless into compositions whose formal characteristics (balance, unity, etc.) can then be admired. In his most compelling illustration of this mistake, a guest in a cabin with a picture window looks out upon a mountain-ringed lake and admires what he sees encompassed by the window frame as a splendid scene. But, by moving back into the cabin, he can spoil the effect of the "picture" by adopting a perspective from which the characteristic of balance is lost as the top of a mountain is lopped off by the frame, as in a bad snapshot. To get the beauty straight and free from forced composition, all he has to do is step outside the cabin and look about.[18] But, look about and see what? It seems to me that, outside the cabin, the guest is indeed freer to look first here and then there, taking stock of this and then that aspect of his surroundings. Yet, if he is to see beauty in nature (and not just gather a general sense of the beauty *of* nature), he may well see it as inhering in a beautiful *something*—a thing, a feature of a thing, a combination of features, or the interplay of some features with others. And for there to be a something there to see, some limitation of his awareness must be imposed.

It is not, contrary to what Carlson suggests, simply to facilitate awareness of formal qualities in nature (which he thinks are destined to be a relatively insignificant aspect of aesthetic appreciation of the environment in any case) that the guest in front of the cabin will frame, or focus, his awareness as he looks at the mountains, the lake, and so on. Rather, he must do something of this sort in order to see what he sees as anything at all, let alone as a possible subject of beauty. One can imagine him gazing out at the natural splendor and saying under his breath "how beautiful!" This exclamation is overheard by another guest, who asks "*What* is beautiful?" To which he responds "Well, all of this" sweeping his arm before him. But gestures of this kind are notoriously ambiguous and uninformative. So his companion presses him for clarification. "Do you mean the mountain? The lake? The play of light on the water? What, exactly?" And at this point we have reached a crucial fork in the theoretic road. If we go in one direction, the inarticulate gestures continue, and there cannot be any prospect of communicating the character or content of his aesthetic experience to his correspondent. In this case the most we can say is that the beauty he perceives seems to be *out there* in a general perfusion of the sensible environment. If we go in the other direction, he considers just what feature or features of the sensible environment present themselves as beautiful—not, or not only, scenic, but beautiful. And in that case, he will abandon the frameless awareness indicated by the sweep of his arm in favor of a more focused, more considered judgment about what counts in a particular beauty judgment. The first path preserves the sense that natural beauty is best understood as unframed, but it does so at the cost of focus and communicability. The second path embraces the idea that beauty judgments require some form of limitation or focal conspectus to make them comprehensible, but it does so at the cost of the dynamic, engaged appreciation of a limitless environment.

THE PARADOX AND ITS RESOLUTION

The paradox of framing derives from the tension that this divergence of paths engenders. We can formulate it this way: On the one hand, it seems that nothing can be comprehended as an object of appreciation unless it is framed or bounded in some way. On the other hand, it seems that appreciative experience of natural environments requires the dissolving and penetrating of all boundaries in favor of a dynamic and engaged experience. Thus, in one sense, frames seem indispensable to aesthetic experience as a precondition of comprehensible appreciation while, in another, they impair proper regard for natural beauty, converting limitless sensible subjects into mere scenes or compositions.

The usual strategy for resolving paradoxes involves taking a closer look at apparently incompatible premises to see whether they really do imply what they are usually taken to imply. If it can be shown that the way in which the premises are formulated disguises ambiguities or possibilities of reinterpretation, then rereading the premises in one way rather than another does away with their apparent incompatibility. That is exactly how we need to resolve the framing paradox. The source of the problem, as I see it, lies in an overly narrow conception of "frame" that has been assumed throughout the debate. Both framists and anti-framists speak of frames as enclosing their aesthetic contents and helping to compose those contents, making possible an appreciation of their balance, unity, harmony, and so on. Framists think this a virtue. Anti-framists think it a vice, at least as it is applied to nature. But neither side fully appreciates the nuanced way in which the other deals with the line between inside and outside.

Although it is certainly true that picture frames facilitate form appreciation in a way that is relatively rigid and impermeable, our experience of paintings, for example, often penetrates the frame by taking stock of undisclosed elements that are part of the painting as much as is the paint on the canvas. To take an obvious example, a proper appreciation of most medieval paintings will require familiarity with the iconographic code that lends significance to some of their elements. That code is not within the frame; it is instead a part of the work that the framed composition calls up. The aesthetic experience one may have in contemplating such a painting—the beauty one might find in it, say—is *focused*, but not *confined*, by the frame. And the same is true of many other features of paintings in all periods and places. Irony, parody, homage, political message, and so on, are important parts of artworks not presented on their framed surface. Nor are the ways in which a particular painting resonates with recent world events. Or the way it unintentionally echoes work done in another age or place. Or the way its display in a particular museum space creates harmony or tension between it and other paintings, and so on. Yet all of these factors can properly contribute to one's aesthetic experience of the painting as it is presented.

The same contrast between focus and confinement is obviously true of other artistic media as well. The novels we most want to read are those that refuse to stay resolutely within their covers. When we buy tickets to watch plays, we hope and expect our experience will transcend the limits of the stage to connect up with other valuable things in our lives. And the same is obviously true of dance, opera, sculpture, gardens, and other art forms. Even though the various ways in which works in all of these art forms are framed do the important work of focusing our regard on a definite *this* to be appreciated, it is rarely ever the artist's intent to restrict the audience's attention to what is displayed within the frame.

In the natural environment, the notion of what is framed and what is not is equally malleable. Our everyday experience of natural objects frequently shows us that framing can provide focus without confinement. Here's a plain and simple illustration. Once, when I was out for a walk on a blustery afternoon in Minneapolis, I came upon a site where the particular contours of the surrounding buildings and trees funneled the wind into a confined space where it swirled around continuously. Having gathered up an assortment of colorful late-autumn leaves and twigs and other miscellaneous things, it swept them along in a huge, oscillating loop, two or three feet off the ground, dipping and bobbing, but never letting up enough to release its hold on them. The shimmering cavalcade of objects winding their way along the loop and back again presented an arresting, delightful spectacle. I was so struck by its odd beauty that I hurried back to summon some friends to share the experience. Fortunately, the wind had not abated, and the freakish whirl of leaves was there for them to enjoy as well. We all stood watching this spectacle for several minutes, grinning admiringly and not saying a word.

Now, if a passing aesthetician had asked us whether we were having an aesthetic experience, I am perfectly confident we would all have said we were.[19] And if she asked whether we found what were observing beautiful—or an example of natural beauty—I am sure several of us, at least, would have assented. I am equally sure that not a one of us regarded the lovely maelstrom as a scene, or composition, or nature-picture set up within some imagined frame. Yet it is clear that in this experience the beauty we discovered depended upon the propensity of wind made visible by the leaves to focus our attention on a certain changing-but-more-or-less-constant space. Within that space, the beauty of the experience was built up by a compounding of the swift and sinuous motion of the leaves, the kaleidoscopic display of their colors as they tumbled about, the patterns that emerged and were immediately eclipsed by other patterns as various bits of things moved past each other, the pulsing, rhythmic pace of it all, and so on and so forth. Appreciation of the beauty of the phenomenon could come about only after a localizing, or focusing of awareness. It hardly matters whether we call it a frame.

Just as artworks sometimes refuse to stay within their frames, so in an aesthetic experience such as this one, intelligence and imagination carry us beyond the immediate phenomenon. That imagination should carry us beyond the natural object itself is quite a proper, let alone an inevitable element of our appreciation, as Hepburn himself is happy to point out:

> [We] delight in the fact that the forms of the natural world offer scope for the exercise of the imagination, that leaf pattern chimes with vein pattern, cloud form with mountain form and mountain form with human form.… Indeed, when nature is pronounced to be 'beautiful'—not in the narrower sense of that word, which contrasts 'beautiful' with 'picturesque' or 'comic,' but in the wide sense equivalent to 'aesthetically excellent'—an important part of our meaning is just this, that nature's forms do provide this scope for imaginative play. For that is surely not analytically true; it might have been otherwise.[20]

Hepburn claims that this fortunate propensity of nature to stimulate our imagination profitably is an asset bestowed on it by its unframedness. Artworks are, relatively speaking, bound in their meaning by the frames and interpretive guides and the like that explain what those frames compose. But I am suggesting that this way of putting things both overstates the controlling function of the frame in art and understates the attention-focusing function of informal framing devices in our experience of nature.

There is, of course, good reason to be cautious about opening the door to imagination in the aesthetic experience of natural objects. As I mentioned in chapter 2, the line between appropriate and inappropriate contributions from this quarter is very hard to draw. That problem, you will recall, lies at the center of my criticism of the non-conceptualist position advanced by Emily Brady, Arnold Berleant, Noël Carroll, and others. Still, it may not be impossible to draw an adequately clear line between appropriate and inappropriate imaginative elaborations of an experience. Indeed, it seems to me that aesthetic grownups generally have a pretty good intuitive grasp of this distinction. To some members of my little band of onlookers, the leaf maelstrom might have called to mind the hectic pace of modern American life, to others the relentless cycle of seasons and years, and to yet others the blessed-and-doomed dance of Paolo and Francesca in Dante's *Divine Comedy*. All of these reflections seem to be capable of intensifying and enlarging the experience without losing sight of its material manifestation. If, in the fugitive imagination of a given spectator, the wind and leaves called to mind the need to answer a flurry of e-mail messages, the messiness of Uncle Henry's wig, or the green swirl of Gladys's gown at the prom, no one—including that particular spectator—would be likely to deem these associations aesthetically pertinent. Undeniably, however, there are many borderline cases and no hard-and-fast rules for discriminating between pertinent and inapt products of imagination relative to a given natural object. This is a problem to which I will return in the next chapter.

If we think of framing simply as concentration of attention within limits—not concerning ourselves with the question of the potential of those limits to control the elements it confines into a composition—we must concede that every aesthetic experience of nature is framed. It is framed because it depends first and foremost upon the senses, and each of these has a limited range. It is easy to make too much of this condition. This sort of framing is a limitation that is, like many other essentially human limitations, generally indiscernible in the conduct of life. But it is also easy to make too little of it. Whether one is standing outside the cabin looking at the vast panorama or standing within it looking through the window, one is looking at what is necessarily only a *selection* from the great inventory of natural phenomena. It obviously follows that nature as a whole cannot be appreciated aesthetically and that we are therefore stuck with finding beauty, sublimity, etc. in parts of nature rather than in a limitless and therefore insensible whole. To this plain fact of limitation, we may add the fact that our limited capacities of attention and comprehension, let alone culturally inculcated limitations on what we may become aware of, inevitably circumscribe our ability to experience natural phenomena. This conclusion flies in the face of at least the most ambitious forms of "aesthetic integralism," the notion that natural beauty emerges when, and only when, we regard the whole of nature (just as the beauty of a poem emerges when, and only when, we regard the whole of the poem).

As Wladyslaw Tatarkiewicz pointed out, aesthetic integralism arose in the middle ages as a metaphysical and religious doctrine.[21] Present-day philosophers are, for the most part, no longer confident of assertions made about nature as a divinely-ordained whole, seen *sub specie aeternitatis*. And for good reason. Unless one takes the implausible position that everything in nature can be available at once to the experience of a human observer, there can be no appreciation of the whole—and *a fortiori* of the beauty of the whole—in the way that there can be appreciation of a poem whose whole is manifest to its reader. But, if nature's beauty is identified with the beauty of the whole, then, lacking the divine perspective, humans will have no access to it. Aesthetic attention to nature must be selective, therefore, if anything in it is to come into focus and qualify as beautiful. Of course, it does not follow that there are no wholes within the whole of nature to be appreciated. Far from it. The view of appreciation I develop in the next chapter makes selection of appreciable wholes (conspecti) from within the larger (and unappreciable) whole a fundamental ingredient in judgments regarding natural beauty.

In the end, the framing controversy is about the variety of limits on attention. Everyone admits that our sensory exposure to the world is limited and that our way of making sense of, or appreciating, the world to which we are exposed is also limited. Not only are the limits inevitable, they are basic conditions of the intelligibility of our sensory world. One person walks along a mountain path turning his head this way and that, listening to the wind, smelling the faint fragrance of high pine needles, feeling the gusts of frigid air on his cheeks. His awareness of all these natural qualities is informally framed, re-framed, and re-framed again as he continues his hike. If his sensory experience were utterly unframed it would be chaotic and unintelligible. Certainly it would be unappreciable. Another person peers through a microscope to examine a volvox colony. She locates it in a dense biotic soup of other animate and inanimate matter, and she isolates it for attention simply by seeing it as a volvox colony, taking its physical limits as the limits of her regard, and pushing all the rest of what appears in her optical field into the background. She has framed the volvox colony for attention—and if she finds it aesthetically interesting, as a potential focus of aesthetic experience, she does so simply by allowing one set of frames (names and physical dimensions of the named objects) to subtend the larger frames of sensory awareness. A third person stops in the course of clearing a debris-clogged gutter to admire the way the oil runoff, surface froth, and slow-moving mud are catching the low-angled winter light to produce a luminous, rhythmic swirl. As he gathers this in, he turns to his fellow laborer and, looking through his hands with thumbs at right angles, says "I wish I had a camera!"

I would insist that each of these persons (and of course the roster of similar examples could be indefinitely extended) is in a position to have an aesthetic experience involving a natural object, and hence to be in a position to appreciate natural beauty (or other natural aesthetic qualities). Those who, like Allen Carlson, insist that the proper course of appreciation lies in the direction of wide open, dynamic, picture-frame-penetrating engagement with nature are, in the end, simply promoting a preferred framing technique. Those who, like Noël Carroll, point out that certain natural expanses have features (e.g., caves, copses, clearings, etc.) that provide natural closure, and other features (e.g., moving water, bright illumination, etc.) that provide natural salience for human beings are acknowledging another framing technique.[22] Those who, like our hypothetical gutter cleaner, *do* want to impose frames—even picture frames—on natural phenomena in order to capture beautiful things in memory or in photographs are turning their backs on the broader splendors of the natural environment in order to train awareness on the aesthetic qualities of a narrower range of objects. Holding up one's hands and imagining a framed photograph is just one more way to pay attention to a limited range of sensible qualities. Each of these ways (and countless others) can be a useful approach to gathering objects of attention into a conspectus for aesthetic delectation and appraisal. Appreciation doesn't just rove endlessly and haphazardly across the sensory panorama. It must be trained on this or that, focused by our interest in taking in objects or qualities in various assortments. We *can't help* limiting our experience of nature by selecting various objects for attention at various times.

Taking an aesthetic interest in a particular natural object is an act of selective attention within other selections of attention that don't disappear in the moment of particular appreciation. They just become temporarily extraneous to the appreciation at hand. Carlson himself acknowledges that this sort of focal framing takes place all the time: "We experience our surroundings as obtrusive foreground allowing our knowledge of that environment to select certain foci of aesthetic significance and perhaps exclude others, thereby limiting our experience."[23] Limits of this sort placed on a given experience obviously do not nullify or denigrate other limits we may choose to accept on other experiences. Aesthetic experience must be experience of *something*—some object, quality, or constellation of objects and qualities—that can be drawn into attention for reflective consideration. As Arnold Berleant has pointed out, the idea that there needs to be some kind of wholeness to the object of aesthetic attention goes back to Shaftesbury, in whose hands it became closely connected with the pictorial virtues of completeness, self-sufficiency, and unity.[24] But the notion that objects of aesthetic attention must be whole (i.e., must be comprehensible foci of aesthetic significance) is detachable from all of these named virtues. To say that an object of awareness is composed is not to say that it is as-if-composed-by-an-artist. Nor that it is formally balanced and controlled, as a person who acts with social grace may be said to have a composed manner. It is, instead, simply to say of a whole that its aesthetic ingredients are (as its Latin roots suggest) *presented together* before us. Not inextricably or permanently together. Not together against all or any rival aesthetic ingredients. Not together in vindication of some claim of inherent affinity or appropriate unison. Just together as the basis of what may be a coherent aesthetic experience.

From what I have said about the variability of the means by which we focus aesthetic attention in regard to natural phenomena and the variety of scope these means provide, it will be clear that the framing paradox is easily resolved in the context of appreciative practice. If by "frame" what is really implied is the selection of this or that object or constellation of objects for aesthetic attention, rival claims about nature being framed and unframed can be seen as no more than variable markers on the endless scale of aesthetic selectivity. To frame a piece of the vast environmental whole need not be to convert the selected portion into a quasi-artwork. At one point on the scale, it can be to do precisely what the conceptualists criticized in chapter 2 said we *should* do, namely to regard natural things as what they *are*, employing the appropriate categories of natural science. Categories of this sort function quite ably as frames, locating what it is that we are observing and presenting it as an integral object against its larger background. Names are also frames. To see the dandelion as a dandelion is to use its name to draw its qualities into focal awareness. At another point on the scale, to frame a natural object can be to form a nameless *experiential conspectus* rather than a scene or nature-portrait. In such a coalescence of awareness, whatever composition occurs should not be thought of as a forced integration of component elements, but rather as a *realization* of their relations in a situation of focused aesthetic awareness. In a way, this view is simply an application to the context of natural objects of the central point of John Dewey's doctrine of aesthetic value. Dewey, it will be recalled, maintained that aesthetic value of any kind emerges in the course of converting undifferentiated experience into experiences. Experiences are, in his account, units, or wholes of lived awareness with distinctive beginnings, middles, and ends. Dewey's way of putting the point has seemed to his latter-day critics to put too much emphasis on organic unity.[25] But his fundamental assertion that aesthetic value invariably arises out of experiences rendered whole and comprehensible by being articulated, i.e., by being separated out from the run of the rest of experience by acts of focal attention, correctly and powerfully expresses the importance of framing in aesthetic living.

In this chapter, I have tried to defuse a threat to coherent natural aesthetics posed by the framing paradox. The resolution I have proposed involves recognition that a) framing is inevitable if any experience whatever is to be had, b) framing need not be regarded as the confinement, as opposed to the focusing, of aesthetic attention, c) framing typically involves more frame-permeability than opposing theorists recognize, and d) rival claims about the nature of framing are generally resolvable into differences of location on the scale of aesthetic selectivity. This resolution clears the way for the important role framing may play in any theory that takes the aesthetic assessment of natural object to turn on the quality of our aesthetic experience of those objects. In the next chapter, I turn to the question of which qualities of natural experience provide a plausible basis for beauty judgments.

NOTES

1 Hepburn, "Trivial and Serious," p. 67. See also his remarks on this point in "Aesthetic Appreciation of Nature," in *Aesthetics in the Modern World*, ed. Harold Osborne (London: Thames and Hudson, 1968), pp. 51-52.

2 Hepburn, "Contemporary Aesthetics and the Neglect of Natural Beauty," p. 290.

3 Ibid.

4 Ibid., p. 291.

5 Ibid.

6 Carlson, *Aesthetics and the Environment*, pp. 35-36.

7 Ibid., p. 36.

8 Ibid.

9 Ibid., p.37.

10 Ibid.

11 Ibid., p. 32.

12 In defending the so-called "arousal model" of aesthetic appreciation, Noël Carroll points out that our emotional response to certain natural objects or groups of objects is predicated on natural closure: "Certain natural expanses have natural frames.... caves, copses, grottoes, clearings, arbors, valleys, etc. And other natural objects have features that are naturally salient for human organisms—i.e., they have features such as moving water, bright illumination, etc. that draw our attention instinctually toward them. And where our emotional arousal is predicated on either natural closure or natural salience, it makes little sense to say that our emotional responses, focused on said features, are impositions." "On Being Moved by Nature," in Kemal and Gaskell, eds., *Landscape, Natural Beauty, and the Arts*, p. 251.

13 The part-and-whole sorting is most commonly done through words and concepts: "This is that sort of thing." "This goes in that file." "No one calls it that; we call it this." And so on.

14 Kendall Walton, "Categories of Art," *Philosophical Review* 79 (1970), pp. 334-67.

15 Still, our judgment that a natural object is beautiful *can* be correct when our classification of it is mistaken. If we mistakenly thought a gladiolus was a lily, we might say it was an unusual and strangely beautiful lily. If we were subsequently to learn that it wasn't a lily after all, we might still be right in thinking that it is beautiful—not *qua* lily, and not *qua* gladiolus, but just as a flower with its very distinctive appearance.

16 Jerome Stolnitz, *Aesthetics and the Philosophy of Art Criticism: A Critical Introduction* (Boston: Houghton Mifflin, 1960), p. 48.

17 George Santayana, *The Sense of Beauty* (New York: Scribner's, 1936), p. 101.

18 Carlson, *Aesthetics and the Environment*, p. 36. He presents a similar line of criticism in "Appreciation and the Natural Environment," *Journal of Aesthetics and Art Criticism* 37 (1987) at p. 270.

19 This is not to say that every nineteenth- or twentieth-century aesthetic experience theorist would concur in our judgment, or that each of the experiences had by the several spectators was alike in all important respects. But that isn't the point. I am using the term here in the conceptually generous way developed at the end of the previous chapter.

20 Hepburn, "Contemporary Aesthetics and the Neglect of Natural Beauty," pp. 292-93.

21 Tatarkiewicz, *History*, vol. 2, p. 287. The point is discussed in chapter 3, sec. 2, above.

22 Carroll, "On Being Moved by Nature," in Kemal and Gaskell, *Landscape*, p. 251.

23 Carlson, "Appreciation and the Natural Environment," p. 273.

24 Berleant, *Aesthetics of Environment*, p. 162.

25 Sometimes we judge a thing to be beautiful not because it draws its various elements into an organic unity but because it presents contrasting or unusually juxtaposed elements in a compelling way.

CHAPTER 7

Syncretic Regard—Part I

JUDGES AND "TRUE JUDGES"

No one who has studied the history of Western philosophical speculation on aesthetic value is likely to believe that a convincing common formula for the measurement of natural beauty (or any other natural aesthetic characteristic) is attainable. After the decline of idealist aesthetics in the eighteenth century, no serious and informed thinker could suppose that there are features common and peculiar to all identifiable natural objects in virtue of which they are beautiful. If we follow the lead of those who made what I have called "the subjective turn," we will regard aesthetic judgments as ultimately dependent on qualities of experience rather than any special combination of qualities in the objects experienced. And for this reason we are bound to conclude that there can never be hard-and-fast general criteria of natural beauty, ugliness, etc. These criteria are unattainable because the factors that play into aesthetic experience are not only complex and variable, but inherently dependent on features of objects that are contextual, unpredictable in their evolution, and resistant to schemes of mensuration.

The easy conclusion to draw from all of this is that aesthetic judgments regarding natural objects are immune to philosophical ordering in the way that judgments of gustatory taste are. Some people prefer vanilla ice cream to chocolate. Others prefer strawberry to both. As philosophy is obviously and utterly incapable of resolving the differences between them by making a principled case that one flavor is actually superior to the others, it is equally incapable of resolving differences among competing claims regarding natural aesthetic qualities. Beauty, ugliness, and all other natural qualities are in the eyes of the beholder, and, as the ancient maxim declares, *de gustibus non est disputandum*, matters of taste are not to be disputed. So, if Aunt Millie, Uncle Moe, and Mandy are affected in a way that makes them think that certain objects are beautiful, who's to say they're wrong? Their being affected in the way they are is enough to settle the question. Those objects *are* beautiful. Not only that: anybody can *make* anything beautiful by experiencing it in a way that supports deeming it so. Likewise, anybody can make anything ugly by experiencing it in a way that supports deeming it so. And if one and the same thing is deemed by some people to be beautiful and others to be ugly, it is both, or neither, or whatever you please.

This is a conclusion that must be rejected. It would not only entail the inapplicability of all aesthetic theory to natural valuation but, more importantly, it would entail the unintelligibility of all discussion in which natural value judgments are compared and assessed. If any claim on any given natural aesthetic quality carries the same weight as any other claim (because it means no more than the expressed feeling or preference of one party rather than another), then there can be no sensible reflection about conflicting or contradictory assessments. And if this is the case, there can be no rational basis of comparative judgments and no basis for criticism in regard to natural aesthetic claims. To skeptics, this conclusion will present itself as the final and fatal *reductio ad absurdum* of philosophical efforts to render natural aesthetics rational and defensible. But the skeptics are wrong.

David Hume was the first philosopher to face up to this problem and propose a solution to it. In "Of the Standard of Taste," his brief but incisive investigation of the problem of reconciling diversity of taste with standards of judgment, he turned the issue of experience into an analysis of the hypothetical "true judge," equipped, through an absence of incapacities and impairments, to settle conflicts of taste. As Hume saw it, the vast diversities exhibited in aesthetic judgments might converge if they were rid of the impediments that prevent open and unbiased apprehension. There is no denying, he admits, that "beauty is no quality in things themselves: It exists merely in the mind which contemplates them; and each mind perceives a different beauty." Yet, at the same time, the experience of all peoples seems to confirm the conviction that some things more than others conduce to our aesthetic satisfaction, whatever individual responses may be. Hume's way of reconciling the individuality of aesthetic response with the demand that some preferences must count more heavily than others was to invoke the hypothetical standard of the "true judge."

Now, Hume's speculative true judge is not a Platonic autocrat, wedded to an immutable standard set for all time and independent of eccentric artistic practices, nor is he or she a pure populist, accepting as valid whatever the community majority may deem. Rather, Hume's position is that there is, despite all the apparent divergence of aesthetic opinion, an underlying tendency toward convergence of opinion, based on inclinations common to mankind but masked by prejudice, inexperience, and local tradition. This underlying tendency can be exposed by systematically negating the conditions that inhibit it. And this leads Hume to his famous declaration that sound aesthetic judgments rely on the joint verdict of true judges:

> Strong sense, united to delicate sentiment, improved by practice, perfected by comparison, and cleared of all prejudice, can alone entitle critics to this valuable character [comparative determinations of beauty]; and the joint verdict of such, wherever they are to be found, is the true standard of taste and beauty.[2]

But, where are such true judges to be found? Clearly the idea is that we are to make them up as philosophically respectable models of judgment. Hume strongly hints that, although the issue is an empirical one, subject to the same modes of investigation open to any other question of fact, it is highly unlikely that all of the capacities (or, equivalently, the lack of judgment-impairing defects and distractions) required of such a judge will be found in any one individual. Thus, our determination to rely on the judgments of the true judge is almost certainly going to turn out to be a theoretic exercise in composition, relying on imagination to project into a hypothetical individual what the hit-and-miss process of human evolution has not yet provided.[3]

It might seem that such a construct threatens ironically to collapse into the very idealism it was meant to displace. We begin with the thought that matters of taste are ineluctably individual. We observe that individual taste judgments may be clouded, distorted, or otherwise defective. To correct these imperfections and get to what the individual judgments really should be (but in the present instance aren't) we defer to the opinions of hypothetical judges whose capacities for sensory response and subsequent pertinent reflection are free of such flaws. Thus, it appears the principles of taste are taken to be grounded in experiences not our own and, indeed, to be attainable only through projections of experience beyond what you or I or anyone else may have actually had. But, if this is so, what is the difference between a standard of taste embodied in a true judge whose capacity for aesthetic appreciation is *ex hypothesi* perfect and a standard of taste embodied in an abstract ideal to which particular correct judgments asymptotically approach?

There is a difference. Aesthetic judgment along Humean lines can be shown not to collapse into idealistic judgment, cognitive or otherwise. In fact, the characteristics that set it apart from its historical predecessors provide the initial building blocks for the syncretic theory of judgment I want to defend. First we should notice that, although the aesthetic judgments of the hypothetical true judges are independent of the experience and pleasure of any individual, they are not independent of experience and pleasure in general. Hume's whole project in "Of the Standard of Taste" is to find a way to acknowledge the authority of aesthetic experience in judgment while admitting the fallibility and hence unreliability of any one person's experience. No standard will do, he says, that would allow that there could be beauty apart from anyone's experiencing it. Equally, no standard will do if it simply endorses the verdicts of everyone's judgments. Hume's great contribution on this issue is to see that a principle of judgment may be external to me in the sense that it is not one whose experiential base I currently share (or acknowledge) while remaining internal to me in the sense that it postulates as verdicts the very ones that I would reach were I freed from defects and impediments. Thus, the judgments of the judges may be seen as no more than an explication of judgments that are latent in me, and in you, and in everyone else.

There are, of course, formidable metaphysical and epistemological problems lurking in Hume's theory, and while these cannot be ignored, they must be put aside if we are to capitalize on its strengths. Hume makes extravagant claims regarding the universality (or near-universality) of correct principles of taste, the durability of objects of high aesthetic merit, and the authority of common sense, among other things. But these unsupportable declarations must not blind us to the central point of importance that emerges from Hume's essay. This is that accepting the foundation of individual experience for principles of taste need not dissolve the resulting theory in personal relativism. My claim that this rose is beautiful and yours that it is tacky are but the beginning observations in an evolving conversation that can lead toward resolution of our differences as we work at understanding and refining our initial responses.

This brings me to the second important Humean point. Just as my conversation with you about our differing aesthetic judgments may lead to the improvement of those judgments, so the pleasurable response I experience in relation to objects I find beautiful, elegant, sublime, and so on can itself propel me to continue to reflect on my initial response, thus improving it. Peter Jones summarizes this aspect of Hume's theory as follows:

> Someone becomes conscious of pleasure in a certain ob-
> ject, and this induces him to pay closer attention to it,
> with the aim of sustaining the pleasure. If the spectator
> can make sense, in some way, of what he perceives, he will
> experience new sentiments that may loosely be described
> as enhancing the original ones.[4]

Because Hume regards the core of beauty judgments as a certain kind of pleasure, and because it is a commonplace that pleasures can be immediate and momentary, we might suppose that those judgments come "in a flash," as it were. This is clearly not the case. Beautiful things don't just draw attention; they reward it. This reward is paid out over time, and in a variety of coin—feelings, thoughts, associations, comparisons, contrasts, and so on. As these elements enhance the initial experience that provided their impetus, the experience of beauty grows and deepens. And as the experience grows and deepens, the judgment of beauty it supports is affirmed and strengthened. This is a process of reflection and reinforcement distinctive of the empiricist tradition and alien to its idealistic forebears. It seems to me that the prospect of experiential growth it entails figures importantly into any account of natural beauty judgment that doesn't trivialize the focal notion of aesthetic experience.

The third point I want to mention is not entirely explicit in the text of Hume's essay; but is clearly implied by the way Hume characterizes the process of judgment committed to the hands of the "true judges." Empiricist that he was, Hume was disposed to regard aesthetic verdicts as reflecting the accumulation of evidence sufficient to pass an agreed-upon criterial line rather than the presence or absence of some qualifying feature or set of features. Accordingly, (unlike the idealists) he did not regard aesthetic judgment as a pass-fail system in which partial compliance with a standard is rendered nugatory. Rather, Hume's view was that determining that a thing is beautiful (or elegant, or ugly, etc.) is a matter of identifying and fastening on the right features of experiential evidence, distinguishing them from others, drawing on the rest of one's experience to make comparisons, observe subtle differences, etc., all of which is a process of cumulative appreciation and a matter of degrees. When the evidence adds up sufficiently, a real (albeit indistinct) criterial line is crossed. Short of that line, there are graded degrees of appreciable qualities that are to be savored as well. Beyond that line, additional degrees of aesthetic commendation are attainable. The graduated virtues of aesthetic acuity peculiar to the true judges are, in a way, a reflection of the need to make scalar and threshold judgments of this kind. The threshold nature of Humean beauty judgment is a point George Dickie applauds in *The Century of Taste*, a study that places Hume at the forefront of eighteenth-century taste theory:

> Hume realized ... that beauty as an overall evaluation of a work of art (or a natural object) is a threshold phenomenon; that is, such an object might have one or more beauty-making characteristics and still not be beautiful. On Hume's kind of theory, an object would be beautiful when it has one beauty-making characteristic in sufficiently high degree to make it beautiful, or when it has two or more beauty-making characteristics, each in high enough degree to suffice to make it beautiful, or when it has two or more beauty-making characteristics that somehow work together to make it beautiful.[5]

This characterization of Humean beauty judgment is perfectly in line with the view I presented earlier about the cumulative-to-a-threshold character of aesthetic experience claims in general (what I called the "sorites" interpretation). It seems to me unavoidable that a satisfactory theory of aesthetic judgment regarding natural beauty will admit of degrees of partial qualification and will deem full qualification to be a determination that, taking stock of all relevant features of a given phenomenon, a threshold has been crossed.

The analysis of aesthetic judgment I present in this chapter is Humean in the sense that it accepts the three foundational premises I have outlined above. First, it acknowledges that judgments regarding natural beauty (and other natural aesthetic qualities) are subjective, but only in the sense that they are tied to aesthetic experience in general, rather than to any one individual's personal experience. This position acknowledges the fallibility of individual experience and yet ties judgment to that experience by maintaining that the correct judgment is that which the individual would have reached (and can be admitted to have already partially and imperfectly reached) were it not for impediments that the individual does admit to be impediments or can reasonably be held to accept as impediments. Second, it acknowledges that natural beauty judgments reflect a propensity in beautiful objects to reward awareness by sustaining pleasurable attention and by enhancing it. This position denies the commonplace denunciation of aesthetic judgment that its claims reduce to tingles and buzzes. The claim that a natural object is beautiful is necessarily more than an assertion that it produces pleasure. A drink of cold water on a hot day produces pleasure, too. The distinctive kind of pleasure involved in the appreciation of a natural object's beauty entails a deepening or reorientation of the initial impression, often involving reflection on similarities (or disparities) between this object and others. And this deepening or reorientation takes time. Third, my analysis acknowledges that the business of aesthetic judgment is conducted on a gradient, where partial contributions accumulate to produce a result that may be deemed to have crossed a threshold. Beneath the threshold, partial contributions can be acknowledged as approaches to the end result, and beyond the threshold, extraordinary contributions can be acknowledged as making a case for exceptional degrees of beauty—magnificence, for example. The notion of partial contributions I have in mind admits the confluence of appraisals from widely divergent points of view. But it supposes, as Hume did, that there are a good number of commonalities that can be discovered beneath the apparent diversity, and that this fact undergirds the rationality of aesthetic judgment.

My theory is Humean in one more, very important respect. As they parse Hume's numerous controversial claims, modern readers of his essay may easily overlook its overall purpose. That purpose was to provide an emerging public who had the means and leisure to indulge aesthetic pleasure with the tools of taste. It was not to cleave between the worthy and the unworthy in the aesthetic world these people encountered. It was to indicate ways of honing skills everyone has to some extent in order to find value in what everyone can experience to some extent. Partial was as important as perfect, and the common judgment was as significant as the king's. This is precisely the spirit in which I offer the following account of natural aesthetic judgment. Its object is to identify features of attention and appraisal most conducive to the kind of aesthetic experience that warrants positive natural beauty judgments without indulging in the endless and pointless quarrel over thresholds.

I should point out, however, that my account is non-Humean in several important ways. It rejects Hume's hypothetical judges as a reference standard. It rejects Hume's extravagant claims about universal agreement on unclouded aesthetic judgments. And it rejects Hume's itemization of the qualities germane to sound judgment. In its conception of aesthetic experience, my account is much more indebted to Dewey, Beardsley, and Stolnitz than to Hume. And, as will become evident, it collects bits and pieces from the entire line of philosophic thought I traced in the preceding chapters. My theory is meant to be syncretic in more than one sense. Its concept of what counts as aesthetic experience is meant to draw together various threads of previous Western philosophical speculation into a coherent scheme acceptable to the modern sensibility. It is also syncretic in that, when it turns to the forum of qualified appreciators, it provides room for a developmental notion of aesthetic apprehension, one that expands and matures in the course of an individual's life. Appreciation has its apt elements at all stages of experience. The apprehension of natural beauty by the third-grader should not be discredited simply because it is not as knowledgeable or as sophisticated as that of the ecology graduate student. We do grow up aesthetically. In what follows I identify prominent elements of appreciation that (among many others) can be learned, amplified, and refined in the course of aesthetic maturation.

THE NATUREWORLD

Claims are cognitive if they state or depict facts and are for that reason capable of being true or false. They are non-cognitive when they function in non-statemental ways, typically by expressing positive or negative attitudes toward things. "The elevation of Mt. Hood is 11,235 ft." expresses a cognitive claim, as does "Most Oregonians find Mt. Hood to be beautiful," whereas "Hooray for redwood forests!" does not. "Subjective" and "objective" mark different ways in which cognitive claims are true, when they are true. A cognitive claim is subjective if its truth is dependent on the beliefs or attitudes of the person making the claim. It is objective if its truth is dependent on something other than these beliefs and attitudes. "Purple seems a more somber color than red" expresses a subjective claim, whereas "the rusty blackbird's song is a split creak like a rusty hinge"[6] expresses an objective one. Accordingly, an aesthetic theory of natural objects is both cognitivist and objectivist if it holds that natural beauty judgments are statements that are true or false, and that they are made true or false by facts independent of the beliefs of those who make them. It is cognitivist and subjectivist if it holds that natural beauty judgments are true or false statements, and that their truth or falsity is dependent on the beliefs of those who make them. And it is non-cognitivist (and therefore necessarily subjectivist) if it holds that these judgments aren't statements of fact at all, but declarations of the feelings or attitudes of those who make them.

Now, which of these descriptions fits the theory of natural beauty I am presenting in this book? None of them and all of them. No one of the positions I have distinguished fits my theory *as a whole* because my theory recognizes natural beauty judgments of importantly different kinds, some of which involve cognitive claims, and others non-cognitive claims, some subjective claims and others objective claims. Equally importantly, my theory holds that aesthetically mature and reflective natural beauty judgments inevitably involve a layering, or nesting, of claims of all of these sorts. So, all of the descriptions apply to *parts* of my account, even if none of them applies to the whole. All of this may seem vague and evasive. But it really isn't. Let me explain.

As I see it, in saying of a natural object that it is beautiful, one might be saying at least five quite different things. First, one might be doing no more than expressing an emotion of a certain intensity. The plum eater, for example, exclaims "delicious," but he might equally have said "beautiful," or just "mmmmmm!" Children who are just learning to appreciate natural objects for their aesthetic qualities are notoriously indiscriminate in their expressions of approval. That is, once they come to understand that "beautiful" is a term of strong approval their elders are disposed to use with respect to various objects, they use it too. But at this stage they mean (and *can* mean) no more by this than something close to "I like it very much!" Let us call natural beauty judgments that amount to non-cognitive declarations of this kind "simple emotive judgments."

Other beauty judgments turn not on the felt quality of one's own reaction to a natural object, but on a determination that its perceivable qualities are such as to qualify it for high aesthetic approval according to beauty standards current in one's culture. A person who declares this particular specimen of *Camellia giulio nuccio* to be beautiful is, in this sense, reporting the fact that this flower is of a kind that her society currently takes to be beautiful (whether or not she is particularly moved by it on this occasion, or, indeed, would be on any occasion). Flower show judges routinely make judgments of this kind, typically refined and sophisticated ones. In making them, they deliberately set aside or restrict their own individual aesthetic predilections (they may actually dislike the larger, looser blossomed camellias) in favor of what they take to be prevailing opinion in the relevant aesthetic culture. Let us call cognitive, objective natural beauty assessments of this sort "descriptive judgments."

A third kind of beauty judgment involves a person's determination that, within the relevant aesthetic community, his being moved in a certain way by a given natural object *counts*—not just because it may reflect agreement with the beauty standards antecedently reached by that community, but because his own aesthetic experience contributes to the evolution of those very standards. Such a person sees his cognitive and emotive responses to natural objects as deeply personal (in that they are subject to the conditions of his own directed awareness) and at the same time as deeply social (in that they are partially formative of his aesthetic culture's notion of natural beauty). The distinguishing mark of judgments of this kind is reflective awareness of the interdependence of personal and social value. Looking at the Crab Nebula through a powerful telescope, an observer may conclude that what she sees is beautiful, mindful in part that her aesthetic community has antecedently established that phenomena of this sort are beautiful (or can be beautiful) and mindful also that, as an "insider" or aesthetic stakeholder in that community, she holds a franchise to declare the quality and power of her own aesthetic experience and make that experience part of the aesthetic community's collective awareness of the aesthetic qualities of this natural object. Let us call cognitive, subjective beauty assessments of this sort "reflective judgments."

A fourth kind of beauty judgment arises when an observer forms an aesthetic assessment about a natural object that puts him or her at odds with prevailing social views or standards of the sort directing descriptive judgments. Such an observer might be powerfully moved by features of, say, dogfish that most folks overlook or deem aesthetically uninteresting. Even if the prevailing view in her aesthetic community is that dogfish are un-beautiful, if not positively ugly, this observer may insist that they are beautiful as a way of urging amendment or revision of the prevailing view. Cultural norms of natural beauty are by no means static, as we have seen. Although changes in these norms tend to be gradual, even glacial, there are occasions where divergent views precipitate radical revisions.[7] The aesthetic dissenter isn't merely declaring his own emotive response. Nor is he simply denouncing a standing descriptive judgment. There is more than a declarative cast to his judgment; its hortative function reveals its fundamentally performative purpose. Just as promises, blessings, and nominations cannot be true or false, urgings have an illocutionary character that renders them non-cognitive.[8] The dissenter wants to draw upon his aesthetic experience to amend the cultural context itself. Let us call prescriptive beauty judgments of this sort "corrective judgments."

Where there is correction there is bound to be counter-correction. The fifth kind of beauty judgment is prescriptive in much the way the fourth is. But it aims at affirming, rather than amending, current aesthetic norms. Put off by corrective declarations that would accord the title beauty to swamp gas or remove it from magma flows, a defender of established cultural judgments might deploy beauty declarations in their defense in the same prescriptive way (but to opposite effect) that the dissenter does. In saying "magma flows *are* beautiful" she is not merely issuing a descriptive judgment, based on standing aesthetic norms. She is instead urging the preservation of those norms against challenge. Again, because the point of the declaration is not to state a fact but to affect attitudes, it is a performative expression that can be neither true nor false. Let us call non-cognitive declarations of this prescriptive type "affirmative judgments."

The important thing to realize about these five forms of natural beauty judgment is that they are not detached and independent modes of evaluation.

Rather, they are nested, or integrated, in the developmental process whereby individuals grow up aesthetically. Simple emotive judgments are the bedrock elements of this process. Without these, there would be no point in making the other judgments. But it would be just as much a mistake to suppose that simple emotive aesthetic judgments are independent and self-substantiating as it would be to suppose that ethical judgments are no more than "boos" and "hoorays."[9] Our simple emotive beauty judgments are born in, and grow up in, a social context. It is through our "insider familiarity" with this context that we come to understand, in a general way, the limits of deployment of all aesthetic terms. In a general way, I say, because aesthetic cultures invariably take reflective beauty judgments to have a creative effect on the evolution of descriptive natural beauty judgments. That is, whatever canons of natural beauty judgment may have become established at a given time in a given aesthetic culture, they are understood to be corrigible and emendable through the accumulation of aesthetic experiences by members of that culture.

To be an "insider" in the sense I have in mind is simply to be aware of and intelligently engaged in this five-fold judgmental process. A person whose natural beauty judgments are all of the simple emotive variety (or, for that matter any other single variety) is not an insider. Likewise, a person who is properly positioned to judge the beauty of artworks must know more than that she likes this one and not that one. As Danto put it, she must apprehend their sensible qualities in an atmosphere of theory and history, an artworld. When, in chapter 2, I raised the question of whether it makes sense to speak of a "natureworld," comparable to Danto's "artworld," I did so to dismiss the conceptualist position that it is the atmosphere of scientific theory and natural history that provides this setting. Now I want to suggest a more positive role for the notion. "Natureworld" can serve as a compendious designation for the complex, protracted interplay of personal and social perceptions that takes place in the five forms of natural beauty judgment I have mentioned. Just as participants—insiders—in the artworld are those who have a stake in art and are appropriately equipped with background knowledge, to make aesthetic judgments regarding artworks, so insiders in the natureworld are those who have an aesthetic stake in the non-artifactual world and who, with a different appropriate range of background knowledge, make aesthetic judgments regarding natural objects. The insider perspective, the view from inside the natureworld, is one in which the various objective and subjective, cognitive and non-cognitive factors I have mentioned are able to respond to each other in the course of committed, and evolving, awareness.

The process of development I am describing here is nothing new or exotic. Consider, for example, the way in which some, but not all, native users of a natural language come to acquire an aesthetic appreciation of that language. At first, language acquisition is simply a matter of gathering what sounds and symbols are aptly used in relation to various situations. A child may, early on, acquire the skill of uttering "boy" in identifying male humans. Later she will learn the refinement that it is only young male humans to which the term applies. And it may be quite some time before she comes to appreciate the ways in which this term can bear illocutionary weight: "Come here, boy!" "Boy, what a finale!" And so on. Appreciation of the possible poetic and other artistic uses of this and other terms comes later, if it comes at all. It will require a willingness to contemplate non-standard uses, tropes, analogy, alliteration, rhyme, and so on. It will require an ability to stand back from current use and see it against the backdrop of evolved language history. And it will involve a willingness to take pleasure in the way words may be artfully and expressively arranged—the *beauty* of the written or spoken word and not just its meaning.

All of this is perfectly familiar. It is the commonplace business of growing up with and into a language. In becoming a language "insider" one must acquire both a solid grasp of current canons of usage and a sense of how to move in and out of, and around, those canons. This is a matter of responding to both individual and social perceptions and classifications. There are objective truths based on facts regarding a language community's usage. And there are subjective responses to these facts that it is incumbent on the attentive langue-user to make or understand. Becoming a language-insider is a matter of finding a fit between these factors. Similarly, in growing up aesthetically with respect to natural objects, one starts by learning current, canonical descriptions (common names, scientific information, etc.). Over time, one may acquire a wide range of ways in which these objects can reward fertile and informed attention. This process will necessarily involve taking natural objects seriously, having a stake in their aesthetic qualities, and giving them prominence in one's attentional life. Again, this will involve both personal and cultural elements that need to be worked into harmony. But, just as there is no one right way of apprehending beauty in language, there is no one right way in which the natureworld insider must marshal the five kinds of natural beauty judgments in appreciating natural objects.[10]

At the end of the day, the difference between aesthetic awareness that is located within the natureworld and aesthetic awareness that is located without it is no more difficult to mark than that between the corresponding awarenesses within and without the artworld.[11] Natureworld is the home of mature aesthetic appreciation of natural objects in the same way that artworld is the home of mature artifactual appreciation. These are homes into which one is not born. One enters either world only after a considerable period of preparation and evolving commitment. It is my view that people grow into their natural beauty judgments in the way they grow into their religions and their politics—gradually, socially, individualistically, but not inevitably.

FUNDAMENTAL ELEMENTS IN JUDGMENTS OF NATURAL BEAUTY

Let us now turn to the issue of how this quasi-Humean, natureworld-based, syncretic approach plays itself out in the practice of making beauty judgments about natural objects. It is important to bear in mind that, in making natural beauty judgments, people are generally less interested in classification, score-keeping, and qualification than in recognizing and cultivating a set of emotive and cognitive ingredients that cooperate in making certain experiences rewarding and worthwhile. Almost always, when people express an interest in gaining *expertise* in making beauty judgments about natural objects, they want to know how to feel confident in the responses they have (or would like to have) to these objects—to be able to savor them more completely, to communicate what they find valuable in them to others, and to defend them against skeptics. They want, that is to say, to establish the *bona fides* of the aesthetic franchise they hold in making reflective judgments regarding natural objects.

In this section, I describe the four elements of natural beauty judgments that are fundamental ingredients in any reasonable response to these objectives. The elements I describe incorporate principles that provide a common platform for rational aesthetic decision making in regard to natural objects, a platform on which different combinations of theoretic commitments and individual predilections will lead to varying outcomes. I discuss some of these difference-making ingredients in the next chapter. At no point in this discussion do I present anything that could plausibly be turned into a formulaic or mechanical basis of value assignment. Nor do I suggest any rationale for reducing matters of aesthetic regard to empirical measurement. The analysis I present here is, I believe, supported equally by the strands of historical thought I have discussed earlier and by common intuitions about the point and promise of aesthetic appreciation.

Three general principles should be borne in mind as we face the problem of articulating a reasonable basis for aesthetic judgment regarding natural objects. First, aesthetic judgments are, as I think the philosophical record has shown, irreducibly subjective in the sense that they are analytically connected to individual responses rather than to some external standard independent of these responses. A thing is beautiful not just because it has certain identifiable features but because people have certain responses to it in virtue of those features. Thus, persistent and sincere beauty claims, however naïve, based on the quality of reported aesthetic experience of natural objects are not to be discounted. If someone whose world view has been shaped largely by commercial television and checkstand newsmagazines glows and gushes when he sees a shooting star, we should take his simple emotive judgment as a legitimate and serious contribution to the ongoing cultural conversation that settles the aesthetic status of shooting stars. We shouldn't take it as the final word. But, equally, we shouldn't take the response of the *New York Times* comet critic as the final word either.

Second, even though many people are more wedded to their aesthetic prejudices than they are to any of their other convictions, it is a mistake to suppose that these preliminary aesthetic positions are as sound as they can become in the light of reflection, comparison, and the adduction of pertinent information. Although we may have been thrilled and intrigued by the sound of piano music before learning how to play, the piano teacher shows us how to hear what we otherwise couldn't have heard in a composition. The astronomer shows us intriguing things about the face of the planet Jupiter we otherwise surely would have overlooked. To be sure, initial convictions are not to be dismissed out of hand. They are, more often than not, very like the convictions to which we return after the refining process of criticism has run its course.[12] The responsible philosophical objective is not to discount perceptions or ideas at any stage of development, but to point out productive connections to ideas we all might want to weave into our own thinking about things. When philosophy gets involved in the business of beauty judgment, it is rarely ever to correct mistakes, so that something deemed beautiful can be shown to be unbeautiful, or vice versa. Rather, it is to show how some natural object, quality, or combination of objects or qualities can reward the protracted attention and deeper response it deserves.

Third, as I explained in connection with my adoption of an overall Humean strategy of judgment, the dependence of aesthetic judgments on individual emotive response must not be taken to be a license for unbridled relativism. However personal or private an individual's response may seem to be, it is ineluctably caught up in the cultural context that makes it intelligible to our society and to ourselves. The deep truth of Aristotle's characterization of the human individual as *zoon politikon*, the political animal, is that we are what we are only in and through our societies. Social context circumscribes not only personal responsibilities but—to a large extent—personal responses. Brilliant sunsets may leave some individuals cold. But if, in a given society, such visual displays have become generally recognized as paradigmatic natural beauties, that fact alone has a shaping effect on the aesthetic awareness of any member of that society. And while it is certainly true that corrective judgments which challenge prevailing patterns of response to natural objects can have the salubrious effect of inducing innovation and eventual change, it is also true that affirmative judgments call upon us to recognize established baselines without which the strength of divergent aesthetic judgments would be impossible to measure. Aesthetic challenges work only against a backdrop of acknowledged acceptance of judgments embraced by the culture or community. Aesthetic vitality entails the constant, creative rivalry of established and unconventional apprehensions of beauty.

In turning now to consideration of what I have called the "platform" elements—four common ingredients of the aesthetic attention that must be paid to natural objects in the making of beauty judgments—I want to point out that nothing turns on the number or scope of the elements mentioned. Admittedly, a different but equally plausible sorting process could identify more or fewer categories, or move some of the factors I describe in the next chapter onto the platform. There is, that is to say, nothing rigid about the analytic picture I draw here. It is the analytic approach, not the arrangement of all the elements, that is crucial.

Selective Sensory Focus

The first demand of beauty judgment is that close and sustained attention be paid to the object or objects, feature or features (or combinations of these) under regard, drawing on the talents of one or more of the senses. Already this demand entails some elements of delineation or framing. There is something about a rock, just *this* rock, that invites a hiker to pick it up. "Beautiful," she says. But *what* is beautiful? It may not be the rock's sensible status *qua* rock that compels her regard. It may instead be its mauve luster, the rhythmic angularity of its edges, the elaborate pattern of mineral veins criss-crossing its surface, or any of a number of other things that captivates her. Whatever it is—the object, its features, or the display of just this constellation of features in just this way—commands her attention, and not just for a moment. If it were merely glanced at alongside the trail in the course of a hike, and not afforded sustained attention, the same rock (and its features) would not support beauty judgments (beyond the simple emotive ones). It would be just one more feature of the world panorama.

As I have pointed out earlier, Noël Carroll's theory takes qualities of attentional directedness as the key ingredients in aesthetic experience. In Carroll's account, design appreciation and quality detection are welded to attention far more closely than they are to affect. This bent is most conspicuously apparent when we contrast Carroll's theory to the most prominent rival theories of aesthetic experience, those of Beardsley and Stolnitz. While my own view is more in harmony with the latter views than with his, I agree emphatically with Carroll's insistence that careful, sustained attention to the constellation of features or objects in question is an unavoidable prerequisite to their being properly judged beautiful. Whatever discrimination, interpretation, comparison, or special delectation might follow from it, the initial act of serious attention must be the foundation.

There is a kind of casual, but positive, attention to natural objects the Chinese traditionally refer to as "looking at flowers on horseback." In the hurried worlds of many Western societies there is no shortage of superficial sensory sampling. Many, perhaps most, folks find it very difficult to pay sustained attention to things that don't have a direct bearing on their financial and social well-being. Unwilling to allot these objects the time their appropriate aesthetic regard demands, they offer a variety of quick-and-easy acknowledgments of what they know is *potential* natural beauty. They comment that the autumn foliage is gorgeous while speeding along the highway because they know that those who do pay attention to it generally find it gorgeous. They buy post cards displaying photographs of beautiful natural objects they never bother to seek out. They decorate their homes with furnishings and artifacts that are fashionable because of their "natural" qualities. In trying to experience natural beauty on the run, on the cheap, these folks fail to experience natural beauty at all because they simply aren't paying proper attention.

So the attentional demand I have identified as the first demand of natural beauty judgment is far from trivial. At the bare minimum, it requires that people pause and train sensory faculties on just this rock, just this flower fragrance, this particular play of leaves against clouds, or this unique pattern in a fingerprint. And not only for an instant. Just as it is analytically true that neither grief nor joy can be experienced in a second, it is analytically true that the experience of beauty requires protracted attention to natural objects. How protracted? Again, this is a question that cannot be answered independently of all the other factors involved in aesthetic experience. I see no point in denying that a field of daffodils can be deemed beautifully yellow in a fairly short time span.[13] But, equally, I believe it is obvious that recognizing the beauty in a craggy lava field, the carcass of an antelope, or a microscopic volvox colony, demands more extended reflection. Some appreciations take more time than others, but all of them take enough time for sense and intelligence to cooperate in the apprehension of separable features of an experience and of their combination in the experience as a whole. Youngsters and busy people are often incapable of taking the time needed to sustain aesthetic attention to a point where simple emotive judgments evolve into reflective judgments.

Just as there can be too little attention given to a natural object for the experience of beauty to take hold, there can be too much. Attention to a natural object sustained over a very long period can exhaust the sensory and cognitive capacities employed. Enraptured as I may be by the beauty of a towering waterfall, restricted attention for hours on end to the waterfall and nothing else will inevitably result in a dulling or dissipation of my initial aesthetic response. In this respect, natural beauty is like beauty in general. As much as I enjoy the taste of Honey Crisp apples, overindulging in them may cause them to lose their savor. Exclusive attention to one art work, one author's work, or even one artistic style can draw down one's critical capacities and undercut one's sense of what is special about such things in relation to others.[14] The more we constrain attention to one thing the less we attend to *other* things. Knowing one thing to be beautiful is not merely knowing what it is, but knowing how it stands in relation to the full inventory of comparable objects of experience. The common stock of value and experience in human life is difference. And the differences among things cannot be properly appraised if our attention is trained exclusively on some narrow subset of them.

If focused attention is a fundamental requisite for natural beauty judgment, it might be tempting to think that *ultimate* attention, perfectly focused, would provide the perfect basis of appreciation. Indeed, something like this thought pervaded medieval aesthetic theory. But, the idea of an indefinitely extended focus of attention that would permit the complete regard of all natural things *sub specie aeternitatis* is simply incoherent. Just as a theory that explains everything really explains nothing, indefinitely extended attention is (from the human point of view, at least) no attention at all.

In regarding a natural object as the potential repository of aesthetic qualities, spatial no less than temporal boundaries must be drawn. In her pleasure at the look of the rock, is it the whole rock, or just this part of it that commands her attention? Is it the play of lines and shadows, or the network of vein lines? Is it the way these features catch the light? Or the color, or the contrast of colors between this part and that? Or is it, perhaps, some choreographic combination of all of these features that leads to her pleasure? The focal boundaries in these instances are flexible and relative to the act of appreciation. There can be no rule for determining which of these counts more than the next. Indeed, in the specific instance, any of these factors can be decisive.

Natural beauty appears only when aesthetic attention falls upon a natural object (or qualities of an object, or concatenations of these) and is sustained. Of course aesthetic attention never, or scarcely ever, falls on just one thing or one aspect of a thing. It is, of its very nature, vagabond. Even though we may start out thinking that some natural object is beautiful just because it has this or that quality, we often find that perceiving it as it is cannot be accomplished without taking stock of its connection to kindred aesthetic objects, both near and remote. Thus, as I aim to show in the next few sections, selective sensory focus is, as a platform component, importantly linked to elements of aesthetic awareness that spread attention beyond any of its particular objects.

Completeness Within Limits

As I have pointed out in discussing the "framing paradox," there can be no successful attention to an aesthetic object without some form of attentional framing, however transient and permeable. This conclusion is inconsistent with some claims made by proponents of the doctrine of repleteness, discussed in chapter 3. The repleteness position entails that the commonality of sensory presentation makes universal natural beauty judgments possible because they connect all of human senses with all of nature, seen as a dense body of unconceptualized content. As you will recall, my rejoinder to the doctrine of repleteness was that limits are inevitable and that discrimination lies at the heart of judgment. When it comes to beauty judgment, however, it isn't enough that the item of attention be isolated. It must be attended to in a way that takes stock of those features, combinations of features, or relations between features, that contribute to its ability to affect us the way it does. Beauty judgment is often a positive interest in the completeness of an object (or combination of objects, etc.) seen as a pleasing concatenation of features that might have fallen apart but don't in this particular instance. These features need not be sensible properties or formal relations among the sensible properties. In many instances, what lends completeness to our interest in a natural object is a combination of sensible, cognitive, and associative features. In a justly famous passage, Ronald Hepburn describes an episode of traversing a tidal flat, a "wide expanse of sand and mud," and experiencing a "wide, glad emptiness ... tempered by a disturbing weirdness" at the thought that this very expanse is a seabed half the day.[15] The tidal flat can be seen to draw its peculiar beauty from the way in which the look of the thing, our knowledge of its geophysical nature, and perhaps our recollection of other desolate, wild, mutating things converge to form a unified focus of appreciation.

Monroe Beardsley was a passionate advocate of the principle that aesthetic appreciation should always involve a sense of wholeness, a sense of completeness within limits. In his early work *Aesthetics: Problems in the Philosophy of Criticism*, he put the point as a psychological tendency conducive to aesthetic experience: "[B]ecause of the highly concentrated, or localized attention characteristic of aesthetic experience, it tends to mark itself off from the general stream of experience, and stand in memory as a single experience."[16] As I pointed out in chapter 5, Beardsley continued to refine and modify his analysis of aesthetic experience and its ingredient notion of wholeness over the course of a long career. Eventually, in his last book, the idea of wholeness took on a deeper sense in which the felt integration of the phenomenal subject transferred itself to the mind of the aesthetic responder, culminating in a certain sense of "contentment, even through disturbing feelings, that involves self-acceptance and self-expansion."[17] This last claim may seem to go too far. It seems clearly possible to have what should count as an aesthetic experience of a natural object in which one becomes aware of that object's beauty without at the same time coming to enjoy a sense of contentment of the profound kind Beardsley describes. Still, it is fair to say that a sense of the wholeness, or completeness-within-limits that episodes of natural beauty can, and characteristically do, foster *can* make the aesthetic observers cognizant of unifying capacities in their own consciousness. And it is not too far-fetched to say that the transference of such a sense of wholeness can have salubrious results beyond the reward of aesthetic pleasure. After all, as we have seen, something like this point lies at the core of Dewey's theory of experience, a theory that ties articulated wholeness to social and personal values of all kinds.

Equally importantly, what is carved out in the discrimination process must be contemplated in its entirety, so that appreciation extends to the whole of what has been delimited. A child might say that a burnt-out forest was beautiful because he had found an unharmed poppy blooming at its edge. On the one hand, it appears that the child has found a natural object (the poppy) worth savoring. On the other hand, it appears that he has wrongly assimilated the positive quality of that object (and possibly the sense of contrast it carries with it) into the less obviously positive aesthetic qualities of the burnt-out forest. I regard this as an instance of the (not uncommon) tendency to allow peripheral features to affect our sense of a whole on which they impinge.[18] If we reject the child's judgment, as I think we should, we should do so because his evaluation is a mistaken read on the relation between part and whole. Although the child's simple emotive

145

judgment was a legitimate expression of a positive aesthetic response, it did not apply to the more comprehensive claim his judgment entailed.

Reflective aesthetic judgment regarding a natural object involves the reasonable circumscription of its features. Sometimes familiar nomenclature gives us a basis for attentional limit. Sometimes the classifications of natural science do this job. And then again, sometimes it is something more subtle or esoteric—a recognition of its displacement from its matrix, say, or a sense of its harmonious relation to a number of other similarly (or contrastingly) featured objects in its sensible environment. But whatever it is, the organizing principle that makes a whole out of the potential prospects of attention is clearly both a cultural object and a personal choice. When a person gathers together the sensory field in a way that makes this or that an object of attention, she cannot do this on her own. She is inevitably making such determinations through the conceptual instrumentalities afforded by her culture, including its inventory of standing descriptive judgments. Yet, at the same time, she is making her *own* choice, her *own* selection among endless potential objects of attention. This is what it means to be enfranchised by the aesthetic culture to make reflective beauty judgments. Just as poets are bound to work with the language their culture provides them, and yet are invited and expected to add to that language by applying it in fresh ways to new experience, so natural beauty judges are invited and expected to amplify and enrich the established base of beauty judgments by declaring and defending their own assessments.

It is the lesson of every great novel that people are captives of their cultures but only to a limited degree, and that the rest is a matter of character. The effect of "character" in this context means that patterns of individual choice may deviate from patterns of social choice in relation to the contingencies of local circumstances and unconventional values. Making an aesthetic object complete within limits is thus a matter of recognizing both the strictures of cultural recognition and the more flexible bounds of personal selection. In order for a natural object to be beautiful, it must first become an aesthetic object. And to do this, it must be a comprehensible whole. A comprehensible whole arises only when cultural recognition and personal judgment come together in reflective attention.

Savoring

No experience of natural beauty is a merely dispassionate recognition that something is both natural and beautiful. It is intrinsic to the idea of beauty response that it *doesn't leave us cold*. It is a species of savoring. When someone declares that the aurora borealis, say, is beautiful, we must take it that she is positively *moved* by her sensory awareness of the aurora borealis. To say that one is positively moved by an aesthetic object is more than to take note of a positive feeling. It is an acknowledgment of a positive disposition to act in favor of this object—to commend it, to protect it, to promote it, or in some other way to support the prospect of its experience by oneself and others.[19]

The generality of the claim that natural beauty judgments are in this way emotively commissive is subject to two qualifications. First, as I have pointed out earlier, any aesthetic judgment is assumed to apply to episodes of aesthetic attention that are neither impaired nor distracted. An observer who knows that he would, under normal conditions of observation, find the Crab Nebula beautiful is warranted in declaring it to be so, even if, on this particular occasion, he has a blinding headache and can't enjoy observing anything through his telescope, or even if he simply doesn't take time to observe it carefully. Natural beauty judgments, that is to say, encompass both present-tense declarations of positive affect and dispositional claims that the observer *would* have been positively affected under appropriate conditions.[20] Second, descriptive judgments that one's culture deems a certain kind of natural object (or would deem this particular natural object) beautiful are factual, objective determinations, and for that reason emotively non-commissive. Here it is important to remember that descriptive natural beauty judgments are no more than acknowledgments of what has come to be accepted as an aesthetic norm in a culture where we may assume that that acceptance is based on the historical accumulation of affirmative aesthetic responses by persons who *weren't* left cold when they made their judgments. So it is fair to say that descriptive natural beauty judgments are dependent on, and ultimately beholden to, subjective declarations of positive affect. And thus, in the end analysis, natural beauty judgments in general do invariably depend on individuals' undergoing the experience of savoring and being positively committed toward natural objects.

What is entailed in savoring of this sort? Does it imply a form of delight that is like the spontaneous olfactory pleasure one might experience in proximity to a kettle of popping corn, or the sharp burst of satisfaction one derives from a cold glass of water on a very hot day? What does it mean to be *moved aesthetically*? As we have seen, the history of Western aesthetics from Kant forward contains a steady stream of efforts to disentangle the special mode of savoring characteristic of aesthetic experience properly-so-called from savoring that is merely pleasant. Following the trajectory of this historical trend, we can agree that being moved aesthetically is *more* than being pleased and positively disposed to act in favor of that which moves one. But how much more, and in what way? From what I said in chapter 5, it will be apparent that no straightforward, formulaic answer to this question is forthcoming. Instead, the *sorites* approach I take insists that a number of disparate emotive factors combine to carry the responding individual across a culturally defined threshold. Moreover, cognitive factors—one's knowledge of basic principles of nebular astronomy, for example—frequently contribute importantly to aesthetic savoring. Scientific knowledge regarding a natural aesthetic object can deepen and intensify our appreciation of its beauty. Imagination, likewise, may contribute significantly to the quality of our positive experience of natural objects by calling up apt comparisons and distinctions from one's repertoire of memories (just as, in judging the quality of a fine bordeaux, a wine expert may rely upon a considerable inventory of past experiences and associations).

The volvox colony, the antelope carcass, the whorled fingerprint, and the Crab Nebula can be (and generally are) savored in different ways—ways that emphasize one combination of beauty-making characteristics after another. In one case, it will be the appreciation of an intricate pattern (and perhaps the way that pattern echoes other patterns in our lives) that will take the lead in inviting a positive response. In another, it will be the recognition of rarity, remoteness, or vastness. And in yet another it will be the harmonious interplay of sensory ingredients and associative ingredients. It is for this reason that the activity of assessing the savory-responsive, beauty-conducive characteristics to natural objects is destined to appear messy in all the interesting cases. Like Wittgenstein's celebrated rope-fibers, the elements draw their strength from their overlap, rather than from sharing a common core running the entire length. The one fiber that *does* run the length of the rope is the commitment of positive disposition. Natural objects we find beautiful are those whose qualities we approve and are disposed to recommend for approval to others.

The relation between our natural beauty judgments and the affective conditions supporting them is similar to the relation between moral judgments and the complex normative conditions in which they are framed in great literature. As Richard Wollheim, Martha Nussbaum, and others have pointed out, the Benthamite ideal of a moral calculus that would turn ethics into arithmetic is a manifestly forlorn prospect.[21] What, after all, should Maggie Verver have done in her peculiar set of circumstances—not just to conform to an abstract moral ideal to which she was initially and fervently committed, but to deal with the interplay of weighty values that rushed in on her from all angles to assault that ideal?[22] Many philosophers today—they may indeed be a majority—concede that the answers to questions of this sort are resistant to formulaic solutions precisely because they involve a personal recognition and sorting-out of innumerable factors that do not succumb to a clean process of comparative weighing. It should not surprise us that the judgments regarding moral plights depicted in great literature have an affinity to judgments regarding the aesthetic qualities of natural objects. That is because the predicaments of judgment—involving multiple, intersecting values, a background of social norms, and an imperative of personal action—are alike in both settings.

Letting Nature Be Nature

As I indicated in chapter 1, the demand that appreciation of natural objects must respect their naturalness—their non-artifactuality—has usually been turned into an insistence that observers regard these objects rightly in just one way. Early on, the imperative was to regard everything that man hadn't made as divinely created, and thus removed from the scale on which we weigh human artifacts. More recently, the imperative has become one of subsuming natural objects under categories provided by natural science. My conviction that both of these imperatives are mistaken is not born out of disrespect for theological or scientific perspectives per se, but out of a belief that any analytical account that respects the variety of our aesthetic experience of natural objects cannot obey a single imperative of regard. Sometimes it is rewarding to look at that rock that the hiker picked up as enjoyable because it is part of God's handiwork. Equally, it may be rewarding to recognize that it is a hunk of gneiss, basalt, or granite and has the features one would expect to see in rocks of such kinds. But what should we say if the hiker says that she finds it beautiful because the pattern of colored veins that criss-cross its surface produces in her an edgy sense of rhythm and harmony very much like the one that she gets from Mondrian's *Broadway Boogie-Woogie* (1942-43)? Is her response flawed because it is not a response to the object qua natural object, but to the object in relation to an artifact? I don't see why this should be so.

The core demand of aesthetic regard for natural objects as natural is that they not be seen as, or measured for merit against, man-made objects. No thoughtful theorist will quarrel with this demand. But it does not entail that the aesthetic gains one has made in the appreciation of artworks be utterly non-transferable into the natural domain. Or vice versa. Malcolm Budd cautions that

> [T]he aesthetic appreciation of nature ... might ... be understood to mean no more than the aesthetic appreciation

149

of anything that is available in nature for aesthetic appreciation.... [T]here is no purely aesthetic requirement that
a natural thing should be appreciated aesthetically as the
natural thing it is or as being a thing of a certain natural
kind or just as being a natural thing; and it may well be
aesthetically more rewarding not to do so but to contemplate it in abstraction from whatever kind it is seen to be
and focus on its shape, textures, and colouring. But just
as artistic appreciation is the appreciation of art as art,
so the aesthetic appreciation of nature should be understood to demand the appreciation of nature as nature.[23]

Budd is certainly right to think that aesthetic attention to natural objects
should not be so abstracted from their environmental settings that all that is
left to admire about them are context-indifferent features such as shape, texture, and color. In regarding natural things as non-artifactual we recognize not
only that humans didn't make them. We recognize that they have come about
through processes that create and shape almost everything there is, including
ourselves. But, aesthetic admiration of natural things is, or can be, distinct
from admiration of environmental process, or of the environment *per se*.

It is a mistake to suppose that aesthetic regard for an object in nature that
doesn't dwell on its being a thing of a certain natural kind is limited to formal
features of the sort Budd mentions.[24] This mistake rides on a false assumption
about what it is to be a natural thing. The assumption is that because nature
consists of things that are instances of natural kinds, i.e., instantiations of
types that arise in the course of the interrelation of all these things, proper
attention to any particular thing (or aspect of a thing) must be paid to it as
a kind-member (or type-instantiation). But there is no one thing a natural
thing is, any more than there is just one thing a house, a car, a totem pole, an
impressionist painting, or a love poem is. Attention paid to a natural object
that does not set its typal status in the foreground is not mis-attention. It is
just one more kind of attention. Or possibly it is a congeries of various kinds
of attention, each with its rewards and hazards. I agree entirely with Allen
Carlson's oft-repeated insistence that the aesthetic appreciation of natural
objects "must be centered on and driven by the real nature of the object of
appreciation itself."[25] It is important to recognize, however, that just as there
is no one thing a natural thing is, there is no one truth about it, and no
one real nature of it. Although it is often appropriate to take cognizance
of a natural object's natural type (as, for example, in reminding ourselves

that whales are cetaceans, warm-blooded, and mammals), there is nothing that requires such a recognition to be the "center" or the "driver" of our appreciation of that object.

Consider one of Hepburn's own lovely examples, the fall of an autumn leaf:

> If we simply watch it fall, without any thought, it may or may not be a moving or exciting object, but it must be robbed of its poignancy, its mute message of summer gone, its symbolizing all falling, our own included. Leaf veins suggest blood-vessel veins—symbolizing continuity in the forms of life, and maybe a shared vulnerability. Thus the thought-element may bring analogies to bear on the concrete particulars: this fall with other falls; and temporal links—this autumn with innumerable other autumns; the deep carpet of leaves in forests; the cycle of the seasons.[26]

What Hepburn here calls analogies produced by the "thought-element" are the modern-day equivalent of Archibald Alison's "trains of ideas of emotion," reflections set in motion by our regarding an object both as what it seems to be and as what it calls to mind. In the falling-leaf episode Hepburn describes, the observer is cognizant of the leaf as a leaf. He's not confusing it with a kindergarten paper leaf, nor imagining that he is watching an art world "happening" in which skilled holographers contrive to remind us of our mortality. Nor is he in the grip of some religious illusion that transmutes this fall into The Fall. It's still a leaf. But the leaf's status as the instantiation of a natural type is neither the center nor the driver in the appreciative reaction Hepburn describes.

Of course, it remains open to conceptualists such as Carlson to deny that the powerful associative themes Hepburn weaves into his account of the episode are proper but relatively minor parts of the appreciation of natural things as natural. They could say that these are all ancillary reflections, while the core of beauty lies in the object of appreciation itself, that being the leaf *qua* leaf—or perhaps leaf *qua* leaf-cum-force-of-gravity-in-autumn. But this strips the appreciative response of obviously rich dimensions (or requires their subordination) for no good reason. The blood-vessel simile may be closer to the core of what moves us in the leaf observation experience than an awareness of the leaf as leaf, i.e., as an instance of, say, *Acer japonica* foliation. To put the point boldly: It is not the nature of the falling leaf to be *just* a leaf. In relation to the human perspective from which alone we may view it, the falling leaf is everything that Hepburn describes and much more. For us, nature is inevitably seen through human nature.[27] Natural objects are not just what they are. They are what we find them to be. Appreciating them as *natural* is a matter of understanding and respecting the fact that they are not products of human concoction. Appreciating them as *beautiful* is a matter of wedding this respect and this understanding to schemes of value and responsiveness distinctive of human cultures. These schemes incorporate a wealth of relations to all manner of things coupled with elements of self-reflection that show us what *we* are in the enterprise of appreciation itself.

TYPAL AND GENERAL JUDGMENT

Before I turn to elements to build on the foundation I have described so far, I need to address an important distinction between two ways in which natural things (objects or aspects of objects) may be regarded. One way involves the comparison of things to standards or ideal members of a recognized type. On such a basis, the question of a thing's beauty is affirmatively settled by the thing's accommodation, or its degree of accommodation, to that standard or ideal. The other way involves a more distributed mode of appreciation in which things aren't measured against any one standard but considered in relation to a range of value characteristics on a broader scale. On the latter basis, the question of a thing's beauty can be settled only after a consideration of the effect on the observer of the display and interplay of a wide range of characteristics.

There are professionally qualified referees who judge the relative beauty of dahlias, dachshunds, and dental array, among a myriad of other natural things. These referees do not take themselves to be executing capricious judgments based on whim or personal taste. Far from it. The fact that a given aesthetic culture empowers experts to make judgments of this sort is an acknowledgment that there *are* established, culture-specific standards of aesthetic merit in these fields. The standards are embedded in tradition, consumer preference, and insurance rates, among a great many other things. The recognized judges are certified as having the skills and experience needed to make intelligent assessments according to standards accepted by those having a stake in their judgments. Acquiescence in typal judgment of this sort is as close as we are going to get to Hume's notion of deference to true judges in popular assessments of natural beauty. That is because verdicts of typal natural beauty judges are assumed to be expert renditions of approval that informed, unbiased, and unimpaired observers would make were they in a position to do so. In the modern world, where people are generally unwilling to defer to the kind of authority I have described as cognitive idealism, widespread popular confidence in standardized judgment by qualified referees embraces this Humean rationale.

Natural beauty judgment of the typal sort is most vividly on display in pet shows. To return to an example I cited earlier, in a schnauzer contest the question of whether a particular dog is beautiful (which we can take to be equivalent to "most pleasing in appearance in the way distinctive of schnauzers") lies in the hands of a tiny band of dog show judges who are poised to make careful, exacting, impartial, and informed judgments about conformity of this specimen to the accepted schnauzer norm. The judgments they make are objective in the sense that they take into account qualities identified in officially stated criteria of schnauzerian beauty. They are subjective in the sense that they reflect the judges' own measurements and interpretations of these qualities. A particularly stunning schnauzer who happened to be pure white, glowed in the dark, spoke Spanish, and struck every observer as "cute as can be" could not be deemed beautiful (or at least as beautiful as the winner) if she had a shorter tail than was required.

Typal aesthetic judgments of all kinds are, of course, both emendable and corrigible. Over time criteria change. Preferred assets are downgraded. Others are newly recognized. This is the way that plants formerly deemed weeds become desirable border plants in fancy gardens. Even as we may complain that floral societies have, in our culture, assumed the autocratic prerogative of deciding gradations of aesthetic merit within varieties of a species, we need to remember how these societies have settled on the standards they apply. They certainly can't have uncritically adopted the standards subscribed to by earlier floral societies. First, this would obviously entail an infinite regress of standards, and a *reductio ad absurdum* of typal beauty judgment for the flowers involved. Second, adopting this posture would provide no means of effecting the changes in standards I have just mentioned, changes that sustain the vitality of the judging (and judge-appointing) enterprise itself.

What happens instead is that, at every stage in the evolution of such societies, enthusiasts who respond to certain varieties and specimens as particularly beautiful contribute their observations. Over time, the accumulated weight of these observations modifies the standards themselves. And that projects a new basis of evaluation that stands until the weight of later views overwhelms it in turn.[28] This process of gradual and incremental evolution is not substantially different from the processes by which other important value notions are fixed and altered in modern American culture. At any given time, officials charged with determining whether something is "reasonably careful," "conformant to standards of good medical practice," "conscionable," "competently argued," as well as whether a given state of affairs should be deemed a marriage, a tort, a valid election, or a nuisance turn first to canonical standards to make their determinations. They are, in fact, duty-bound to do so. But even as they appeal to these standards as "received," "well-established," "authoritative," and so on, they know that the standards are historically malleable and subject to the shaping influences of a community's desires, concerns, aspirations, and evolving values. No competent lawyer would argue that what counts as "reasonable" today is what counted as "reasonable" fifty years ago. Every act of subsuming new instances under old categories is an incremental shaping of those categories. This is as true in aesthetics as it is in law.

Suppose that some typal canon—a standard identifying the features that count toward making a mountain peak beautiful, say—were to have established itself in our culture in such a way that qualified judges could make certain and expert discriminations between any two mountain peaks as to their beauty. Assume that these judges have come to have the same authority in their specialized field of expertise as labor arbitrators, district court judges, and baseball umpires have in theirs. Suppose further that, on the basis of this standard, Mont Blanc is found to be, all things considered, more beautiful than the Matterhorn. Now along comes someone who, notwithstanding the judges' determination, finds the Matterhorn more beautiful than Mont Blanc. He addresses them, saying, "I know that the Matterhorn just doesn't measure up in some of the ways we have come to think of as important in mountain beauty. But just look at the wonderful, stark angularity of that rise! And look at the wonderful shadows that spill so dramatically down the south face! It just *gets* me. The long and the short of it is that I am moved much more powerfully and positively as I gaze at this peak than I am when I gaze at Mont Blanc. So, despite your acknowledged expertise, and despite your admittedly correct application of the received standards, I nevertheless find that the Matterhorn is the more beautiful mountain." On first blush, this looks like a plain judgmental blunder. The dissenter seems to have missed the point of making categorial determinations expertly. But do we think the dissenter simply *has to be* mistaken? What kind of a mistake is it he is making? Is it like getting the elevation of the peaks wrong? Is it more like getting the pronunciation of "Mont Blanc" wrong? Or is it something else entirely?

Here again we need to distinguish between beauty judgments that are meant to be *objective*, in that they report or take as correct the received beauty norms for a given aesthetic culture, and those that are *subjective*, in that they express individual reflection respecting these norms. Dissent from aesthetic authority in the Matterhorn-Mont Blanc example need not be seen as a misunderstanding of mountain-peak-beauty. Nor need it be regarded as a misapplication of the ingredient notions of beauty and natural beauty. Instead, it might be understood as a proposal for amendment of an aesthetic culture's beauty norms by one who is already an "insider," one who, for that reason, has a genuine stake in them. In the natureworld as in the artworld, non-standard, aberrant views and usages play important roles in sustaining the growth and vitality of judgment. When the Matterhorn admirer states his opposition to prevailing standards of beauty, he is less like the baseball spectator who disagrees with the umpire's safe call at third base and boos in the hope that the call will be revoked than he is like a stockholder who recommends a change in business practices in a corporation in which he has a substantial investment. Cultural aesthetic standards count. Individual experiences at odds with those standards also count. And we might hope that dissent in the natureworld is at least as effective in renewing and revising authoritative standards as it is in other institutional contexts.

A bias in favor of typal beauty judgment pervades a good deal of natural aesthetics. It is easy to see why cognitive idealism is partial to such an approach. If a thing's aesthetic merit is welded to an ideal and that ideal is something knowable only by a select body of qualified experts, the connection of beauty to type boils down to a tautology, as it did, effectively, in the theories of Plato and Aristotle. But a similar bias can be seen to infect more recent natural-environmental approaches that enshrine the categories of natural science. Modern conceptualists generally insist that models of appreciation of natural objects that resist the framing power of natural science are defective. Why? The rationale Allen Carlson has consistently repeated over the years is that we need to respect natural objects for what they *are*, and that natural science gives us classifications that fit natural objects in an expert way, thus telling us with certainty what they are, and that therefore science's taxonomy is the functional equivalent of art-historical taxonomies that provide the means of seeing artworks for what they are.[29] Science, as he sees it, presents a uniquely clear path to the objective truth about what the natural object is, and hence marks the way to that object's proper aesthetic appreciation. The order in which the object properly is to be considered is therefore the natural (scientific) order. The forces to be considered are natural (environmental) forces. The place it occupies is its natural place. The right account to rely on in making natural objects intelligible is that of natural science.[30]

Despite its prominence, it is easy to exaggerate the role of science in Carlson's natural aesthetics and many of his critics have done just that. Carlson has made it abundantly clear that he thinks it proper to admire beautiful natural things for a wide range of reasons other than that they are excellent exemplars of their natural types. He certainly doesn't suppose that science provides a type as a norm of beauty for each of the objects it classifies such that a proper natural beauty judgment is always of the form "x is beautiful *qua* y" (where x is an object token and y is its type). This particular orca, for example, might well be found to be beautiful for its extraordinary swiftness and sinuous grace in the water, and not for its exemplary embodiment of qualities distinctive of orcas. Accordingly, on Carlson's view, an informed observer's determination that a particular orca is beautiful is far less conceptually constrained than a referee's determination that a particular schnauzer is the best of its breed in the show.

Still, Carlson insists that appropriate appreciation of natural objects entails that we not only begin by getting straight on what these things *are* but rely on science (or, in some instances, proto-scientific common sense) to tell us their types. Even though our judgment that a given orca is beautiful need not be a measure of its qualities against the orca-type, it *does* presuppose knowledge that it is a token of its type, an orca. This view seems to me to imply an undue restriction on our appreciation of natural beauty. There are, of course, times when it is useful, or even necessary, to know what a natural object is (i.e., to know its type) in order to apprehend its beauty. But there are also times when it is neither useful nor necessary to do so. An observer might be filled with delight and awe at the spectacle of a huge black-and-white mass throwing off a vast and delicate mantilla of spray without knowing that she is seeing an orca breach. Here, the appreciation of beauty precedes any typal knowledge. If she is subsequently informed that what she has seen is an orca—a cetacean, an air-breather, and warm-blooded—her experience and the judgment born of it may well be deepened and intensified. But the independence of her initial beauty judgment from the subsequent information shows us that the former is not contingent on the latter. Furthermore, as I will demonstrate in the next chapter, there are clear instances of natural beauty judgment in which information not only fails to enhance, but actually impedes appreciation. Suppose our observer has an intense, religious-based phobia regarding killers and anything related to killing. Her initial delight in the spectacle of the breach itself is nullified when she is informed that it was an orca she saw because she already knows that orcas are commonly known as killer whales. For her, the beauty of the breaching event is nullified in much the way someone else's experience of the beauty of a grand architectural monument (a pyramid, say) would be nullified by knowledge of the immorality of its construction.

This last example may seem disingenuous in that the hypothetical phobia is clearly a perceptual impairment, and thus (on Humean grounds) a disqualification of aesthetic judgment. But we should not be hasty in drawing this conclusion. It is not only through phobias that knowledge can get in the way of experience, as I have argued earlier. If we tone down the notion of phobia to encompass aversion, resistance, cultural discredit, and so on, the claim that aesthetic appreciation is always enhanced by what we *know* about its objects is diluted to the point of implausibility.

Non-typal beauty judgments are, of course, less constrained. Cognitive, formal, and associative factors may play significant roles in them, with none enjoying necessary privilege. Putting aside the thought that the breaching orca is an *orca*, what might be involved in a beauty judgment regarding this event? It is possible to comprehend the *beauty* of the orca breach as nothing more than flashes of white and black thrown momentarily together in a series of patterns, in the way that a beautiful jazz riff brings its parts together in an unexpected and wonderful way. It is possible to take the whole experience as a revelation of the intimate connection between power and grace. And it is possible to see this event as a reflection on or intimation of the larger majesty of the environmental system in which the orca plays its part. In fact, there are hosts of nameless features associated with this orca-breaching experience that are susceptible to aesthetic regard but escape typal analysis: The peculiar confluence of sunrays and spray against the backdrop of seascape. The dramatic concord of sound and sight throughout the episode. The echo of one's own vitality that one hears in the orca's bold ascent and fall. I take it that these can be real and important aspects of a person's aesthetic experience of this aquatic event. They may, in a given instance, assume more prominence than anything tied with typal recognition in justifying a natural beauty judgment.

NOTES

1   David Hume, "Of the Standard of Taste," in *Eighteenth-Century British Aesthetics*, ed. Dabney Townsend (Amityville, NY: Baywood, 1999), p. 232.

2   Ibid., p. 238. There is some controversy over whether "such" in this passage refers to the critics mentioned above or to the qualities enumerated above. The conventional scholarly view is that Hume here subscribes to an "ideal observer" theory, in which the judgments of a hypothetical appreciator, abstracted from the positive characteristics of normal appreciation, are taken to be canonical within their cultural context.

3   In a way, this proposal for theoretic composition is reminiscent of Zeuxis's famous notion that artistic representations of beautiful beings (especially patron gods and goddesses) are best achieved by selecting the best features from this and that existing beautiful person and creating a composite more beautiful than any one individual. Although Zeuxis's combinatory method does rely on empirical subject matter, it ultimately responds to a standard of beauty that was allegedly independent of, and beyond, any material manifestation. By contrast, Hume's theory stays stubbornly in this world and regards beauty judgments as tied to historically evolved pleasurable reactions universal only in the sense that they may be imputed to observers always and everywhere.

4   Peter Jones, "David Hume: Survey of Thought," *Encyclopedia of Aesthetics,* vol. 2, p. 426.

5   George Dickie, *The Century of Taste: The Philosophical Odyssey of Taste in the Eighteenth Century* (Oxford University Press, 1996), p. 130.

6   This is the identifying characterization given in Roger Tory Peterson's *Field Guide to Western Birds,* 2d. ed. (Boston: Houghton Mifflin, 1961). Although the simile invoked requires a hearer-dependent determination that this sounds like that, the claim remains objective because it is intersubjectively validated and not dependent on any one hearer's views or beliefs.

7   One can imagine a band of early romantics strenuously urging mountain-dwellers to see the surrounding peaks as beautiful, despite the long-standing contrary conviction.

8   The theory of performative expression was one of the major accomplishments of twentieth-century ordinary language philosophy. It is given its fullest exposition in J.L. Austin's *How to Do Things With Words* (Oxford University Press, 1965).

9   The emotive theory of ethics is sometimes caricatured as espousing this position. But no serious exponent of that theory ever held that positive and negative emotive expressions were *all there is* to the matter.

10   I might add that the process of natural aesthetic maturation closely parallels the development of ethical judgment in moral cultures and individuals. The bedrock in both cases is affirmation or disapproval. Moral standards evolve in social settings to the point where it is possible to say, descriptively, that in a given culture it is a fact that, for example, a woman's failing to cover her hair is taken to be wicked. Here again there is a subjective element (moral judgments "don't leave us cold") and an objective one

(there are facts about prevailing moral rules). We all know that morals, like mores, change over time as a result of the systole and diastole of critical reaction.

11 This is not to say that both demarcations are free from critical contention. Far from it.

12 This was really Mill's point in *On Liberty* (London: Oxford University Press, 1859). The good and worthwhile beliefs are the ones that grow out of uncritical contexts but are then subjected to the refining fire of critical commentary. Those that survive are re-affirmed and have the credit of criticism added to that of intuition.

13 The standard account of beauty judgment in regard to just those qualities that natural objects might have in various qualitative degrees and in which the amplitude of these degrees is decisive in the assessment of them is to be found in Guy Sircello's *A New Theory of Beauty* (Princeton University Press, 1975).

14 This is the very point Plato has Socrates score against over-attention to a single artistic subject matter in *Ion*.

15 Hepburn, "Contemporary Aesthetics and the Neglect of Natural Beauty," p. 61.

16 Beardsley, *Aesthetics: Problems*, p. 528.

17 Beardsley, *Aesthetic Point of View*, p. 289.

18 In this respect, it is a bit like deeming Mozart's works beautiful because they are usually performed in such handsome settings.

19 Sometimes, but very rarely, acting in favor of aesthetic objects may imply an imperative to withhold them from general attention (as with certain Native American sacred vestments) or even to destroy them (as with Tibetan sand paintings).

20 The latter pose obvious problems of verification. But these problems are no different from those that attach to art critics, drama critics, music critics, et al. who may not, on a given occasion, be in the properly receptive frame of mind yet can still make expert judgments about a work's aesthetic merits. A record of judgments based on unimpaired positive responses can give us confidence that judgments based on beliefs about hypothetical responses are reliable.

21 The idea of a felicific calculus is a notion no one since Bentham has really taken seriously—with the possible exception of Richard Posner.

22 This issue is taken up with great subtlety in Martha Nussbaum's *Love's Knowledge: Essays on Philosophy and Literature* (Oxford University Press, 1990).

23 Budd, *Aesthetic Appreciation of Nature*, p. 2.

24 If this were so, the only intelligible alternative to Carlson's natural-environmental model of natural appreciation would be the formal model, and not even Carlson is such a radical reductionist.

25 Carlson, *Aesthetics and the Environment*, p. 12.

26 Hepburn, "Trivial and Serious," p. 67.

27 In "Icebreakers: Environmentalism and Natural Aesthetics," (*Journal of Applied Philosophy* 11 [1994] pp. 15-30), Stan Godlovitch presents a powerful argument for an "acentric" environmental vision, one that insists that nature be taken on its own terms, rather than ours or anyone else's. However sensible such a view may be as it regards the contemplation of environments as a whole, it seems inapplicable to the localized and particular business of forming beauty judgments. This is because, for reasons indicated in chapter 5, to the extent that these judgments turn on aesthetic experience, they are inevitably tied to factors of consciousness that are indelibly human and which frustrate any effort at acentricity.

28 Human beauty *is* a species of natural beauty. So, it is possible for what are usually called "beauty contests" involving human contestants to be comparisons of physical characteristics judged by experts in current and contextual aesthetic standards. This possibility is seldom, if ever, realized. Comparing human to animal competitions does, however, highlight the issue of externalities. It has been argued that in human contests non-sensible features such as "congeniality" count toward a person's physical beauty. There is nothing intrinsically wrong with extending the denotation of "beauty" to cover such features. Indeed, current English usage tolerates the extension of its denotation to all manner of admirable characteristics. The worry such usage invites is that the *primary* sense in which aesthetic attention to the sensible is the key element can be obliterated by a host of secondary senses. It was a need for just such a distinction that led Richard Sclafani and George Dickie to distinguish between the primary, secondary, and tertiary senses of "art," and to limit their aesthetic analysis to the first of these. I think it is important to insist that not every admirable quality of a thing is part of its beauty. Remembering this exclusionary principle may immunize us from some of the over-reaching claims of theorists who want to wrap every aspect of every natural object in the cloak of beauty.

29 Carlson presents this point very clearly in chapter 7 of *Aesthetics and the Environment*.

30 Carlson, "The Aesthetics of Art and Nature," p. 220.

CHAPTER 8

Syncretic Regard—Part II

GENERAL FACTORS

*L*et us begin the turn from typal to general aesthetic judgment by thinking about clouds. Why clouds? Because they are paradigmatic examples of natural objects that are sometimes beautiful and sometimes not, that can be beautiful both singly and in multiple formation, that frequently constitute elements of larger aesthetic conspectuses, and—most importantly—that are observable pretty much everywhere. Clouds are as available to the city child as to the back country trekker, as familiar to the farmer as to the meteorologist, and as prominent in the art and folklore of most cultures as they are in the six-thirty weather report.

It is distinctive of modern cultures through much of the world that questions about what a cloud *is* are turned over to scientists. The science of clouds has burgeoned over the last century and now comprises a very considerable body of empirical data and theory. American children usually get their first taste of this science when they learn the standard taxonomy of cloud types (stratus, cirrus, cumulus, cumulonimbus, etc.) in school or summer camp. In the course of looking at the sky to detect the stated differentia, many children pay closer attention to clouds than ever before. This attention sometimes leads to an increased appreciation of clouds' aesthetic qualities. What we learn in this way gives us a basis for regarding some remarks we make about clouds as right or wrong. If, looking at a huge, compact, fluffy-looking pile, you say it's cumulus and I say it's cirrus, you are right and I am wrong. That is so because a person who fails to recognize the type to which a token cloud belongs makes a category mistake. Similarly, if in looking at a dark configuration of clouds on the horizon I say "that means rain" and you dissent, one of us can be right and the other wrong. Here it's a question of seeing how events play out, taking the clouds not as exemplars of types, but as testable clues about future outcomes.

If, however, I say that an odd, angular concatenation of features in a cloud formation is a "W" and it stands for Wittgenstein, and you say it's an inverted "M" because it stands for Malcolm, it would be boorish or foolish, or both, to insist that one of our opinions is right and the other wrong.[1] This is because there is, in such a case, neither an applicable category that controls regard nor an implied prediction as to an outcome. The experience of most people who have given any prolonged attention to clouds confirms this fact. A formation that looks like a duck to one party may well look like an angel to another, and a map of Wisconsin to a third. Experiences like this show us that while some of our judgments about clouds are clearly true or false some of them are neither.

Now suppose that the question is not whether a given cloud is of this or that type, not predictive of this or that result, not "W" or "M," but simply whether it is *beautiful*. Historically, responses to questions of this sort have run to excess along two divergent paths. One path leads in the direction of rigid, canonical standards. A good many theorists have supposed that, if judging the cloud to be beautiful is to be anything more than a purely subjective and therefore uninformative declaration of personal delectation, it must invoke a fixed, knowable criterion of cloud beauty. Cognitive idealists, as we have seen, generally took the position that determining that a thing is beautiful is the same thing as determining that it is a perfect exemplar of its type. To Plato the question of what a cloud truly is and the question as to whether it is beautiful are the same question. Many later thinkers less comfortable with conflating metaphysical and normative issues in this way have nevertheless often insist-ed—in the interest of reaching a reasonable level of determinacy in aesthetic claims—that judging a cloud to be beautiful must be substantially *like* a typal judgment. There must be, they say, some recognizable, intersubjectively acces-sible measure of the cloud's beauty if disagreements about its aesthetic status are to be resolvable. Just as atmospheric scientists can agree upon something like a model cumulus cloud, so, they urge, aestheticians should be able to agree upon something like a model of cumulus cloud beauty (or of back-lit cumulus beauty, twilight cumulus beauty, etc.). Reference to such a cloud beauty model would then settle the question of particular aesthetic merit in much the way that the taxonomic model settles the question of its type. Youthful nature-observers sometimes carry with them reference cards bearing images of cloud types.[2] Mightn't they carry with them similar reference cards bearing images of cloud-beauty types?

If we thought that cloud beauty judgments were like schnauzer beauty judgments, such a strategy might make sense. But we don't, and it doesn't. First, the prevailing modern unwillingness to hand over final authority about clouds to standards and experts reflects our post-Kantian conviction that the intensity and quality of individual aesthetic experience is of more importance in regard to most natural objects than the identification of any criteria-satisfying characteristics they may have. However beholden our personal aesthetic responses may be to the descriptive judgments established within our nature-world, we generally insist on retaining the authority to amplify or amend them in forming our own reflective, corrective, and affirmative judgments. Second, even if we were—in a Humean spirit—to take cloud beauty models to embody the very judgment we *would* have reached were our appreciations undistorted and unimpaired,[3] the more model-judgment becomes like typal-judgment, the more prone it becomes to the latter's failings. Not least of these is the obvious fact that there are many natural objects, or combinations of objects, for which there is *no* type. The thing that might strike us as beautiful in a particular early evening sky is the peculiar way a thick bank of fluffy, reddening cumulus clouds is juxtaposed against a jagged mountain outcropping, casting long shadows on the plain below. Here, the appreciation of clouds as clouds, outcroppings as outcroppings, and so on, is dissolved in the more comprehensive grasp of a conspectus without a name. Third, the more appreciation is impelled in the direction of typal analysis the more it fastens on a thing's claim to exemplariness rather than on its impressive particularities. Just as, in our experience of human faces, the features that make them especially fine exemplars of their types (whatever types we may select) are often not those that lead us to find them especially beautiful,[4] what makes a given cloud beautiful may well be something about it that involves a departure from, rather than conformity to, its type.

The second path leads in the anarchic direction of giving any response as much aesthetic authority as any other. Where the other course suffered from a fatal form of conceptual stinginess (its restriction of attention to what fits types or something like them), this one suffers from an equally fatal form of conceptual profligacy. To begin with, if we take aesthetic appreciation to be as open to idiosyncratic appraisal as is a dispute over whether a given cloud is seen as an M or as a W, we risk breaching the law of non-contradiction and entering the logical morass that yawns behind it. Nothing can be both an M and a W at the same time and in the same respects, and that is because W is taken to be a form of non-M, and nothing can be both M and non-M. Denying this last claim, by alleging that you are right in claiming that the cloud is

M while I am right in claiming that it is W, leads to the absurd implication that anything follows from anything. Second, even if we don't think of the difference between my judgment and yours as one of logical incompatibility, the more an account of natural beauty judgment runs to unbridled personal preference the less it provides a basis for impartial discrimination between our rival views. If saying that this particular cumulus cloud is beautiful means no more than that you like it because it is fluffy and tinged with aquamarine and I don't, natural aesthetics dissolves into the sociology of personal preference. Third, if beauty judgment is seen to be an enterprise dominated by an endless diversity of likes and dislikes, whims, and fancies, the more its fundamental seriousness—its connection to the other important value considerations in our lives—is lost. Such a view reduces natural beauty discussion to a survey of wordless and irrefutable feelings that defy appraisal, criticism, or interpersonal comparison. If beauty is to have currency as a social value, it cannot be so tightly bound to individual perspective that the question of whether this cloud is more beautiful than that is the equivalent of whether its shape invokes Wittgenstein more than Malcolm.

Disconnection of aesthetic judgment from any disposition to act with respect to the objects judged is a potential consequence that looms at the end of either of the paths I have described. If judging a cloud to be beautiful is ultimately taken to be a matter of checking a perception against a concept, model, or type, there is no reason to think that this undertaking necessarily implies any incentive to act one way or another according to its results. Equally, if judging a cloud to be beautiful is simply a matter of registering various emotive responses in a vast, unranked display, there is again no implied incentive to act. If we think, as I believe we should, that natural beauty judgment *does* entail a positive disposition to act in some way regarding the objects judged, we must reject both conclusions.

When an observer declares that this particular cumulus cloud is beautiful, she is doing more than joining her knowledge about cumulus clouds to her knowledge of beauty. She is making a *choice* regarding this cloud, a choice that declares one path in life more acceptable than another. She is saying, in effect, that interrupting her quotidian activities to admire the aesthetic qualities of this particular cloud was not only a good choice for her, but a choice she would recommend to others. She is making a case for *acting* one way or another in the natureworld.[5] Like moral judgment, natural beauty judgment is wedded to behavioral disposition on a broad scale of intensity of commitment. Sometimes, in saying that a natural object is beautiful, we imply no more than that we are positively disposed to enjoin others to appreciate its sensible qualities.

At other times, saying that a natural object is beautiful implies a more active willingness to preserve, protect, celebrate, or otherwise enhance the status of that object in the natureworld. In saying that natural beauty judgments, like moral judgments, don't leave us cold we are saying that they are always more than notations on a checklist of approvals. They make a difference—sometimes small, sometimes large, but always a real difference—to the way we lead our lives.

The two extreme paths I have described lead, as such paths almost always do, to dead ends. Yet, one of the most powerful lessons of history is that the pendulum of theory has to swing to one extreme and then to the other in order to make plain the place for a plausible middle ground. There *is* a plausible middle ground to be taken here. I lay out its essentials in the remainder of this chapter.

Intensive Beauty

Sometimes, but not always, what we find aesthetically appealing in a natural object is the prominence or intensity of a sensory quality it displays. This quality may have nothing to do with the object's type and nothing to do with its propensity to any future outcome. *Lantana*, exposed to the warmth of a sunny day, exudes a rich fragrance that many people find beautiful. If we walk by a planting of *lantana* and catch a whiff of this aroma, we may be pleased without coming to any aesthetic conclusion. But if we are tempted by that whiff to stop and attend to the aroma more carefully, focusing on *it* instead of all the other things that are going on in our lives, the very intensity of the fragrance may impel us to conclude that it is beautiful. It's not the quality of the *lantana* as a specimen of its type that counts. And it's certainly not how this plant and its characteristic fragrance fits into some larger scheme of things. Its scent is not beautiful because it calls up ecclesiastical incense or expensive perfume. What we are finding beautiful in this instance is the experience of a particular fruity, spicy aroma, emphatically presented to our olfactory sense.

As this example shows, the sheer intensity of a fragrance (or presumably any other sensible quality) can on its own provide a reasonable basis for a natural beauty judgment. In declaring that the *lantana* fragrance is beautiful, I am saying (at least) that I am positively moved by it in a way that sustains attention and deepens with it (or, if I am not now smelling it, that I would be moved by it under appropriate conditions). I am also saying that I would expect that other people with unimpaired olfactory senses would be similarly moved and would find the fragrance beautiful. By insisting that my beauty judgment here does not terminate in a declaration of personal pleasure but implies the imputation of similar judgments to others, I am agreeing with Kant that such a judgment contributes to our conviction that aesthetic connections bind people together. This does not, however, commit me to following Kant in regarding such a judgment as implicitly universal, calling on a set of responsive characteristics shared by all sentient beings. Rather, it is enough that the judgment imply an expectation of agreement on the part of a large portion of one's cultural community, a large enough population to insure that the judgment is genuinely social and contextual. This population will certainly include the natureworld "insiders," but it is likely to include others as well, others who don't yet have a serious stake in the aesthetic qualities of natural objects, but may be inspired by intense beauty to develop one.

The leading proponent of the view that intensity should be a prominent factor in aesthetic judgment is Guy Sircello. In *A New Theory of Beauty*, he argues that the beauty of both artifactual and natural objects should be assessed in relation to their propensity to display "properties of qualitative degree" to an especially pronounced extent. One of his paradigm examples is the craggy, dentate appearance of the Santa Ana Mountains as seen when the sun comes up behind them. This ridgeline is not, Sircello insists, beautiful on most occasions. It cannot compete in craggy splendor with many of the ridges in the Dolomites, for example. Instead, the Santa Ana ridge *becomes* beautiful just when the sun is in the east, illuminating its planes and contours in a particularly striking way.[6] This example shows us three things. First, it shows us that a beauty judgment about a natural object can reasonably be grounded in the degree to which that object exhibits a given beauty-making characteristic rather than in the mere presence or absence of that characteristic. Second, it shows us that a natural object can be understood to become beautiful (or presumably to become un-beautiful) in the course of changes that affect the way we see it. It is a peculiar confluence of atmospheric, meteorological, and observational features rather than something about the craggy ridge itself that makes it beautiful on those occasions when it is. Third, it shows us that the *degree* of presence of any one beauty-contributing quality does not make a thing itself beautiful. An intensely yellow mushroom might be beautifully yellow without being a beautiful mushroom. Yet a daffodil can be beautiful because it is beautifully yellow, even though it is not an excellent specimen of its species.[7]

Just as the intense presentation of certain aesthetic characteristics may make a natural object beautiful, a lack of intensity in those same characteristics can prevent its being beautiful. An otherwise splendid crystal might be disqualified as beautiful because it doesn't show sufficient clarity or color. Qualities that may be *individually* beautiful because of their intensity may, in combination with other qualities in a group of natural objects, become *jointly*, or *cooperatively* beautiful because of the patterns, compositions, or designs that they create. It can also happen that the very quality of intensity that contributes to a thing's beauty when taken individually works against the formal beauty of a larger whole. (It may clash with other elements of that whole, or stand out in a way that makes it seem out of place, etc.) Moreover, the relative prominence or intensity of a given sensory quality may *emerge* only in the context of its relations with other qualities and things. So there is a close connection between the natural-beauty-making features mentioned here and those mentioned in the next section.

Formal Beauty

Where intensive natural beauty is an effect of the emphatic presence of a sensed feature or features, formal natural beauty is an effect of relations among a thing's various features or of the relations of its features to features of other things in an aesthetic grouping somehow framed or composed into a whole. It is in virtue of these relations rather than the presence of any one feature or set of features that a thing is deemed formally beautiful. In the fading hours of a winter afternoon the low-angled sun may catch a lake's countless ripples and troughs, casting them into a pulsating, shifting-but-repetitive pattern that we are likely to find delightful and captivating. It is clear that the dominant effect here is not that of typal beauty, as I have presented it above. For while we are perfectly aware that what we are seeing is a lake, that the ripples are upswellings of water, the glint a product of the sun's reflection, and so on, our aesthetic awareness doesn't focus on any of these things as exemplars of their types. Nor is the effect contingent on typal recognition. In finding this vivid spectacle beautiful, we may well be largely oblivious of the roles its various components play in the natural order and simply get caught up in the *look* of these things as they form an experienced whole.

The ingredients of formal natural beauty may be, and often are, sensible characteristics beautiful in themselves on account of their intensity or prominence. But again, this need not always be the case. Snorkelers in a tropical lagoon may be struck by the beauty of the spectacular confluence of two schools of reef fish—that beauty being mainly a delight in the arrangement and interplay of colors, shapes, and motions—without finding any characteristics of the fish themselves beautiful for their intensity or relative prominence. This is not to say that intense beauty cannot complement and amplify formal beauty. If the fish in one of the schools had been beautifully yellow tangs and those in the other beautifully blue parrotfish, the intersection of the schools is likely to have been all the more stunning. And if that intersection should occur, the intense beauty of component features would enhance the formal beauty of the whole constellation of features in their interaction, rendering the pattern or design created by its component elements more vivid, more emphatic. Yet the formal beauty that attaches to this constellation of natural objects would remain even if, due to a sudden overcast, its ingredients should lose the beauty that attaches to them through their color intensity.

The components of formal natural beauty are endlessly various. Certain arrangements of tastes, sounds, smells, tactile qualities, shapes, colors, and movements conduce to sustained and deepening aesthetic pleasure, and others don't. The reasons why some do and some don't are lost in the deep shadows of evolutionary history. Useful work in the direction of exposing some of the evolutionary roots of aesthetic value has been done by Jay Appleton, Evelyn Dissanayeke, Gordon Orians, Grant Hildebrand, and others.[8] This research appears to show, for example, that our common aesthetic preference for certain configurations of limbs on trees may be traceable to the accessibility of some limbs and not others to our remote ancestors as they fled from predators. But no one imagines that this work could eventually lead to a complete explanation of our modern notion of natural beauty. At most, it would explain how we came to think of some things as beautiful and others not, leaving untouched the question of why we persist in thinking this way and why we defend our judgments with reasons that have little or nothing to do with our prehistoric past.

How certain elements in our experience came to be valued is one question. The status of their value in relation to all the other elements of present-day life is quite another.[9] It may strike us that the combination of features we find beautiful here are appealing and important because they connect to, or resonate with, recurring wordless features of our everyday experience—features we know and value, but which come vividly to mind only when brought to the foreground of consciousness by aesthetic presentations such as this. When we pause to reflect on it, it may even occur to us that our emotive lives are replete with elements analogous to these glints, pulsations, and patterns. It may also occur to us that a fair measure of what makes a life rich and rewarding involves both the delectation of these various components and the enterprise of coaxing them into a harmonious pattern or design. Because the components of

formal natural beauty are so various, the causal influences of their evolutionary sources so obscure, and their interconnection with other patterns in our
lives so multifarious, we should regard efforts to pronounce general principles
of formal natural beauty as futile. In this, we are once again agreeing with
Hume, who chose to leave the topic of formal beauty as an unanalyzed tangle
of connections between perceptions and pleasure contingently related to the
various responsive means members of aesthetically aware cultures have come
to have.[10]

The thought that formal beauty is ineffable and destined to remain so was
later emphatically embraced by the nineteenth-century formalists, led by Clive
Bell and Roger Fry. Bell declared that "for a discussion of aesthetics, it need be
agreed only that forms arranged and combined according to certain unknown
and mysterious laws do move us in a particular way."[11] Here he was speaking
of visual art, rather than natural beauty, or beauty generally. But there is little
question that he intended the point to apply more broadly. The formalists who
subscribed to Bell's notion of "unknown and mysterious laws" and the doctrine of "significant form" they generated were quick to apply these ideas to
beauty judgment in all contexts.

The hazards of this campaign are obvious. If principles of formal beauty
are available only to intuition and expressible only through example, there is
no uncontroversial way of knowing whether one has got them right. Suppose
that Able is a world-renowned, much-decorated cabinetmaker. Able insists
that the wood on the table Baker is contemplating buying has an extraordinary
granular pattern, the beauty of which makes the piece worth the price being
asked. Baker isn't so sure. Everyone says Able is an acute and reliable judge of
the aesthetics of wood grain beauty. But, when it comes down to it, the grain
pattern on that table doesn't inspire Baker. In fact, it leaves him cold. If the
grain is either beautiful or unbeautiful, one of them is right and the other is
wrong. Where can we turn to settle the issue?

One easy answer is "nowhere." Aesthetic skeptics and emotivists regard the
mystery invoked by Hume, Bell, and Fry as a cloak for ignorance and conceptual disarray. The reason natural beauty judgments look mysterious, they will
say, is that there is nothing under the magician's hat. They declare the idea of
"true judges" bankrupt on the grounds that everyone has his or her own preferences regarding arrangements of form—no one better than another—and
any convergence among these preferences should be regarded as coincidental,
or at most reflective of social fads. "Formal beauty," they will say, is just a fancy
word for "I like it" (seen as a simple emotive judgment) or "That's what's in
vogue" (seen as a descriptive judgment).

An equally easy answer leads in the opposite direction. This is the idea that the principles of formal beauty are, *pace* Hume et al., neither mysterious nor ineffable but ultimately reducible to canonical norms. This is a view that has more adherents in schools of design than it has among philosophers. Still, there have been sporadic, bold attempts by philosophers to state general aesthetic principles meant to apply equally to any arrangement of elements. One of the best of these is to be found in Stephen Pepper's *Principles of Art Appreciation*.[12] As Pepper sees it, the four central elements of design, or formal beauty, are contrast, gradation, theme-and-variation, and restraint. Although Pepper's primary focus is on aesthetic qualities in the arts, he lays out principles that involve "aesthetic likings" generally—likings that apply equally to artworks and to all manner of other things in a responsive life. One might quarrel with his inventory, and it is not difficult to make a case for exceptions to his principles. Still, as Pepper illustrates in instance after instance, artworks that exemplify combinations of the principles he has identified move us by tapping values important in our lives outside the museum, the concert hall, and the sculpture garden.[13]

What makes accounts like Pepper's appealing is the sense they express—and that most of us, I believe, have—that there *should* be a close connection among the forms or relations of forms we find beautiful in nature, in art, and in our lives generally. What may make them ultimately unconvincing is the conspicuous thinness of their stated principles. Contrast, gradation, theme-and-variation, and restraint can be found here and there and everywhere, arguably as often in settings we find ugly as in those we find beautiful. So, even if these qualities should be regarded as individually necessary elements in the composition of formal beauty, they cannot be regarded as its jointly sufficient elements.

The harder, but more promising, solution lies between the extremes of skepticism and subscription to stated principles. To reach it, we turn again to the Deweyan-Beardsleyan notion that formal elements in any context (natural or artifactual) are admired usually, if not always, just when they are framed or composed into a savorable, appreciable, whole of experience. On this account, it is neither the components of formal array nor the designs or patterns they create *per se* that should direct our thinking about formal beauty. Instead, it is their effect on the resultant aesthetic experience, whose own bounds and inward organization are pleasing for their integrating effect in our lives.

As I mentioned in chapter 4, Dewey regarded the conversion of experience-at-large into the having of *an* experience as life's fundamental value producer. Formal unity, on Dewey's terms, entails the concrescence of sensed elements. Formal beauty, as he presents it, is the beauty of the whole-ness or unity of the experience itself, clarified and intensified by its traits

of continuity, rhythm, contour, and what he called the "consummatory quality." Beardsley, as we saw, amended Dewey's analysis with his own inventory
of aesthetic experience-making characteristics. It is fair to infer from what he
says on this score that one aesthetic experience is held to be superior to another
if it demonstrates a greater number or intensity of those characteristics—object directedness, felt freedom, detached affect, active discovery, and a sense
of wholeness. In chapter 5, I argued for a cumulative, "sorites" approach to
qualifying an experience as an aesthetic experience. Now I want to extend this
same approach to the issue of comparing aesthetic experiences in establishing
gradations of formal beauty.

A little while ago, I claimed that the components of formal natural beauty
are endlessly various and that the most we can say about them is that certain
of their arrangements please us and others don't, for reasons we will likely
never know. But this doesn't mean that any natural object can be as formally
beautiful as anything other. Nor does it mean that elements of formal natural
beauty can't be taught. Consider again the example of the conflict between
Able and Baker over the beauty of the pattern of grain in a tabletop. In first
describing this example, I said that it would *seem* the grain is either beautiful
or not and that therefore it would *seem* one of the two is mistaken. But this is
the wrong way to look at the situation. When Baker looks at the grain pattern,
deploying both sense and intelligence, his reaction may or may not amount
to an experience of the kind Dewey, Beardsley, and I had in mind in speaking
of aesthetic experiences. In saying that he finds the grain pattern beautiful,
we can now take it that Able means to convey the idea that it *does* move him
in that way (or perhaps, more circumspectly, that it is such that it would so
move him under proper conditions of appreciation), and that he invites Baker
to join him in being so moved. The difference between the two isn't really a
difference about formal properties of the wood. It's a difference of opinion
about how regarding these properties in this way or that ends up elevating and
intensifying the experience. Able may succeed in bringing Baker around by
pointing out characteristics of the grain arrangement he may have overlooked,
or didn't have the training to see, or couldn't see from his perspective. There
is no loss of meaning if we put the point another way in saying that Able may
succeed in teaching Baker how to see the beauty in the wood. And of course it
remains open to Baker to persuade Able that he is making too much of this or
that characteristic in the wood, and overstating its beauty.

This is the familiar dialectic of formal beauty interaction between people
who initially disagree, and it underscores the common human impulse to
induce in others positive experiences one has had. From one initial point of

view, the wood grain wasn't beautiful. But it can *become* beautiful as the quality of the aesthetic experience one has regarding it deepens. Degrees of formal natural beauty are nothing more than notations of the comparative strength of cumulated elements in the experiences of those who find these experiences rich and rewarding. For the most part these are the same elements that contributed to qualifying these experiences as aesthetic experiences in the first place. Natural objects become formally beautiful as we have positive aesthetic experiences in respect to them. One natural object will be more beautiful than another just when the experiential quality (a cumulative effect of factors such as those I have mentioned above) outstrips the experiential quality of the other. As we grow up aesthetically, and as we learn more facts about the natural world, our responses become clarified and intensified. Teachers, natural scientists, artists, poets, and lots of other folks help us shape our experiences of natural objects in ways that make our formal judgments more confident. Equally importantly, in growing up aesthetically we come to see the ways in which similarities and contrasts between formal elements of natural beauty, formal elements of artifactual beauty, and formal elements in the intentional design of our own lives contribute to each other.

Formal Beauty and Formalism

Lately, formal beauty has not been treated very sympathetically as a component in the aesthetic appreciation of natural objects and environments. There are two reasons for this. First, there is the conceptual hangover that Bell, Fry, and their *ars gratia artis* allies induced in the aesthetic community through overindulgence in the idea that form is all-important in painting. These early advocates of form-over-subject insisted that the only point in attending to the formal qualities of artworks was their capacity to effect extraordinary emotions (Bell spoke of them as a form of ecstasy) cut off from ordinary life. From what I've said already it should be clear that the appreciation of formal beauty, whether in nature or in art, need not be seen as an impetus for any manner of transcendental departure from everyday experience. Quite the contrary. As I have presented it, formal beauty can play a significant formative role in framing and organizing life's important elements generally. There may be no more perfect expression of the formal beauty of tones in time than Bach's *Kunst der Fuge*. But the forms woven into that masterpiece do not stand apart from our lives like a shrine to be visited when we are feeling musically reverent. They are instead beautiful because we can hear—if we listen attentively—myriad ways in which these same patterns are woven into our emotive and social lives.

The second reason for denigrating formal beauty is a species of naturalistic puritanism that has attracted some modern-day conceptualists. Its central tenet is the belief that attention to formal beauty is a perversion of the proper role of appreciation. Proponents of this belief insist a distinction be drawn between viewing natural phenomena as scenes (whose appreciable qualities may be determined by their relation to others within some kind of frame) and regarding them as the unbounded, unorganized things they *really* are. A dazzling display of swooping terns against a coastal cliff may make a pretty picture. But these shapes and motions are the shapes and motions of *living birds*, doing the things birds of their kind do naturally. So, it is argued, any account of their beauty that neglects these facts misses the whole point of the appreciation of natural beauty as natural, reducing displays of birds in flight to something analogous to bird patterns in quilts, dance movements, or birdsongs in tone poems.

Anti-formalism's most vigorous champion is Allen Carlson. But Carlson is by no means an out-and-out enemy of formal beauty. Nor is his view puritanical in the sense that it would both deny any positive role to formal beauty in nature and regard those who do embrace such a role as misguided extremists. Carlson has no quarrel with taking formal qualities as relevant factors in the determination of aesthetic value in the art world, including that portion of the art world that portrays or depicts nature. He is happy to concede that formal aspects such as balance, proportion, and organization "are rightly appreciated in, and contribute significantly to the aesthetic value of" landscape paintings and postcard reproductions of the natural objects they portray.[14] The mistake that must be avoided, he cautions, is to "assume that formal qualities have at least the same place and importance in our aesthetic appreciation of the natural environment as they have in the appreciation and evaluation of art."[15] That mistake is compounded if one assumes that formal qualities are *exclusively* relevant in determining aesthetic qualities in the natural environment. Carlson reserves the term "formalism" for those who make the latter mistake.[16]

Carlson thinks that the root of the problem with formalism is a pernicious reductionism, a tendency to regard all aesthetic appreciation of natural objects as something like a transformation of the environment into an arrangement of lines and colors.[17] But this is a misleading characterization of what defenders of formal natural beauty actually think about the appreciative process. Formalism is indeed fatally flawed if it is defined as a position that neglects all other aesthetically relevant aspects of a thing to focus only on form and arrangement.

But, on that construal, no one, or practically no one, is a formalist. To say that something has a beautiful shape or an harmonious composition is not to say that it is beautiful or admirable *only* in those ways. Affirming that a certain configuration of tree limbs, stars, and sounds is beautiful because these elements form a compelling and pleasing pattern need in no way denigrate the environment in which they have their place.

The appreciation of formal beauty in nature as I have portrayed it certainly doesn't reduce nature to scenery or "views," or framed-feature-displays alienated from an environmental matrix in the way that a Claude-glass or camera viewfinder does.[18] It simply takes stock of two aspects (that a thing is natural and that its sensible properties are configured in a certain way) of one sector of our experiential perspective without denying the importance of other aspects. For that matter, no aesthetic mistake can properly be attributed to a person who enjoys the look of a detached configuration of natural features in a Claude-glass so long as she is cognizant of the fact that the beauty she is enjoying is the beauty of selected aspects, rather than of the whole, of a subject that could be otherwise and more comprehensively perceived.

Finally, it is worthwhile remembering that Carlson's anti-formalist argument is focused exclusively on *environmental appreciation*, excluding all appreciation of natural objects considered apart from their environment. Clearly, not all appreciation of the beauty of natural objects need be an appreciation of those objects as situated in natural environments. I may, for example, be powerfully impressed by the intricate, glittering formation of lavender-tinged quartz crystals in a geode resting on a library mantel. What would be the point of denying that I can find this thing beautiful as a natural object even though it is no longer situated in its basaltic matrix? Indeed, in its matrix the geode would be impenetrable to the aesthetic regard to which it is now open. Nor can I see the point of insisting that its manifest formal qualities (the complex pattern light refraction, the odd-angled layering of rectilinear planes, etc.) should be disqualified as contributing to the geode's beauty just because they are so conspicuously *framed* by the aperture that reveals the inner crystals. To be sure, observing natural objects in their rich environmental contexts can produce different and additional appreciative effects. But it is pointless to deny that some natural objects have formal characteristics that contribute to their beauty quite independently of an environmental setting, and that, at the same time, remind us emphatically of their natural—i.e., non-artifactual—status.

I am not alone in opposing anti-formalism's denigration of the role of formal beauty in the appreciation of natural objects. In *The Aesthetic Appreciation of Nature*, Malcolm Budd attacks anti-formalism along lines similar to my own.[19]

Recent formalist counterattacks have been mounted by Patricia Matthews, Ira Newman, and Nick Zangwill, among others.[20] The common strand that runs among their arguments is an insistence that, in some circumstances at least, attention to sensible features of natural objects altogether detached from attention to the type or category to which those objects belong is a necessary (although possibly not a sufficient) condition of the appropriate appreciation of their natural beauty. This "new formalism," as it has been called, differs from the kind Bell, Fry, et al. proposed ("traditional" or "extreme" formalism) chiefly in that it reduces the importance of specifically *compositional* elements (i.e., designs organized by frames or informal framing strategies) and also restricts the ascription of formal beauty to parts, rather than the whole, of the domain of natural objects.

In *The Metaphysics of Beauty* Nick Zangwill presents a particularly vigorous defense of new formalism (which he prefers to call "moderate formalism"). He argues that the conceptualist restriction of aesthetic appreciation of natural objects to what they are seen *as* under appropriate categories is oblivious to the fact that "nature has purposeless beauty" that can, and sometimes should, be regarded as category-independent.[21] Moreover, he points out, some living natural objects are readily found to be beautiful in ways that have nothing at all to do with the kinds of natural beings they are. His example: "the elegant and somewhat dainty beauty of a polar bear swimming underwater."[22] This is, he says, an "incongruous beauty," an illustration of the fact that nature is full of surprises.[23] The general lesson to be derived from examples like this is that we shouldn't be trapped by conceptualization into failing to take stock of all kinds of unexpected and complex features natural objects present to our senses. The formal beauty of biological nature emerges when we unblinker ourselves from the spell of categories. I agree with him entirely, of course.

Zangwill's position on inorganic (i.e., non-biological) natural beauty is more conceptually aggressive, and is meant to cut more sharply against anti-formalism. He says:

> Extreme formalism about inorganic nature seems obvious to me. Surely, where a natural thing has no purpose, we need only consider what we can immediately perceive, and we need not know about its origin. The beauty of an inorganic natural thing at a time is surely determined just by its narrow non-aesthetic properties at that time. Anything else may be interesting, but it does not (or should not) affect aesthetic appreciation.[24]

There is, he says, nothing wrong with regarding Hepburn's celebrated sea-bed mud flat first one way, then another—just as Hepburn described himself as doing. But it's important to see both that the beauty uncovered by one description doesn't annihilate the beauty uncovered by another and that the beauties presented in the experience are *all* formal beauties, different only in *scale*. They are formal beauties because they are free from historical and functional dependence on natural types, environmental matrices, etc. And they are *all* formal beauties because the only aesthetic properties that count in an a-historical, function-free context are those that are presented to our senses for immediate delectation.

This is where my agreement with Zangwill ends. Although I endorse many of the ingredients in Zangwill's version of new formalism,[25] I cannot endorse the conclusion which he constructs from these ingredients. From the fact that various natural objects are, as non-living things, cut free from organic environments it does not follow that their beauty is always and only formal beauty. Unless, of course, the concept of formal beauty is exploded in such a way as to make Zangwill's claim trivially true. But it shouldn't be trivially true that all inorganic natural beauty is formal beauty. Not everything that is non-conceptual (i.e., category-free) natural beauty should be regarded as formal beauty. It is not only Zangwill who ventures down this mistaken path. By expanding the notion of formal beauty to cover a great deal more than was covered under traditional formalism, the new formalists in general lose sight of the importance of retaining the sense in which aesthetic viewing is selective and multi-optional. To regard all inorganic beauty as formal beauty is to rule out ways in which the same natural object can be variously beautiful. The rock crystal that impresses us visually as a wonderful concatenation of planes, angles, and reflective surfaces can be regarded as formally beautiful for that reason. But this judgment doesn't preclude judging it to be a superb exemplar of its type (amethyst, say), and beautiful for that reason. Nor does it preclude judging it to be beautiful on account of the intensity of its color, or on account of its affinity to crystalline elements in our lives to which it is tied by elaborative imagination.

If the strategy of rescuing formalism amounts to expanding it so generously as to make natural formal beauty synonymous with beauty free from the constraints of concepts and categories imposed on natural appreciation by conceptualists, then it has gone too far. Such a strategy purchases sweep at the price of discrimination. What the traditional formalists were trying to establish was a basis for recognizing the importance of non-narrative, affective arrangements of ingredients in an organized, appreciable whole. If everything perceptible that escapes the covering-law influence of natural categories gets counted as formal, the distinctive aesthetic point the traditionalists were trying to establish is lost in the welter of other aesthetic factors. It shouldn't be. The syncretic theory I am presenting insists that natural beauty judgment needs to be both open to the multiplicity of reasonable aesthetic perspectives and discriminating enough to locate disparate aspects of a natural object's beauty within a given perspective. Some of a crystal's beautiful qualities are formal qualities. Although they should redound to the judgment that the crystal is beautiful, they shouldn't be regarded as exclusively controlling that judgment.

Predictably, anti-formalists have mounted a counterattack on the new formalism. The powerful first blow was struck by Glenn Parsons and Allen Carlson.[26] They argued that formal aesthetic qualities cannot be central in our appreciation of natural objects because, to the degree that aesthetic attention focuses on the object, it must attend primarily to the "aesthetic properties that are characteristically related to it, belonging to it as the thing that it is. But formal aesthetic properties, locked as they are within the sensory surfaces of things, are not of this kind."[27] Moreover, they argued, the new formalist view fails to meet the criterion of significance, understood as an ability to provide powerful explanations regarding natural objects. To the first complaint, the easy response is that there is nothing about a natural thing's sensible qualities that makes the formal ones less central than the typal ones. If I find an halite crystal beautiful, it is certainly no less likely that I will do so because I find the glinting surfaces impressive than that I will do so because I appreciate this quality as characteristic of crystalline halides. To the second complaint, the somewhat-less-easy response is that it is not the objective of natural beauty judgments, as the new formalists understand them, to identify properties that are explanatorily powerful (unless "explanation" is given an extremely broad, non-standard denotation). "Significance" is an accordion concept. It expands and contracts according to one's other conceptual demands. The notion of significance Parsons and Carlson deploy seems to me to be unduly narrow. Who is to say that the intersecting flashes of light reflected by the planes of an halite crystal are less significant than the fact that the crystal is a variety of salt? Aestheticians shouldn't be too quick to circumscribe the business of signification.

For all its avowed moderation, Zangwill's version of formalism goes too far. It overstates the bounds of formal beauty. And for all its concessions to the new formalism, the rebuttal mounted by Parsons and Carlson doesn't go far enough. Each position, in its eagerness to defend the centrality of its own perspective, fails to recognize the full legitimacy of alternative perspectives.

In the enterprise of aesthetic appreciation this kind of theoretical antagonism is pointless. As I have argued above, the legitimacy of taking formal values in natural objects as important components of their beauty is something no one will deny. Taking these same formal values as the *exclusive* determiners of natural beauty is something everyone should deny.

Connective Beauty

Some natural objects are beautiful because they are connected to other things. A patch of soft green moss may be found beautiful because it spills down over a hard, dark, basaltic cliff face. The moon may appear to be more beautiful tonight than last night because it is now seen low against an alpine horizon. A row of sycamore trees on campus may be regarded as beautiful because they are connected in thought to the student soldiers whom they memorialize. Of course, the moss patch, the moon, and the sycamores may be found to be beautiful apart from their relations to other things and ideas. But there is no denying that their relations to other things and ideas *can* have an important impact[28] on the quality and intensity of their beauty. This impact is a function of the aesthetic quality of the relational wholes they help to compose.

The key question for the notion of connective beauty is: are some natural things beautiful *just because* they are connected to other things? We should be disposed to answer this question affirmatively because we have plenty of evidence in favor of the parallel proposition in the field of artifactual beauty. An arch may be beautiful only in connection with an edifice, an adagio only in connection with an allegro; a chocolate sauce only in connection with a raspberry torte. When we turn to connections between natural things and other natural things, or natural things and artifacts, the issue becomes less obvious. If some natural things are beautiful just because they are connected to other things, that is often because our experience of the one is dependent on an experience that incorporates both it and the other. We may, for example, find a sinuous orange strand in a fragment of malachite beautiful not for its color and sinuosity taken alone, but for the striking contrast these present to the blue-green of the malachite matrix. The limb of a contorted filbert may be seen as anything *but* beautiful until it is connected in thought to contours of human aspiration.

When the beauty of a natural object (or a feature of that object) is a func-tion of (or is enhanced by) its perceived connection to another (natural or artifactual) object (or feature of that object), the result is *connective* beauty. Connective beauty comes in two varieties: If the perceived connection is one of physical relation between two or more things, the resultant connective beauty is one of juxtaposition. If the perceived connection is one of mental relation between a thing and an idea or ideas relating to that thing, the connective beauty is one of association. In both of its varieties, connective beauty involves sensory awareness of relations between things (or things and ideas) as well as sensory attention to the things themselves.

The key to connective beauty is time. No matter what kind of regard— typal, intensive, formal, etc.—dominates in a natural beauty judgment, that judgment involves an experience in which attention to an object or objects is sustained and rewarded. The appreciation of natural beauty is never mo- mentary.[29] It necessarily extends over a period of time during which a first impression can be amplified or clarified in response to various cognitive and imaginative influences. The fact that it has captured and *sustained* my atten- tion makes it possible to take stock of those connections that may transform and enrich my initial impression. Connective beauty is dependent on the propensity of aesthetic attention to cultivate awareness of the relations among things, as well as the relations between things and ideas about them, during the sustained awareness of natural objects.

On my way to work, I notice a spider web strung across limbs of a rose bush, and I find it attractive. A glance is enough to register its attractiveness, but probably not its beauty. For that, the spider web should hold my attention long enough for me to *reflect* on its appearance, to savor it in a way that attaches my initial attention to its relations to other things in its perceptible context, to thoughts and impressions it may evoke, or to both.[30] If I come to recognize it as a web of the sort only a certain kind of spider makes, I may connect the web to its type and find it a beautiful example of that particular web-type. If I see it instead as part of an ecological network in which spider webs are integrally connected with a host of other processes, I may deem it beautiful because I connect this particular to a beautiful whole in which it is involved. If I am struck by the way a pattern of iridescent dew beads on the web plays off against the underlying, dark green pattern of rose leaves, I will have discovered a beau- tiful juxtaposition. And if I am struck by its rigid, symmetrical pattern, I may find that the web's design elements are beautifully reminiscent of steel-truss bridges. Not every connective reflection that follows my initial impression of the spider web will contribute relevantly to my judgment that it is beautiful. The fact that the web abuts a rubberized garden glove I dropped next to the rose bush yesterday is a juxtaposition that is likely neither to add nor to detract from the quality of aesthetic experience of the web. Nor should a connection between the knowledge that this is a *spider's* web and the guilty thought that I haven't picked up the *Spider-man* video I promised my family.

There are two quite different ways in which we might understand juxtapositive connective beauty judgments. It is plausible, for example, to think of them as rudimentary formal beauty judgments. Here, rather than regarding a constellation of natural objects as composing a complicated pattern or design, we are considering the way a very limited number of members (often only two) of a larger whole relate to each other. Relations of parts to parts are often aesthetically different from relations of parts to wholes. Consider the possible disparity between the visual impact of any two patches in a large, patchwork quilt and the impact all the patches make when conjoined in the quilt's overall design. But, as different as part-to-part and part-to-whole formal judgments are, they share the quality of formality. That is, the basis of the beauty judgment in either case is the sensible impression a certain arrangement of qualities makes, rather than the relation of those qualities to knowledge about what they are. On this view, juxtapositive connective beauty poses no new problems of analysis or explanation since it reduces to formal beauty. It is equally plausible, however, to regard the juxtapositive beauty judgments as simply expanding the field of aesthetic attention. Our appreciative attention is now trained on A+B where previously it was trained on only A or B. But, as I have indicated earlier, the ontology of natural aesthetic objects is infinitely malleable. A is an object. B is an object. A+B is an object. And any constellation of A's and B's that can be brought into a conspectus by some act of framing or quasi-framing is also an object. If the sensible effects of A's being juxtaposed to B are not different in *kind* from the sensible effects A and B individually present to our aesthetic experience, juxtapositive beauty doesn't collapse into some other variety of natural beauty. Rather, it opens itself to the explanations and analyses available to *all* varieties. One way or the other, connective beauty in juxtaposition appears to raise no special problems of analysis because it reduces to forms of judgment subsumed under other rubrics.[31]

It is associative connective beauty that poses the serious problems. As we have seen, philosophers have long disagreed about the way in which natural objects may be connected to ideas in such a manner as to affect their aesthetic quality. Archibald Alison spoke of the series of associations that ensue when disinterested attention fastens on an object as "trains of ideas of emotion." Kant spoke of the "free play" of our mental faculties as generating the distinctive kind of pleasurable response we call beauty. John Dewey spoke of "trains of ideas" following from an experience in which the "ideas form a train only because they ... are phases, emotionally and practically distinguished, of a developing underlying quality; they are its moving variation."[32] In the same vein, an important component of Arnold Berleant's theory of aesthetic engagement with environmental beauty is what he calls "place memory," in which personal and cultural associations and meanings persist in the locations to which our aesthetic attention is drawn, imbuing them with resonance and richness.[33]

Skeptics who would deny or restrict the role of connective beauty in the aesthetics of natural objects have a disparaging way of describing these contents. To them, all these chains, trains, and resonances are mere "flights of fancy," "free association," or "idle reveries." The common charge is that nothing in particular, nothing substantial, holds the contents of connective beauty together. Whatever trains of thought may have set out from the station, they say, the tracks lead in an infinitude of unpredictable directions. According to this charge, it is as likely that reflection on a beautiful natural object will set in motion ideas that lead to irrelevant and purely personal concerns as that it will lead to associations that improve our understanding or intensify our aesthetic regard of the object.

It cannot be denied that if there is no principled way of distinguishing between beauty-pertinent elements (such as seeing the web as a web of a certain type) and beauty-irrelevant sidetracks (such as seeing it as a reminder to buy a video tape) then the idea of associative connective beauty is a shambles. But this conclusion has met with resistance at every stage of the development of aesthetic theory. Alison, for example, sought to allay this concern by insisting that only certain ideas will qualify as fitting and as sensibly extending an original aesthetic experience, by insisting that patterns of association entrenched in our animal nature and social convention be respected, and by requiring that linkages of thought be generally consistent.[34] Kant described the operations of imagination and understanding as forming an interlocking relation such that the nameless perceptual representations offered up by the former are brought into synthetic unity by the latter's conceptualizing effects.[35] Dewey thought of the ingredients in his "trains of ideas" as being marshaled into a unity by the consummatory conclusion toward which they are moving, a conclusion that imparts to them "internal integration and fulfillment."[36] And Berleant insisted that, in infusing exceptional occasions with deep resonances of association and meaning, environmental experience doesn't diverge from our perception of the natural objects of attention, but enlarges that perception and attaches to it an opportunity for self-discovery as well.[37]

Which side has it right? Is connective beauty a conceptual dead end or a vital element in the appreciation of natural objects? Even conceptualist skeptics like Carlson and Eaton concede that taking an object of attention to be a thing of a certain type often involves reflective response to one's original observation of it and may entail a succession of ideas through which the identification of the object is amplified by recalling and then attending to features proper to its type. "My goodness, would you look at that splendid creature leaping from the surface in a fountain of spray! It's a whale! In fact it's a right whale, unusual in these parts. It's probably part of a pod, because these whales travel in pods. Whales are warm-blooded and suckle their young—maybe there's a baby whale out there too!" And so on. No part of this train of ideas takes us away from the object of appreciation, understood—as present-day conceptualists so often insist it must be understood—as what natural science tells us it is. No part of this train gets sidetracked into reverie and irrelevance.

But, beginning with the same initial perception, another train of ideas might do just that: "My, would you look at that splendid creature leaping from the surface in a fountain of spray! The dark mass looming up in the midst of all those silvery water droplets reminds me of an oil well geyser. So powerful, so spontaneous, so spectacular. That reminds me in turn of the wealth, energy, and world turmoil that oil brings in its wake. And that reminds me in turn of folks I know who have lost children in wars in oil-rich regions. How sad." Most of this series of associations has *no* bearing on the beauty of the breaching whale. There is plenty of room for disagreement here over the question of what should count as a connection between natural things, or between natural things and thoughts. There is also plenty of room for controversy over the line that must be drawn between connections that count and those that don't. The business of becoming an aesthetic adult is in large measure a matter of learning how to draw these lines. That job is assigned to elaborative imagination—a conceptual domain where much is accommodated, but where not everything goes.

Elaborative Imagination

The surest means of rendering connective beauty coherent and useful as a component of natural beauty judgment is supplied by the imagination. But any deployment of imagination in the theory of the aesthetic appreciation of natural objects is bound to be risky and controversial. For one thing, imagination is a notoriously murky, unruly concept and for that reason might seem to be of dubious worth in clarifying a notion already murky and unruly. For another, as we have already seen, even its earliest proponents were aware that when we enfranchise the associative powers of imagination in relation to beauty judgments we run the risk of subverting beauty by encumbering it with all manner of incidental and irrelevant impressions. Nevertheless, I think we may tease out from among the many aspects of imagination (or, if you prefer, from among various imaginations)[38] one that will be clear enough to avoid the main thrusts of the murkiness critique, one that will focus on factors that escape the charge of aesthetic irrelevance.

What I have in mind is a power of interpretive response to objects that begins with the act of initial sensory awareness and carries forward an elaboration of that same response, rather than a free reaction to it. I will call this "elaborative imagination." I am not suggesting that all imagination is elaborative in this sense. Nor am I denying that other forms of imagination might contribute to the appreciation of natural objects.[39] But I believe that elaborative imagination can be shown to be importantly at work in developing a reasonable ground for natural beauty judgments of the kind I have described earlier. And I believe it can do so in a sufficiently disciplined way to permit connective beauty to function as a plausible element in natural beauty judgments generally. In such a view as this, of course, everything turns on what "elaboration" means, and what it means for an idea to elaborate a response rather than merely being associated with it. I will try to make clear what I have in mind.

To begin with, we need to remember that, even in Kant's epistemology, imagination is taken to have a profoundly *connective* role in determining what a thing is for us, and thus in making sense of experience. In the act of perception, imagination is assigned the role of putting together information provided by the senses into a coherent object, an object that is later to be brought before the understanding. As Kant conceives perception, the heterogeneous impressions that occur to us in the act of sensory acquaintance with, say, a bullfrog—a certain shape, various colors, distinctive movements, a croaking sound, and all the rest—are assembled by imagination into the presentation of a particular, continuous object. Before the understanding is put to work in determining that these impressions belong with the idea "bullfrog," they are taken to be *connected* in our apprehension of something as a coherent object, and thus ready for subsumption under a concept.[40] Hume, too, acknowledged that imagination is required in the joining together of impressions to create ideas of things. And he went on to identify certain uniting principles (resemblance, contiguity in space and time, and causal connection) that were supposed to inspire imagination to produce coherent rather than random ideas of such things.[41] In short, for Kant and Hume, as well as many other epistemologists, imagination is taken to function as a kind of pre-conceptual *glue* holding the elements of awareness together in our consciousness in readiness for cognitive processing (by categories, names, logical relations, etc.).

But if elaborative imagination is to lend coherence to the contents of connective beauty, it must do more than bind together the disparate bits of evidence provided by the senses in unifying the objects of perception. It must provide a basis for continuing on *beyond* the act of perception to bind together the mental contents (images, associations, ideas, etc.) that are called into play by the act of perception and those which attach to it, or flow from it, in a way that clarifies the place of these contents in relation to other elements in the framework of perception. And if it is to do this, it must have a way of keeping the train of ideas initiated by perception on its tracks. This is a job that would seem to be a lot easier in relation to art rather than nature. As Susan Feagin points out, an artwork places some limits on the lines of interpretation to which it opens itself depending on the intention and skill of the artist:

> Value-laden language or style of writing in a novel, the
> colors and spatial arrangements or images in a painting,
> music and camera angle in a film, will prompt some trains
> of imaginings and discourage others, provided one has a
> sensitivity to these sorts of properties of an artwork.[42]

But nature lacks an artist and hence lacks any intentional ingredients that might serve to constrain interpretive imaginings. Is there anything else that can do the job?

Although it may seem to be the very nature of imagination to be free, and although those kinds of imagination central to artistic (and other forms of) creativity do seem to repel constraints of all sorts, unbridled freedom is not characteristic of *all* kinds of imagination. Elaborative imagination, as I speak of it, begins its work by combining elements of perception into comprehensible wholes and maintains its momentum by drawing together images and ideas to amplify and clarify the place of these wholes in our experience. Amplification and clarification are importantly different from free association. Consider again our spider web example. The spider web is a complicated visible structure. It is a home to a spider. It is similar in its stress-geometry to certain other objects of our acquaintance, including steel-strut bridges. And it is reminiscent of the lacy coverlets well-to-do people put on their tables. As our thoughts proceed from one of these considerations to another, they are free in the sense that they can range over all manner of mental material that might help make this experience comprehensible, intelligible, and appreciable.

But they are not free in the sense that they can link up with any other thought you please while still being *about the spider web*. If, in looking at the web, I am reminded that Fiat used to make a Spider roadster that was long the object of my youthful desire, the chain of thoughts that leads off in that direction makes no contribution to the comprehension of the spider web experience for all that it is. The difference between elaborative and unconstrained imaginations is very like the difference between *ratio decidendi* and *obiter dictum* in judicial opinions. The former illuminates the course of reflection the court takes in deciding a case. The latter uses the case material as an impetus to offer remarks that—however interesting on their own—have no direct bearing on the issue at hand.[43]

What is it, then, that holds elaborative imagination to its target experience? One promising way of answering this question has been suggested by Mary Warnock. As she sees it, imagination of the kind in question is not something that begins to react to experiences once they have occurred. Instead it is partially *constitutive* of them. Experience itself, as she sees it, is indelibly interpretive, and imagination is directly involved in calling up and carrying forward the interpretive connections that make any experience an experience of its kind. She says:

> I certainly wish to assert ... that in any intelligible experience there are elements of other experiences which ... have 'gone into retirement'. These add up to an awareness of the past, the future, and the hidden aspects of what we are now experiencing, and they can be said to be the thoughts about our present experience, though also forming a necessary part of the experience itself.[44]

I take it that the "hidden aspects" of which she speaks are not—or not only—dark, mysterious associations buried in the depths of our unconscious. Rather, I believe she is referring here to a repertory of images, lingering sense associations, recollections of past experiences, ideas, beliefs, customary connections, and so forth, through which we habitually and continually make sense of the world we experience. So, when we call out of "retirement" the mental elements we need to interpret a target of awareness, we are deploying imagination to render that thing or collection of things intelligible in the framework of a current conspectus. The spider web is not *just* a spider's web. It is the sort of thing that has an intricate bridge-like structure, catches dewdrops and sunlight, and brings capture and death to unlucky insects. To say these things about it is not to run out a string of incidental associations. It is instead to explain to ourselves the meaning imbedded in a conspectus of awareness. Moreover, it is to lay a sound foundation for a judgment as to its natural beauty.

As Warnock herself puts it:

> [M]eanings spring up around us as soon as we are conscious. The imagination is that which ascribes these meanings, which sees them *in* the objects before us, whether these are the ordinary three-dimensional furniture of the world, diagrams in a text book, pictures, music, or images in the mind's eye or ear. At an everyday level we must use imagination to apply concepts to things. This is the way we render the world familiar, and therefore manageable.[45]

On this view, there is no mystery about what holds elaborative imagination to its experiential target. Imagination of this kind is already at work in creating meaning in everyday experience. It creates the target. And when the experience is not everyday—when it is the encounter with an *extraordinary* beautiful natural object—then imagination may be called upon to continue further than usual the process of meaning-amplification it has started. As an *elaboration*, rather than a *reaction*, it is a continuation of the process of interpretation with regard to one object of awareness. This focus lends coherence to the sequence of thoughts that follow upon an initial aesthetic impression.

Earlier, when I alluded to non-conceptualist defenses of the role of imagination in the aesthetic appreciation of natural objects, I did so to point up problems of limit-setting inherent in these views. On the basis of these problems, I offered the *reductio ad absurdum* argument that if we subject nature to the "unrestricted province of imagination" then there are no bounds on what we make of it, so "a river can be a bookmark and a star can be a good luck charm." But now we can see that imagination's province need not be seen as unrestricted. This recognition clears the way for an improved defense of the role of imagination in appreciating natural beauty.

The leading proponent of an imagination-based natural aesthetic is Emily Brady. The main thrust of her approach is opposition to the cognitive bias in science-based conceptualisms. Recognizing the fundamental problem of finding a satisfactory substitute for natural science categories as frames for aesthetic interpretation, she presents a "loosely Kantian" account that combines disinterestedness with an emphasis on perception's role in guiding imagination.[46] While her opposition to mainline conceptualism centers on its relative neglect of imagination, she insists that a proper approach should not go to the other extreme and take all imaginative responses to natural objects to be aesthetically appropriate. She distinguishes four modes of imaginative activity that can be useful in appreciating natural objects, modes which she styles exploratory, projective, ampliative, and revelatory imagination, respectively. It is the first and third that, taken together, come closest to describing the work I have assigned elaborative imagination.

In Brady's formulation, exploratory imagination is closely tied to the act of perception. As she puts it, "imagination explores the forms of the object as we perceptually attend to it, and imagination's discoveries can, in turn, enrich and alter our perception of the object."[47] On this point, we are bound to ask what counts as a "discovery" as opposed to inappropriate association or fantasy. The illustrative example she offers gives us some idea of what she has in mind:

> [I]n contemplating the bark of a locust tree, visually, I see the deep clefts between the thick ridges of the bark. Images of mountains and valleys come to mind, and I think of the age of the tree given the thickness of the ridges and how they are spaced apart. I walk around the tree, feeling the wide circumference of the bark. The image of a seasoned old man comes to mind, with deep wrinkles from age. These imaginings lead to an aesthetic judgment of the tree as stalwart, and I respect it as I might a wise old sage. My interpretation of the locust tree is tied to its nonaesthetic qualities, such as the texture of the bark, as well as the associations spawned by perceptual qualities.[48]

In stressing that exploratory imagination reaches beyond perception in a "free contemplation of the object," Brady doesn't appear to rein in its associative powers very much. The locust tree example, however, shows us that her idea of discovery involves linkages among ideas that remain reasonably close to the initial perception. They appear to be a string of interpretations of the original experience, rather than a series of unfettered associations it provokes. The tree is wrinkled; so it is like an old man; so it is owed respect due the venerable. Not: the tree is wrinkled; so it is like my bed sheets; my bed sheets are wrinkled because of tax worries that denied me sleep; I've got to reduce my debt; maybe I should sell my car.

Brady's notion of "ampliative imagination" is somewhat more removed from the perceived object. Here, "heightened creative powers" are unleashed, enabling us to expand upon what is seen through the invocation of narrative images. This mode of imagination is clearly meant to be more active, more extensive, and hence more creative than the other. But, once again, the example she gives us suggests that the linkage between object and interpretation is still not very loose:

> In contemplating the smoothness of a sea pebble, I visualize the relentless surging of the ocean as it has shaped the pebble into its worn form. I might also imagine how it looked before it became so smooth, this image contributing to the wonder and delight in the object. Merely thinking about the pebble is not sufficient for appreciating the silky smoothness which is emphasized by contrasting its feel with an image of its pre-worn state.[49]

In this example, reflection begins with an object (the pebble) and ranges out to touch on things other than the object—the action of the sea and the imagined earlier state. But these are not furtive or capricious associations. They are tied to appreciation of the smoothness of the pebble because they are reasonably comprehended in the interpretation of that smoothness itself.

Brady identifies two guidelines for averting the excesses of associative fancy. The first guideline invokes a more-or-less Kantian notion of disinterestedness. This notion, as we have seen, has been variously conceived in the course of its theoretic evolution. In Brady's hands, it is trained on two tasks: First, it is held to free the mind of distractions so as to clear the way for the appropriate deployment of imagination. Second, it is taken to prevent attention from veering away from the aesthetic focus to personal, self-indulgent concerns that might undercut appreciation.[50] These are both important restraints. If we are distracted, we can't get to the aesthetic object clearly. If, in reflecting on the object, we indulge byways of interests, worries, aspirations, fears, and so on that are peculiar to ourselves, we go beyond the object. This seems to me to be a useful and relatively unproblematic rendering of the historical implications of disinterestedness as they apply to the role of imagination in the aesthetic appreciation of natural objects.

The second guideline is described as a skill, born of practice, at "spotting aesthetic potential," having a sense of what to look for, and knowing when to clip the wings of imagination. The effect of the "wing clipping" element is to prevent shallow, naïve, and sentimental imaginative responses from impoverishing appreciation.[51] Brady calls this skill "imagining well," echoing

Aristotle's notion of "living well," a matter of learning virtue by acting in a social context and coming gradually to acquire habits of awareness in which excesses are routinely avoided and sensible choices made. The locust bark and sea pebble examples cited above illustrate the enterprise of imagining well. Just as we can imagine well, we can imagine poorly. As an example of imagining poorly, Brady proposes the image of a lamb in baby clothes as an emblem of innocence. The relative poverty of this imagining is, she says, a reflection of its shallowness and sentimentality.

Marcia Eaton's attack on Brady's term of "imagining well" focuses on the apparent lack of knowledge-born restraints this mode of appreciation involves. "Concepts such as imagining well," she says, "make no sense unless one knows what the object is that one is talking about, something (in fact, as much as possible) about the object, and something (in fact, as much as possible) about the context in which the object is found."[52] But here I believe Eaton overstates the role of knowledge in the aesthetic experience of natural objects. At the very least she overstates the role of knowledge in relation to elaborative beauty if she thinks that any beauty judgment necessarily demands knowledge of the identity (i.e., scientific information about what it is) of its object. Suppose that I present you with a viewing tube and invite you to look through it at something without telling you what it is. What you see is a brilliant milky-white spiral glowing against a pitch-black background. Do you think you could say whether the thing is beautiful before I divulge to you whether what you are looking at is a spiral nebula or a microscopic organism? If all natural beauty were typal beauty or beauty in any way dependent on recognition of a thing's type the answer would be no. Many—perhaps most—people would think that awareness of the beauty of a natural object of such a kind could legitimately precede knowledge of that object's typal identity. And that is because other, less cognitively regimented aspects of natural beauty that I have been discussing count as much as seeing the object as a token of its type.

It is a mistake to tie elaborative beauty judgments to the factual claims of one kind of knowledge—natural science—while denying the pertinence of other kinds of knowledge—such as information about similarities and differences among objects of experience and the awareness of one's own prior acquaintance with such objects. Consider again Brady's locust tree example. She reports that when she looks at the bark she finds its surface to be like the serrations of mountains and valleys. Let us assume she is observing the bark both scrupulously and extensively and that she is not impaired in any way in her powers of observation. On these assumptions, the similarity observed becomes a new *fact* (not a fiction) about the bark. That fact is just as pertinent a piece of information about the tree as its scientific name when the issue at hand is aesthetic appreciation. The initial perception that launches imagination's connective endeavor is itself a form of knowledge—knowledge by acquaintance. A good many elements in the succession of ideas that follow upon the perception are forms of knowledge—knowledge of what belongs with what in our repertory of experience, knowledge of comparison classes, knowledge of the past, knowledge about how our society parses perceptions, and so on and so forth. In the end, it hardly matters whether we call these mental ingredients knowledge or not. They are nature-appreciation equivalents of interpretive resources that constitute the basis of sound aesthetic judgment in film criticism, literary interpretation, dance appreciation, and—Aristotle was right about this—the art of living well. There is no reason for holding knowledge of these kinds to be less pertinent than scientific knowledge to the objective of beauty judgment.[53]

Nevertheless, even if we should agree that experiential contents of the kind Brady has in mind *are* to be counted as knowledge, it remains unclear whether she has provided a satisfactory means of marshaling these contents into a coherent account of natural beauty. Despite her guidelines and restraints, the inventory of plausible imaginative contents seems potentially limitless. And the concept of "imagining well" seems too vague to insure that only apt associations adhere to an initial aesthetic impression. To confirm the useful role of elaborative imagination in supporting judgments of natural beauty, we will need to supplement Brady's account in four ways. First, remembering Warnock's point about the constitutive role of imagination, we should affirm that the initial aesthetic stimulus isn't simply a raw fact to be grasped by the senses. Instead, it is what it is because the faculty of imagination has made it possible to apprehend it in the way it is apprehended. There is no naked sensing. Imagination cloaks perception before we cognize its products. Second, we should acknowledge that various sensible features of natural objects bear affinities in form or function to sensible features in other natural or artifactual objects. The furrowed contours in a piece of bark are close cousins to wrinkles in human skin. The periodic eruption of spray from a geyser is similar to cardiac systole and diastole in its coordination of pressure and release. Finding a natural object to be beautiful for things it resembles is interpreting the object—elaborating its meaning—and not merely attaching to it haphazard associations. Third, we should remember that imagination is contextual. In one aesthetic culture, the patterns visible on the surface of the full moon may be closely tied in spiritual or mythic tradition to the image of a hare. In another, it may be closely tied to the image of a fox, or of a human face. When elaborative imagination connects the thought of the moon's beauty to the aesthetic qualities of these associated images, it is reminding the observer of his or her place in an aesthetic culture. The descriptive judgments that belong to that aesthetic culture may, in due course, generate reflective judgments and corrective judgments that diverge from established patterns of association. But those patterns persist in the re-configuring of any given aesthetic response, much in the way the musical patterns imbedded in late baroque compositions remain present in the reactive compositions of the early romantic period.

Fourth, and most importantly, the capacity for successfully elaborating an initial impression is something that is developed gradually, unsystematically, and incrementally in the course of growing up aesthetically. An apt sense of what connections between natural things and ideas contribute to the things' beauty is—like taste itself, or proficiency in art criticism—acquired in the context-dependent course of an observer's evolving awareness of the aesthetic domain of natural objects. That domain is, of course, affected by traditional perceptions. But it is also shaped by evaluative expectations and creative aspirations. Like poetry, music, dance, science, worship, baseball, politics, and family vacations, it is tied to a respect for history on the one end and a desire for novelty on the other. Poetry, for example, succeeds as an art form only because it links impressions together in ways that make sense against a mutually understood background of prior usage and previously drawn connections. What I call elaborative imagination is the application of an acquired skill of the very same kind in the domain of natural objects, rather than words.

The underlying notion of connectedness involved in this analysis may seem mysterious, but it isn't unfamiliar. Think again of the skill of the movie critic. We don't expect her to make the case for a given movie's greatness simply by describing its plot, montage, character development and so on, or simply by reporting the conformity of these features to received canons of film excellence. Rather, we expect her to connect features we have noticed with features we may have missed. We expect her to build a basis for our appreciation of the film by laying out a chain of reflections that will connect with our own reflections on the movie in such a way that we can judge the movie's aesthetic worth and the critic's critique. What shapes and constrains the trains of ideas the critic provides? Part of the answer has to be the by now familiar Humean requirement that associations not be derailed by distortion or distraction. Hepburn gives us another part of the answer: Where perceptions are inattentive, undiscriminating, or lazy, and where the reflections consequent to perception are feeble, stereotyped, immature, or confused, he says, the result is trivial, rather than serious appreciation.[54] A third part of the answer lies in the distinction knowledgeable review-readers can draw—and commonly do draw—between an extended interpretation of a given object or event on the one hand and a series of prismatic reactions (and reactions to reactions) that that object or event might inspire on the other. An inept, self-indulgent, or polemically motivated critic might allow his review to stray from the former mode to the latter. A competent, expert critic develops chains of ideas that hang together because they all are tied to the movie—chains of ideas that are arguably in the movie or rooted in the movie and for that reason tied to its appreciation. People who care about movies—who view them regularly and who pay attention to movie criticism—know the difference between solid and inept comparisons. I believe people who care about natural beauty can make the same kind of distinctions.

My point here is not to sketch out a preliminary theory of movie criticism. It is rather to suggest that, in this context, we are already familiar with the *kinds* of constraints that are fitting for reining in the imagination as it responds to natural beauty as much as when it responds to movies. Again, I am not suggesting here that we look at nature as we look at art, or that the critical theory that fits the one will comfortably fit the other. Rather, I am pointing out that, when a significant portion of our judgment (that a natural object is beautiful) involves the connecting of an initial impression with a series of subsequent reflections, these reflections can make a difference to what that object is taken to *be*. They do so by elaborating the initial impression in a way that reveals aspects of it that were not at first wholly apparent. If the critic is doing her job properly, the series of reflections she presents will not be erratic, fugitive, or incoherent. Instead, they will be connected to the film in a way that gives us a richer, deeper understanding of what it is we observe. In sound movie criticism—and in sound criticism in the arts generally—we have a good model of the positive objectives and companion constraints that enhance aesthetic appreciation. In the natureworld as in the artworld, the process of growing into mature understanding demands recognition of associative objectives and associative constraints as well as the development of a feeling for the limits of both.

ART AND NATURE

The preceding analysis puts us in a good position to reassess a contentious issue that has plagued natural aesthetics for centuries. This is the question of whether the modes of appreciation we habitually adopt with respect to artworks can contribute to, or must inevitably interfere with, the modes of appreciation we need to adopt toward natural objects. As we have seen, historical opinions have fallen on both sides. Classical thinkers generally regarded beauty in nature as the model and standard for beauty in art. Romantics—or at least some species of romantics—preferred to think of artistic beauty as teaching us the way to appreciate and assess natural beauty.[55] Some modern theorists think of the two domains as entirely separate in the sense that nothing that can be said about beauty in the one can have any bearing about what can be said about beauty in the other. Finding nature and art incomparable, they reject both of these approaches.[56]

An extreme version of modern romanticism is advanced by Anthony Savile. Far from denying that it is appropriate to regard natural objects as if they were works of art, he argues that it is precisely because we have learned how to look at works of art that we are in a position to make intelligent judgments about natural beauty. As Savile sees it, our apprehension of beauty in art is a function of confronting and overcoming problems intrinsic to the artwork, and whatever beauty we may find in nature must be a correlate of this pragmatic, problem-solving virtue. On this account, if there is natural beauty, it must be a product of our regarding natural objects as if they were fashioned as solutions to problems of composition, harmonic arrangement, etc.[57]

This extreme view is implausible. Even if we conceive of the successful execution of artworks as necessarily involving the overcoming of conceptual and stylistic problems, it is far from clear that there is any strict correlate to this process in our appreciation of natural beauty. When I find the bright coloration of the fallen maple leaf beautiful, I don't—and shouldn't—regard the leaf as the quasi-artifact of a hypothetical autumn-leaf-crafter who has worked hard to get them just right. As Malcolm Budd observes, such a view is simply "untrue to the phenomenology of the aesthetic experience of nature."[58]

And even if we concede that some (or even *most*) of our modes of aesthetic appreciation are born of our experience with artworks, it doesn't follow that we have no way of appreciating natural beauty independently of these modes. If we lived in a world in which there were no artworks, that fact alone would not imply that we could not experience natural objects in the ways I have described above as conducing to appreciation of their beauty. This is just another way of saying that there is nothing about the particular kind of aesthetic experience we call the experience of beauty that precludes its being attained through means other than the conventional means of art appreciation.[59]

The opposite extreme position is historically defunct. It is the idea that artistic beauty is derivative from and completely dependent upon the canons of natural beauty, an idea wedded to the mimetic theory of art. If artistic excellence were a matter of representing natural objects (including human beings and human activities, seen as exemplifications of human nature) aptly and accurately, then the aesthetic worth of the artwork would inevitably depend on the aesthetic worth of the natural object portrayed. But we all know that it doesn't. Abandonment of the mimetic theory has made it hard to find philosophical proponents of the extreme position in our own day. Still, there is no shortage of artists and theorists who take the view that artistic values are deeply responsive to the real world, responsive to the degree such that the artwork is good only if it is a faithful rendition of a beautiful object. Countless Sunday artists have complimented themselves for their aesthetic achievement when their buyers have told them that "That flower looks so real I could smell it!" If there are any lessons to be learned from contemporary Western artistic practice they are that an artwork can be beautiful or not altogether independently of the beauty of its subject and equally that a natural object can be beautiful or not altogether independently of any artistic rendition.[60]

A less extreme position takes it that while art is largely incapable of teaching us about natural beauty, nature remains capable of teaching us about art, or at least about the beauty of natural objects as depicted in art. The usual support offered for this position is, once more, that the integrity of natural beauty depends on its being freed from the classificatory conditions of art appreciation. Allen Carlson has argued that the concept of beauty in art is so caught up with design appreciation that any effort to assimilate the concept of beauty in nature to it is destined to end up in a "theoretical mistake and an appreciative pity."[61] Art, he reminds us, is appreciated for its qualities as a human creation. These include successful execution of the artist's intention, the location of the work within its artistic category, the story we tell about it that connects it to other works of its kind, etc. Nature, by contrast, is simply what it *is*—unintended, undesigned, and (in a sense) alien. Its story is what natural science tells us, because natural science provides the best available knowledge about natural objects in their home environment. On this account, art can't help us appreciate nature because art and nature draw upon discrete knowledge bases and cognitive objectives. Carlson says:

> If to aesthetically appreciate art we must have knowledge
> of artistic traditions and styles within those traditions, to
> aesthetically appreciate nature we must have knowledge of
> the different environments of nature and of the systems
> and elements within those environments. In the way in
> which the art critic and the art historian are well equipped

to aesthetically appreciate art, the naturalist and the ecologist are well equipped to aesthetically appreciate nature.[62]

But this exclusionary posture reflects a false dichotomy. It may be true that only the naturalist and ecologist are in a position to observe everything about a duck that makes it a duck, an example of its type, an excellently adapted component of its ecosystem, and so on. Still, the question of whether this duck is beautiful may remain unresolved by anything they say. And if it seems useful in trying to answer *that* question to take stock of aesthetically compelling visual qualities displayed in, say eighteenth-century avifaunal painting, doing so need neither belie the duck's status as a natural object nor regard it as though it were an artwork. When Carlson says that the naturalist and ecologist are specially equipped to appreciate nature aesthetically, he must mean that they are appropriately trained and situated to apprehend the beauty *of* nature; i.e., the qualities of nature as a whole (or at least of entire environmental systems) in virtue of which they are aesthetically admirable. The naturalist and the ecologist are no more capable than any other attentive, alert, aesthetically mature observer to apprehend beauty *in* nature—the beauty of this particular duck, say, in these lighting conditions, seen against this backdrop, and colored by whatever duck-associative factors the natureworld incorporates. The duck may be beautiful as a mallard. It may be beautiful for its intensely brilliant blue neck. It may be beautiful for its striking contrast to a driftwood background. It may be beautiful because it splendidly invokes an idea of graceful presence in a space. Then again, it may be beautiful because it so perfectly epitomizes some lovely duck features captured in an eighteenth-century landscape painting.

Reciprocity: Learning from Each Other

The fundamental puzzle in regard to the question of whether aesthetic regard for nature teaches us aesthetic regard for art, or vice versa, is why there should be a rivalry here at all. It is easy to see why naturalists and environmentalists might resent artists and aestheticians telling them what they think they already know about their subjects. It is just as easy to see why museum curators and art critics might resent scientists telling them how to look at artworks. But where experts from each perspective stand to benefit from expertise fostered in the other perspective and thereby improve their overall appreciation of an object, it is hard to see what stands in the way of reciprocal profit. The idea that beauty judgment respecting art objects has a bearing on beauty judgments respecting natural objects and vice versa is as venerable as Western philosophical reflection on both subjects. Plato, we may recall, regarded certain numerical relations in the physical world as causal factors in the production of musical beauty. And he thought that the beauty in a sculpture by a master sculptor could reveal a harmony of bodily composition we might otherwise never understand. Leonardo da Vinci is but one among hundreds of artist-scientists who embraced and capitalized on the interpenetration of discoveries on both sides in their creative work. Many present day artists are fond of puncturing borders between nature and artifact to show us what we have missed in thinking about both of them. Robert Smithson's *Spiral Jetty*, for example, disturbs and reorients the way we perceive water and shoreline in the Great Salt Lake, making us aware at once of the beauty of the intruding design and of the beauty of the natural elements incorporated by it and surrounding it.

It is pointless to think of natural beauty and artistic beauty as antagonists or isolated from each other if they can be mutually nourishing. The account I have presented above makes room for their productive reciprocity by center-ing the analysis of natural beauty on the aesthetic experience of the observer, an experience in which various confluent factors accumulate over time in the acts of response and reflection. The beauty of a natural object is, as I have said, not apprehended all at once, although the membership of that object in a class of natural objects may be. Time, again, is the crucial factor. Reflective judgment, exercised by members of an aesthetic community, requires a kind of attention that draws upon both natural and artifactual resources. It cannot but draw upon both because the human agent who makes this judgment is both natural and artifactual. There is no way of observing natural subject matter except as human conditions prescribe. And these human conditions are, by the time we are old enough to begin to make confident beauty judgments, already informed by aesthetic responses to artifacts. The notion of beauty we deploy in relation to natural objects cannot be wiped clean of artifactual influence because nature and artifact are built into it, piece by piece, from its organic creation. Like law, language, and literature, the natureworld is one more social institution necessarily incorporating a framework of received perceptions, a mutually intelligible language that makes possible communication of judg-ments among members of a community, and an institutionally sanctioned policy for change that empowers reflective judgment.

Whoever holds a stake in the natureworld is *ipso facto* viewing nature through an artifactual lens. Of course the converse is equally true. Whoever holds a stake in the art world is necessarily already a living part of the natural world, and destined to perceive artifactual beauty through a living, natural lens.

At this fundamental level, the interplay of natural and artifactual awareness is obvious and inevitable. At a less fundamental level—the level where one's aesthetic appraisal of a natural object may be open to a conscious comparison to the aesthetic appraisal of artifactual object—the interplay of natural and artifactual awareness may *seem* less inevitable. But it isn't. It is certainly true that I can, in appreciating the beauty of a sunny hillside covered with daffodils, invite (or refuse to invite) reflection on features it shares with a Monet painting. But I cannot undo the dispositive effects of aesthetic discriminations that I have made throughout a life lived amid natural and artifactual objects and that I have inherited from my cultural community's store of similar discriminations made throughout *its* history.

If we are inclined to deny that the Monet painting should have any bearing on our aesthetic appreciation of the daffodil-bedecked hillside as naturally beautiful, that is likely to be because we have forgotten what made us think that the Monet painting was beautiful in the first place. Artworks—at least, important artworks—aren't beautiful because they embody some arcane, self-contained value that pleases us in the way that deciphering an ancient code pleases us. Rather, their aesthetic power is connected to a recognition they inspire in us that the sensible elements they present have an important place in the living of a life—the artist's life, her aesthetic culture's life, my aesthetic culture's life, my life. The art of living is the ultimate aesthetic enterprise in which we are all involved. It is both natural and artifactual. If the materials on which we draw to create aesthetic value in our lives come from both of these worlds, we would be foolish to ignore the ways in which their interaction can intensify that value.

In 1503 Albrecht Dürer painted a masterful watercolor rendition of a clump of grass and weeds now called *The Great Piece of Turf*.[63] Dürer was devoted to making realistic studies of plants and animals on his travels, studies that are famous for precision in their rendition, and this is one of them. *The Great Piece of Turf* is a handsomely composed work, the lower half of which presents a dense population of vegetation against an apparently marshy substrate and the upper half of which shows stems (one apparently broken) and flowers and slender blades reaching into a gray-brown sky. We know that Dürer, in painting this work, was well aware of the naturalness of his subject and of the beauty it enjoyed as a natural arrangement for he once wrote "in truth art is implicit in nature, and whoever can extract it has it."[64] He was, of course, also aware of the demands of the medium and the canons of excellence in nature art in his day.

When, after spending some time admiring a reproduction of *The Great Piece of Turf*, I step into my back yard and find clumps of the same grasses and weeds Dürer portrayed, I am completing a circuit by extracting lessons from his work that allow me to find "art implicit in nature." Now, I hasten to say that I don't take nature as art here. Nor do I take my dandelions, oat grasses, and plantains as quasi-artworks. Rather, I am drawn to them in a different and aesthetically richer way because I have been led by Dürer's watercolor to see things I might not otherwise have noticed—the graceful curves, the rhythmic patterns, the interplay of color shades. Reflecting on that work may also have led me to connect the upsweeping lines of these fragile plants to notions of hope, heliotropism, finitude, and seasonal renewal, among other things. And that broken stem line reminds me of the fragility and impermanence of living things. Seeing these art-related features in them strengthens, rather than diminishes, my appreciation of the plants as natural. It underscores my awareness that this wonderful combination of beauty-making features is a product of natural processes independent of human design. Yet I am reminded that the independence of those processes from human agency does not imply that the factors making this experience aesthetically valuable are alien to human enterprise; for it is caught up in similar processes. We are natural beings. And we make things. It should not surprise us that our roles as natural beings and as makers of things play with each reciprocally. And it should not surprise us that the appreciation we have for beauty feeds on both sources and profits from their mutual reinforcement. Dürer said that whoever can extract implicit art from nature "has it." To this we should add that whoever can extract implicit nature from art also "has it." Or at least, that in the historically demonstrated cooperative interchange between the two, both sides can have it.

Inhibition: Getting in Each Other's Way

There is an opposite side to the reciprocity claim. It is that just as, in supporting beauty judgments, art and nature can reinforce each other, they can also impede each other's appreciation. On the one hand, an aesthetic appraisal of an artwork may be discounted when someone discovers a fact that cuts against its value. So, for example, Arnold Toynbee argued that we should deny that the Great Pyramid of Cheops is beautiful on the grounds that it was the product of slave labor.[65] Similarly, when we learn that works of literature are plagiarized, that films misrepresent their putative historical subjects, or that earthwork installations damage the environment, this knowledge can undercut otherwise favorable aesthetic appraisals. On the other hand, as we have already acknowledged, appreciation of natural objects as natural is undercut if we regard them exclusively as though they were artworks. To regard a stretch of rolling hills and meadows as beautiful because it would, in the right hands, lead to a beautiful landscape painting is not to regard its beauty as natural. A public agency policy that managed portions of the natural landscape by emphasizing design qualities (such as form, distance, color, light, and angle of view) over elements supportive of habitat and ecological equilibrium might end up doing that landscape considerable harm.[66] Artworks that incorporate natural elements such as plants and animals without regard to their status as living, environmentally-situated beings can denigrate and even destroy life for the sake of aesthetic effect.[67]

Evaluative dissonance of this kind does not lie beyond remedy. Where art and nature have gotten in each other's way, they simply need to get out of each other's way. To achieve this, we need to return them to the appropriate relation I have described above, where the benefits of knowledge peculiar to each can be reciprocally shared. Artists whose work incorporates parts of the environment or imposes significantly on it (beyond the trivial sense in which every artwork necessarily draws upon natural materials and changes the natural order) should be reminded of aesthetic values in the environment as a whole (the beauty *of* nature) as well as of non-aesthetic values (e.g., moral respect for living beings) that impinge on such artistic practices. Officials charged with aesthetic responsibilities respecting the natural environment should be reminded that design features readily available for aesthetic evaluation because of their ongoing function in the art world are by no means the only (and needn't be the dominant) values to be considered in assessing its overall aesthetic worth. And so forth. The lessons here seem obvious.

There is a deeper dissonance that may be thought to underlie some of these conflicts, a dissonance that appears more resistant to easy resolution. This is the clash between cognition and delectation I alluded to in chapter 2, the apparent fact that our aesthetic experience of natural objects is itself sometimes disturbed or nullified by what we have come to know about them. As I pointed out there, we *sometimes* seem better off in our awareness of a natural object's beauty when we aren't conscious of the correct categories into which it fits, scientific knowledge about its composition, its relations to other natural things, and so on. In a similar vein, we are *sometimes* more able to enjoy the rich texture of sound in a symphonic performance if we aren't constantly aware of the mechanics of the instruments playing it, the challenges in the score, the acoustic limitations of the hall, or the CD player, or the car radio, and so on. This isn't a matter of nature getting in art's way. It is a matter of a certain kind of mental process getting in the way of another mental process to the detriment of our experience of art and nature equally.

Allen Carlson, who has vigorously opposed the idea that cognitive experience poses any threat to the aesthetic experience of nature, draws our attention to a marvelous passage in *Life on the Mississippi* in which Mark Twain expresses the sentiment that this sort of dissonance is both real and corrosive:

> The face of the water, in time, became a wonderful book— a book that was a dead language to the uneducated passenger, but which told its mind to me without reserve, delivering its most cherished secrets as clearly as if it uttered them with a voice.... In truth, the passenger who could not read this book saw nothing but all manner of pretty pictures in it, painted by the sun and shaded by the clouds, whereas to the trained eye these were not pictures at all, but the grimmest and most dead-earnest of reading matters.
>
> Now, when I had mastered the language of this water ... I had made a valuable acquisition. But I had lost something, too. I had lost something which never could be restored to me while I lived. All the grace, the beauty, the poetry had gone out of the majestic river! I still kept in mind a certain wonderful sunset which I witnessed when steamboating was new to me. A broad expanse of the river was turned to blood; in the middle distance the red hue brightened into gold, through which a solitary log came floating, black and conspicuous; in one place a long, slanting mark lay sparkling upon the water; in another the surface was broken by boiling, tumbling rings, that were as many-tinted as an opal. I stood like one bewitched. I drank it in, in a speechless rapture.... But, as I have said, a day came when I [saw it] after this fashion: The sun means that we are going to have wind to-morrow; the floating log means that the river is rising,... that slanting mark on the water refers to a bluff reef which is going to kill somebody's steamboat one of these nights,... [and] those tumbling "boils" show a dissolving bar and a changing channel...
>
> No, the romance and the beauty were all gone from the river.[68]

Carlson contends that a proper reading of Twain's account of his transformative experience does not warrant the conclusion that aesthetic and cognitive experience are in conflict here. That conclusion, he argues, is reached only if we wrongly assume the applicability of certain aesthetic theories to this natural setting. Two theories are involved. When we try to apply the first, it lands us in incoherence. And when we try to apply the second, we find that its key operative element is as likely to nullify aesthetic experience as it is to nullify cognitive experience. Carlson argues that by eschewing both theories we can avoid the loss-of-beauty upshot Twain describes.[69] Carlson's response to this passage is worth considering in detail here because it epitomizes cognitivist opposition to the approach I take to the role of non-cognitive elements in aesthetic experience. Although I agree with the conclusion that there need be no irresolvable conflict between aesthetic and cognitive experiences in most contexts, I do so for reasons that are altogether different from Carlson's.

On Carlson's reading, Twain's remarks about the river's colors, lines, and shapes, together with his report of the bewitching effect and "speechless rapture" it induced, tip us off that the aesthetic theory tacitly assumed here is the formalist theory of art. As we have already seen, Carlson takes formalism—or at least the "traditional" version of it made familiar to us by Clive Bell—to be utterly hostile to the cognitive element of aesthetic content, which it regards as "at best irrelevant and at worst harmful to aesthetic appreciation."[70] It is the application of this theory in the natural context that leads to the mistaken view that knowledge diminishes our appreciation of natural beauty. Carlson argues that even in artistic contexts it is impossible (possibly both psychologically and conceptually) to make sense of, let alone interpret, the formal elements in an object without reference to its content.[71]

The second theory Carlson considers seems to be more promising in that it doesn't, on any standard interpretation, lead to flat-out incoherence. It is the view that aesthetic experience necessarily involves *disinterestedness*, a state of mind in which some potential features of awareness are put out of gear so that others can be appropriately and fully engaged.[72] At least in some of its versions (Stolnitz's, for example) the requirement of disinterestedness is taken to necessitate conflict between aesthetic awareness and cognitive interest. If we construe Twain's remarks about "mastering the language of the water" and the like as the intrusion of informational interest on what had been a purely detached aesthetic appreciation, his account of the river experience might be thought to endorse the view that cognitive awareness has its inevitable aesthetic costs. Carlson thinks that there is no real evidence that Twain ever entertained such a view. And even if he had, Carlson says, the kind of blank-mindedness apparently required by the strong versions of disinterestedness theories provides no basis for aesthetic experience. This is because it just doesn't make sense to conceive of aesthetic appreciation (whether of art or of nature) as independent of factual information about the object being appreciated.[73]

I certainly agree with Carlson that Twain's river narrative provides no basis for the claim that an experience of natural beauty once had could be forever lost due to the countervailing influence of knowledge. But I don't think that this failure cuts against the impressive value of formal beauty presented in Twain's account. Nor does it cut against the conviction, so vividly expressed there, that some aspects of the appreciation of formal beauty in an environmental setting can be muffled or obliterated by awareness of facts concerning those aspects. It is clear from what Twain says in this passage and elsewhere that he does not *really* think knowledge of the river excludes aesthetic appreciation of the river altogether and forever.[74] His glowing appreciation of the beauty-making aspects of the river scene in this passage tells us that he has his tongue in his cheek, and that the grace, beauty, and poetry he despaired of losing have not gone from the river. As so often is the case in Twain's work, hyperbole sharpens the more moderate, unstated point he really wants to make. Even if we all know that knowledge doesn't altogether obliterate beauty, he is telling us, it *can*—in a way, and for a time—undercut and obscure it. The interference can work both ways. Focusing on a floating log as a hydrological indicator of river height can, for a while, distract us from appreciating various aesthetic elements of that dark, undulating form. And focusing on that dark form against a background of interwoven, streaming reds and golds may distract us from awareness that the river is rising.

First, it is important to remember, as I have pointed out earlier, that acknowledgment of the aesthetic relevance of formal features doesn't require subscription to formalism, let alone to the extreme version endorsed by Bell. Carlson is mistaken in thinking that what Twain says about the river commits him to formalism. While what Twain says shows us that he is keenly aware of certain aesthetically pertinent formal components of the river scene that contribute to its overall beauty, there is nothing in what he says that suggests that these formal elements *alone* make this complex natural object beautiful. Carlson is disposed to take a very broad view of formalism. He seems to regard almost any intrusion of design or pattern considerations into natural beauty judgments as formalistic and therefore inappropriate. But there is no reason why beauty in nature shouldn't share *some* of the formal features of beauty in artifacts. In fact, it is apparent to many observers (Twain among them) that formal elements constitute an important and irreplaceable part of the aesthetic experience of nature. The contours, colors, and intertwining motions of the river can be formally appealing without requiring us to see these elements as derivative from, or aesthetically responsible to, man-made designs. Again, it is often appropriate and fruitful to approach the qualities of things in nature as in art through lenses we have developed for regarding aesthetic qualities at large.

Second, it is simply undeniable that there are circumstances in which, in the experience of some people, attention to the sensory conspectus takes cognition out of play for a time. We don't have to agree with Bullough that there is, in such moments, a dramatic rupture between the items of aesthetic awareness and all the rest of one's life's concerns. But we can't deny that there is a way in which a river scene can catch us up in its majestic beauty so as to make a fair range of our quotidian concerns recede. As we have seen, the historical philosophical quarrel over disinterestedness revolves around differing conceptions of what is cut off from what in the process of appreciation. On the one extreme, philosophers have suggested that disinterested attention means obliviousness to anything but the look, smell, taste, and feel of a thing. On the other, philosophers have held it requires no more than a deflection of personal and practical concerns sufficient to allow imagination to act sensibly on its subject. There is nothing about the notion of disinterestedness itself that makes one interpretation decisive against another. Carlson's critique of the view that knowledge can inhibit aesthetic appreciation depends on one extreme interpretation being correct. Disagreeing with him leaves open a substantial range of alternative interpretations between that extreme and the other. Some of these accounts leave more room for cognitive awareness than others. To the extent that disinterested awareness of a natural object is compatible with recognition of that object as an object of its kind, Carlson's objection to disinterestedness as a feature of aesthetic appreciation can be dismissed.[75]

Carlson's claim that we cannot make sense of the formal elements in the river scene save by taking stock of the cognitive content attached to these elements denies the effectiveness of non-cognitive framing or conspectus-forming devices. In what I have presented above, I have made the contrary case that a variety of elements can provide the basis for regarding a natural object or constellation of objects as a focus of aesthetic appraisal. There are, as I pointed out, various constellations of natural objects for which we may have no names and which, nevertheless, can be formed into wholes of awareness by familiar, informal framing devices. In looking at wind-driven, twilit clouds through a gap in oak tree limbs, it might be neither the clouds nor the limbs and the quaking leaves, but the mobile counterpoint of shapes and colors that I find to be beautiful. It may be the way the leaf falls and not the leaf itself that is beautiful. A daffodil may be intensely, beautifully yellow without being a beautiful daffodil. I may have no idea what birds there are in that flock that flashes black then white as it turns and turns again in the sky, but I can certainly find that look—the flashing, flickering, rhythmic alternation of shapes and colors—beautiful.

Twain's portrait of the river is particularly useful because it highlights differences between conceptualist theories such as Carlson's and syncretic theories such as my own. This story expresses a deep truth conceptualists persistently ignore. This is the truth that the aesthetic appreciation of natural objects isn't all of a piece, with knowledge of the object a constant quality and other sensible features simply variables that find their experiential places as knowledge accommodates them. Rather it is, like aesthetic appreciation in general, a complex, unregimented process in which, over a period of sustained awareness, a rich variety of elements—some cognitive, some emotive, some associative—may accumulate to produce in the observer an experience that warrants a beauty judgment. In this process, formal elements may for a while obscure cognitive awareness of an object's typal identity. Likewise, cognitive elements may, for a while, obscure the formal elements. Sometimes it is recognition that an object is a wonderful exemplar of its type that counts most in supporting a beauty judgment. Sometimes impressive design features make typal recognition nearly irrelevant. Sometimes a powerful aesthetic response arises only after a series of connective thoughts has brought to light analogies or affinities in virtue of which a natural object's own beauty becomes evident. There is nothing simple or formulaic about all of this. As observers acquire and refine capacities to know and notice things about the objects they observe, and as they develop lines of imaginative association linking what they see to what is otherwise pertinent in their aesthetic lives, they come to make more confident and more telling beauty judgments. But even the naïve child can rightly claim that a natural object—a golden, translucent agate found on the shore, say—is beautiful. And all that her declaration may mean is that, on its own rudimentary terms, her experience of this object (about which she may know next to nothing, and with which she associates next to nothing) is the first step toward an aesthetic future that is positive and gratifying.

NOTES

1   Connoisseurs of philosophical biography will recognize this example as a slight distortion of an anecdote Norman Malcolm reports in his fond memoir of Ludwig Wittgenstein. In the story, it's stars rather than clouds that are the topic; but the point is the same. As the two were walking across Jesus Green at night, Wittgenstein pointed to Cassiopeia and

made the "W" claim. When Malcolm responded with the "M" claim, Wittgenstein solemnly assured him he was wrong. Norman Malcolm, *Ludwig Wittgenstein: A Memoir* (Oxford University Press, 1958), p. 32. Here, of course, the solemnity is mock-seriousness, and the point is made all the more effective for the underlying irony.

2   We may assume that these images are attained by creating a single, computer-generated, composite image from a vast sampling of natural specimens—the cyber-equivalent of Zeuxis's method of distilling partial beauties into a singular ideal.

3   This would mean that reflective judgments would confirm the aesthetic culture's descriptive judgments, leaving no room for corrective judgments. But it wouldn't mean that reflective judgments reduce to descriptive judgments. There is an important difference between agreeing that it's true that a cloud is beautiful and being moved in a way that warrants one's declaration that it is beautiful. Just as "you can't get an ought from an is," you can't derive an emotive, dispositive judgment merely from a fact about one's aesthetic culture.

4   Consider the aesthetic impact of Marilyn Monroe's mole. As an anomalous departure from standard facial beauty norms, it should have been regarded as a serious aesthetic detriment if those norms were taken as the final, typal, determiner of facial beauty. But it wasn't. Far from it.

5   Notice that this declaration doesn't entail what one might call "cloud-preservation activism" or anything of its kind. Instead it entails a general invitation to others in the cultural community to move the agendas of their lives in ways that would provide opportunities to have aesthetic experiences of the kind she has had with this cloud. One's claim that this cloud is beautiful should, for that reason, be regarded as an important contribution to one's aesthetic culture. Natureworld is created, piece by piece, out of judgments of this kind.

6   Guy Sircello, *A New Theory of Beauty* (Princeton University Press, 1975), pp. 46-47.

7   The fact that the intensity of color, fragrance, or taste in a given natural object is one of its conspicuous features can certainly be a contributing factor in its overall aesthetic appraisal. One way of understanding this is to say that that object is beautifully purple, or pungent, or tangy without conceding that it, itself, is beautiful. But this way of thinking seems to me to be an evasive and unilluminating approach to the problem. It is evasive because it ignores the fact that it is often one intensely presented characteristic that draws us to the conclusion that a given natural object

is atypically beautiful or that the combination of objects of which it is a part is beautiful. It is unilluminating because it brushes aside the question of how prominently presented characteristics may cooperate in making a natural object beautiful.

8   Important contributions in this direction include Jay Appleton, *The Experience of Landscape* (London: Wiley, rev. ed., 1996); Evelyn Dissanayeke, *Homo Aestheticus* (NY: Free Press, 1992); Grant Hildebrand, *The Origins of Architectural Pleasure* (University of California Press, 1999); Stephen Kaplan and Rachel Kaplan, *The Experience of Nature: A Psychological Perspective* (Cambridge University Press, 1989); Gordon Orians and Judith Heerwagen, "Evolved Responses to Landscape," in *The Adapted Mind*, ed. J. Barkow, L. Sosmides, and J. Toobey (Oxford University Press, 1992), and Carl Sagan and Ann Druyan, *Shadows of Forgotten Ancestors* (New York: Ballantine, 1992).

9   This point was recognized by Dewey in chapter 1 of *Art as Experience*, where he points out that in order to understand advanced forms of the aesthetic, one must begin with the raw, and that the vital needs and interests of humans derive from a long line of animal ancestry. "Because," he observes, "experience is the fulfillment of an organism in its struggles and achievements in a world of things, it is art in germ. Even in its rudimentary forms, it contains the promise of that delightful perception which is esthetic experience" (p. 19).

10   Leaving aside his controversial claims regarding the ontology of "the internal fabric" that mysteriously aligns our aesthetic inclinations, it is hard to disagree with Hume's belief that, at the end of the day, our beauty judgments regarding the forms and qualities of things depend on the degrees of aesthetic pleasure they evoke in us owing to our being the natural and cultural creatures history has made us. However enigmatic this conclusion may seem to be, it should not be thought to be elitist. It doesn't reserve secret wisdom of beauty judgment to an authoritative elite. Indeed, unlike Plato and his idealistic followers, Hume supposes that everyone in a cultural community has the latent capacity to make correct aesthetic judgments and that sensory defect and distortion are all that stand in the way of this result. Yet he insists that the basis of their judgments *is* ultimately mysterious.

11   Clive Bell, "Art," in *The Philosophy of Art: Readings Ancient and Modern*, ed. Alex Neill and Aaron Ridley (New York: McGraw-Hill, 1995), p. 101.

12   Stephen Pepper, *Principles of Art Appreciation* (New York: Harcourt, Brace and Co., 1949).

13 Pepper links musical rhythms to emotional patterns of order and disorder. He finds in the repetitive folds of the Virgin's cape in Fra Angelico's *Madonna of Humility* a rhythmic analog to a biblical Psalm; he sees in the blurry vase of flowers in Renoir's *Madame Charpentier and Her Children* an illustration of enjoyable dissonance cast against a background of "good manners."

14 Carlson, *Aesthetics and the Environment*, p. 32.

15 Ibid., p. 33.

16 Ibid., pp. 28-29.

17 Ibid., p. 31.

18 The Claude-glass was a small, portable mirror-dome mainly employed by aristocrats in the heyday of the grand tour to convert the raw look of the natural surroundings into a postcard-like compact spectacle. Carlson describes and criticizes this practice in *Aesthetics and the Environment* at p. 32.

19 Carlson's attack on formalism so construed turns on two claims. First is his insistence that to attend to formal qualities it is necessary to perceive orders or arrangements within bounds imposed by a frame (or equivalent delimiting device), whereas appreciation of the natural environment is importantly *unframed*. Second is his insistence that looking at environmentally situated natural objects as if they were a combination of lines, planes, colors, textures, etc. is ultimately to deny their naturalness. It is to turn ever-changing, multidimensional waterfalls into lifeless, static scenes, such as one might find in a tourist guide-book. On the strength of these two claims Carlson concludes that "the natural environment cannot be appreciated and valued in terms of formal beauty, that is, the beauty of formal qualities; rather, it must be appreciated and valued in terms of its other aesthetic dimensions."

It will be apparent from what I have already said that I do not find this argument persuasive. The grounds of my disagreement with the first claim—the effect of frames in our regard of natural objects—are set out at some length in chapter 6; I needn't repeat them here.

To Carlson's second claim—the idea that attention to form denigrates the aesthetic appreciation of natural objects by turning them into quasi-artifactual objects—an equally direct rebuttal is available. This rebuttal involves coupling the obvious point that formal features are common to natural and artifactual objects with the less obvious point that appreciation of formal features in one aesthetic domain doesn't imply anything about the appreciation of formal features in another.

The fact that painted pictures of cockatoos are meant to be appreciated as paintings, framed and composed by their painters, full of man-made ingredients, and so on, shouldn't lead us to think that the way we picture cockatoos when we see them in person is framed or otherwise composed in a way that is painting-like. As I have argued above, we do typically frame and compose natural objects in the process of appreciating. But the way we do this need not (and typically does not) mimic *artistic* framing and composition. Budd, *Aesthetic Appreciation of Nature*, p. 133.

20 Patricia Matthews, "Aesthetic Appreciation of Art and Nature," *British Journal of Aesthetics* 41 (2001), pp. 395-410; Ira Newman, "Reflections on Allen Carlson's Aesthetics and the Environment," *AE: Canadian Aesthetics Journal/Revue canadienne d'esthetique* 6 (2001) at <www.uqtr.uquebec.ca/AE/Vol_6/Carlson/newman.html>; Nick Zangwill, *The Metaphysics of Beauty* (Cornell University Press, 2001).

21 Zangwill, *Metaphysics of Beauty*, p. 114.

22 Ibid., p. 116.

23 Ibid., p. 118.

24 Ibid.

25 It will come as no surprise that I warmly endorse Zangwill's doctrine of "indefinite framing," his insistence that nature is "aesthetically complex," and his view that, because the same *kind* of aesthetic judgments are made about nature and art, neither art nor nature has aesthetic priority (ibid., pp. 120-26).

26 Glenn Parsons and Allen Carlson, "New Formalism and the Aesthetic Appreciation of Nature," *Journal of Aesthetics and Art Criticism* 62 (2004), pp. 363-76.

27 Ibid., p. 373.

28 The impact can be either positive or negative. The green moss might be seen as less beautiful juxtaposed to blue-green mold on a discarded oil drum. The moon might look less beautiful juxtaposed to a neon "half-moon" casino sign.

29 The exception to this rule lies in the initial stages of simple emotive judgments. A child's delight in the beautiful, kaleidoscopic coloration on the surface of a soap bubble might be quite evanescent. But we must remember that it is just the first stage of a process of aesthetic maturation in which more time will be taken as reflection expands.

30 This seems to be a necessary element in what Berleant takes to be the fundamental requirement of "engagement."

31 I don't mean to suggest that the concept of aesthetic appreciation of relations is free from ontological or epistemological problems. But there is an important difference between the idea of finding beauty in the relation between A and B and finding A and B beautiful in their relation. The former notion seems to imply a mysterious third thing between the juxtaposed entities. The latter implies that it is the things themselves, now apprehended differently because of their juxtaposition, that are the objects (or joint object) of aesthetic appreciation. No third thing need obtrude to offend our Occamite sensibilities.

32 Dewey, *Art as Experience*, p. 37.

33 Arnold Berleant, *The Aesthetics of the Environment* (Philadelphia: Temple University Press, 1992), pp. 27-29.

34 Alison's proposals for constraining the contents of legitimate trains of ideas elaborating aesthetic experiences are presented in more detail in chapter 3, above.

35 The application of this part of Kant's complicated account of beauty to natural objects is presented with unusual clarity in chapter 2 of Malcolm Budd's *Aesthetic Appreciation of Nature*.

36 Dewey, *Art as Experience*, p. 38.

37 Berleant, *Aesthetics of the Environment*, p. 29.

38 The ontology of imagination is highly controversial. For my purposes here, however, it doesn't matter whether we consider the mental capacity required to unify the contents of connective beauty to be a species of imagination, an isolated aspect of the general power of imagination, or even some other characteristic or set of characteristics of mental activity for which "imagination" is a name of convenience.

39 Useful analyses of the varieties of imaginative experience in relation to aesthetic value generally can be found in Susan Feagin, "Imagination: Contemporary Thought," vol. 2, *Encyclopedia of Aesthetics*, pp. 471-73, and Roger Scruton, *Art and Imagination: A Study in the Philosophy of Mind* (London: Methuen, 1974).

40 Kant's account of this role of imagination appears in *Critique of Judgment*, pp. 50-54 and 77-81. An illuminating discussion of Kant's position on this issue is to be found in Budd, *Aesthetic Appreciation of Nature*, pp. 31-34.

41 Hume's discussion of imagination's role in perception can be found in his *Treatise of Human Nature*, Part I, section 4.

42 Feagin, "Imagination: Contemporary Thought," p. 472.

43 However, Obiter dicta may well be interesting and important in their own right. Their inclusion in judicial opinions is generally meant to lay a

groundwork for thinking about legal matters not raised in the present case but likely to be at issue in a range of future cases it in some way anticipates.

44 Warnock, *Imagination*, p. 180.

45 Ibid., p. 207.

46 Brady, "Imagination and the Aesthetic Appreciation of Nature."

47 Ibid., p. 143.

48 Ibid.

49 Ibid., p. 144.

50 Ibid., p. 145.

51 Ibid., p. 146.

52 Eaton, "Fact and Fiction in the Aesthetic Appreciation of Nature," in Carlson and Berleant, eds. *The Aesthetics of Natural Environments*, p. 152.

53 Natural facts become scientific facts (i.e., facts comprehensible within scientific explanations of natural phenomena) only when they are understood under covering descriptors or categories. But knowledge by acquaintance is just as legitimate a form of knowledge as knowledge by description. Gary Iseminger makes non-inferential knowledge of the former sort central in his account of aesthetic experience: "Aiming to perfect the exercise of our sensibility can be construed as aiming to see what is, in some sense, really there to be seen, hear what is really there to be heard, and understand what is really there to be understood—experiencing correctly." "The Aesthetic State of Mind," in *Contemporary Debates in Aesthetics and the Philosophy of Art*, ed. Matthew Kieran (Malden, MA: Blackwell, 2006), p. 108.

54 Ronald Hepburn, "Trivial and Serious," p. 68.

55 For a balanced and sensible discussion of relations between these views in regard to contemporary aesthetic debates see Donald Crawford, "Nature and Art: Some Dialectical Relationships," *Journal of Aesthetics and Art Criticism* 42 (1980) pp. 49-58.

56 Donald Crawford critically assesses the view that nature and art can't be compared aesthetically in "Comparing Natural and Artistic Beauty," in Kemal and Gaskell, *Landscape*, pp. 183-98.

57 This is the position taken by Anthony Savile in chapter 8 of *The Test of Time* (Oxford University Press, 1982). The echoes of Kant's view that beauty judgment entails regarding its objects as having "purposiveness without purpose" are evident.

58 Budd, *Aesthetic Appreciation*, p. 94.

59 David Carrier urges the view that people in a world without art could not experience nature aesthetically. Stephen Davies (who agrees with Carrier

that "we experience nature aesthetically through the prism of art") argues at length against his conclusion in *Definitions of Art* (Cornell University Press, 1991), pp. 143-51.

60 This discussion should make plain why the historical conundrum of
whether art is properly seen through the lens of nature or nature through
the lens of art is a non-problem.

61 Carlson, *Aesthetics and the Environment*, p. 114.

62 Ibid., p. 50.

63 The original is in the Albertina Museum in Vienna, but good reproductions can be found in many anthologies.

64 Albrecht Dürer, quoted by Francis Russell in *The World of Dürer* (Alexan-
dria VA: Time-Life Books, 1967), p. 7.

65 Arnold Toynbee, *Civilization on Trial* (Oxford University Press, 1949),
p. 26.

66 Allen Carlson discusses the role of formal qualities in Forest Service policy
in *Aesthetics and the Environment*, chapter 3. Marcia Eaton discusses
methods used by the Army Corps of Engineers to measure aesthetic
values in the natural environment (as well as the broader challenges of
quantitative aesthetic appraisal of natural environments) in *Aesthetics
and the Good Life*, chapter 4.

67 A notorious example of art of this kind is Marco Evaristii's *Eygoblack*, in-
stalled in February 2000 in the Trapholt Art Museum in Kolding, Denmark. It consisted of ten electric blenders containing water and goldfish;
museum guests were given the option of switching on the blenders, and
many did, killing the fish. Other works have caused the death of various
other animals, including rats and canaries, as well as serious (and possibly permanent) damage to the living environment.

68 Mark Twain, *Life on the Mississippi* [1883] (New York: Penguin Books,
1984), pp. 94-96, cited in Carlson, *Aesthetics and the Environment*,
pp. 16-17.

69 Ibid., p. 26.

70 Ibid., p. 19.

71 We cannot, for example, begin to decide what elements count as what
shapes and how many there are in a composition like Aubrey Beardsley's
Peacock Skirt (from *Salome*) unless we see the number and nature of these
elements as conditioned by the work's representational content. Because
formalism can be shown to lead to incoherence, it cannot support claims
that attention to formal features of a thing excludes or nullifies consideration of cognitive experience regarding that thing. Ibid., pp. 18-23.

72 The evolution of this notion from Shaftesbury, Hutcheson, and Alison through Hume and Stolnitz is traced in chapters 3 and 4.

73 Carlson, *Aesthetics and the Environment*, p. 26.

74 Twain presents rich, detailed appreciations of the aesthetic qualities of river scenes not nullified by knowledge elsewhere in *Life on the Mississippi* and in *Down the Rhône*. The second work, written later than the former, contains numerous passages that reflect appreciation of the very aesthetic features that Twain claimed "could never be restored to me while I lived."

75 The line of attack that looks formidable against Bullough's conception of disinterestedness, say, looks far less formidable against Brady's.

CHAPTER 9

Patterns of Appreciation and Aesthetic Development

*A*s we have seen, Western philosophical reflection on natural beauty has ancient roots and a tangled pattern of growth. Only very recently have scholars sought to present anything approaching a comprehensive taxonomy of theories of the aesthetic appreciation of nature. The most prominent and widely respected effort in this direction is Allen Carlson's inventory of what he calls "models for the appreciation of nature," presented in his book *Aesthetics and the Environment*.[1] In this chapter I present a brief description of the models he identifies together with some observations about their most conspicuous strengths and weaknesses. I then discuss the relation of my own theory to this taxonomy, pointing out ways in which it diverges from rival models as well as ways in which it preserves some of their positive virtues.

CARLSON'S INVENTORY

Carlson distinguishes ten approaches to the aesthetic appreciation of nature. They are: 1) the natural-environmental model; 2) the object model; 3) the landscape (or scenery) model; 4) the arousal model; 5) the aloofness (or mystery) model; 6) the engagement model; 7) the non-aesthetic model; 8) the postmodern model; 9) the metaphysical imagination model; and 10) the pluralist model. As Carlson describes them, the fundamental differences among these models are disparities in the ways they portray "the essence of appropriate aesthetic appreciation of nature."[2] There is no denying that several of the models overlap somewhat in their approach to this objective. And at least one (the pluralist model) seems to work its way across many conceptual boundaries at once. But the lines that divide the aesthetic perspectives these models embrace are now clearly enough drawn to make plain their comparative strengths and weaknesses.

Carlson's own theory is the leading example of the natural-environmental model. Its guiding principles are that a) nature must be appreciated "as what it is, that is, as natural and as an environment," and that b) it must (for that reason) be appreciated in light of knowledge provided by the natural sciences.[3] Although I certainly agree that appropriate appreciation of natural objects begins with the recognition that these things are not man-made, let alone artworks, I can't agree that all natural objects are, in the usual sense, environmental. Our delight in the cool beauty of a comet, the graceful swirl of the Crab Nebula, or the glowing brilliance of the aurora borealis has nothing to do with earthly ecosystems. If I should find the patterns in fingerprints, crystals, or even tabletop wood grains beautiful, that may be because patterns of these kinds move us whether they appear in nature, art, or elsewhere in life. Malcolm Budd points out that "trees planted in towns, for example, can be aesthetically appreciated as being natural objects even though they are located in and have grown up in a non-natural or partly non-natural environment, … as can—to take an obvious case—the flowers in one's garden."[4]

I have made the grounds of my disagreement with the natural-environmental model's second principle—its demand that natural science be the dominant guide to the aesthetic appreciation of natural objects—amply clear in chapters 2 and 7, and I need not repeat my arguments here. Suffice it to say that I am convinced there are many appropriate natural beauty judgments in regard to which scientific information is irrelevant, unilluminating, or even distracting. Here again I find that I am entirely in agreement with Budd, who points out that this model fails to make clear what pieces of scientific knowledge figure in what ways in a natural object's appreciation. It doesn't appear that much astronomical knowledge about the relation of the sun to the earth is involved in our aesthetic delight in a sunset. It doesn't appear that knowledge of the sexual physiology of a zinnia plays a major role in our appreciation of its beauty. Nor does our knowledge about the natural function of a zebra's stripes (which seems to be a mystery anyway) have much bearing on the aesthetic appeal of their design.[5]

Even within the general scope of this model, it seems to me wrong minded to insist that scientific categories provide the uniquely correct basis of aesthetic evaluation. The common teasel (*Dipsacus fullnum*) grows a floral head in which twenty or more spiraling rows of firm, gladiate petals curve upwards in a tight formation to form a pineapple-like crown. Seen up close, this formation is visually arresting, in large part due to its intricate geometry and to the way that patterning transforms itself in changing light conditions. Looking at a teasel flower, it is very easy to be reminded of similar, luminous visual patterns in Roman mosaics. We have no difficulty in retaining the thought that this is a natural object (and being pleased and impressed by the awareness that something like this exists free from human fabrication) while finding that its design, intensity, and associative characteristics count heavily in our reckoning that it is beautiful. In departing from exclusive reliance on natural-environmental categories of appreciation, we are not making this object over into a quasi-artifact. Rather, we are recognizing that in it, as well as in such artifacts as it may call to mind, we find features that commonly contribute to a thing's beauty and which may enhance our appreciation through the intensification of reciprocal attention. It seems to me that Carlson's insistence on the unique appropriateness of the natural-environmental model is built on a concept of appreciation that comes close to confusing beauty with respect. Respecting the world of nature by being mindful of native environments, the interdependence of natural beings, the values of endurance and sustainability, and so on is an enormously important and worthwhile mission. But respect for nature no more entails or circumscribes natural beauty than respect for a national flag entails or circumscribes its artifactual beauty.

The second and third approaches, the object and landscape models, go to the opposite extreme. They downplay the naturalness of natural objects, re-conceiving them as if they were sculptures or landscape paintings, respectively, and fastening attention on the perceptible design characteristics (color, shape, pattern, etc.) we appreciate in artworks of those kinds. These views are taken to be untrue to the environmental character of natural objects, the object model purporting to "rip objects from their larger environments," while the landscape model "frames and flattens them into scenery."[6] While I agree entirely that natural objects should not be appreciated as if they were artifacts, I do not agree that all of a natural object's sensible features need to be appreciated in its native environmental setting.[7] Nor do I concede that design features are irrelevant to a natural object's beauty if they happen to be shared with artworks or if we first come to value them in the artworld context. In earlier chapters, I have traced the historical support for the reciprocity thesis. I can see no reason why the idea that our appreciation of art informs our appreciation of much nature as our appreciation of nature informs our appreciation of art should not be considered just as sound today as it was taken to be in the eighteenth century.

Carlson contends that the landscape model wrongly imposes a framing requirement on natural objects or constellations of objects. I argued earlier that it is a mistake to suppose we cannot, or should not, ever impose framing conditions in the course of appreciating natural objects. I believe we do so habitually and unproblematically as we draw natural objects into frames of awareness or conspectuses in order to give them the aesthetic attention that is appropriate to them. For this reason, I find no reason for disqualifying from beauty judgments regarding natural objects such elements as may also appear in framed, deliberately designed artworks so long as we remember that the natural objects are natural and that the formal features they share with arti-facts are not, in fact, designed. Neither the object nor the landscape model will suffice on its own. But their failure is not that of identifying features irrelevant to a natural object's beauty. It is that of overstating the prominence of those features in relation to others.

The arousal model, most forcefully defended by Noël Carroll, centers on the phenomenon of being emotionally "moved by nature," a response that doesn't spring from, but may take place coincidentally with, scientific aware-ness of the sort required by the natural-environmental model. This response has its cognitive as well as its non-cognitive side. In being powerfully struck by the grandeur of a towering waterfall, for example, one can be well aware of its scale relative to certain other objects of one's acquaintance without having learned this fact from science.[8] The strengths of this view are that it seems to square well with widely shared convictions about common experiences involv-ing natural objects, and that it points to a wide range of appreciative responses not easily discounted or reduced to other responses. Some of these responses, at least, appear to be largely detachable from environmental contexts and scientific categories. Its weaknesses are a (perhaps inevitable) imprecision in the central notion of emotional arousal, and a lack of clarity about when and why such a response should be regarded as a specifically *aesthetic* mode of ap-preciation. It is, after all, no easy matter to mark the threshold where positive attention to a natural object involves a sufficient amount of positive emotive response to warrant calling it appreciation. And it is no less difficult to dis-tinguish clearly being moved aesthetically from other ways of being moved emotionally. An unexpected clap of thunder may provoke sudden fear. The sight of an animal corpse may provoke misery. The odd-looking gyrations of certain birds in courtship displays may provoke hilarity. Each of these might or might not be the beginning of an aesthetic experience that ends up being appropriately appreciative; but (as so far developed) the model itself doesn't draw the needed line between when it is and when it isn't.

It is precisely because the arousal model is grounded in experience rather than knowledge that I am generally sympathetic to it (despite the inherent weaknesses I have mentioned). But, once again, this model seems incapable by itself of accommodating the full range of appropriate aesthetic experience of natural objects. There are times when we correctly deem a natural object beautiful when it doesn't emotionally arouse us, or arouse us very much. On such occasions, a different element of appreciation moves to the foreground. It may be that we recognize a particular tulip as an extraordinarily fine exemplar of its type, or that we are struck by the overall balance and harmony among parts in a tangle of driftwood, or that we are aware a lake is brilliantly and deeply blue without being moved in the way the arousal model requires.[9] In all these cases, if we are still warranted in judging the objects to be beautiful—and I think we should be—that will be because we have amended this approach by poaching on others. And that is exactly what we *should* do.

In some ways, the fifth and sixth models seem like polar opposites; yet seen from a certain angle, they are variations on a common theme. The aloofness (or mystery) model demands that appreciation of natural beauty be wrenched away from the confining human perspective and made *acentric*; i.e., freed from any point of view. The engagement model takes the position that in appropriate appreciation the human perspective will be magnified and enhanced by becoming so immersed in the natural environment that familiar critical distinctions (e.g., between subject and object) dissolve. Thus both models promote a dramatic redirection of awareness, one that, at the very least, nullifies the outside-observer mentality with which many people habitually approach nature. They both defend the conviction that getting things straight requires a *dissolution*, rather than a finer resolution, of distinctions the other models draw.

Stan Godlovitch is the leading exponent of the aloofness model. He urges us to avoid both the smugness of science and the reductionism of reverence in our attitude toward nature, arguing that to give the natural world its due, we need to adopt a "frame-free perspective, a move behind the manifold of perception."[10] This view, he insists, is ultimately a concession to mystery; for nature and natural beauty are just *there* in a way that is bound to frustrate our efforts to apprehend or evaluate them. "Nature is aloof, and in this aloofness we come, not so much to understand or revere, as to attempt to mirror or match, and thus to grasp without capture."[11] Beginning from quite different initial premises, Arnold Berleant, the leading defender of the engagement model, reaches similar conclusions. He says:

The boundlessness of the natural world does not just sur-
round us; it assimilates us. Not only are we unable to sense
absolute limits in nature, we cannot distance the natural
world from ourselves in order to measure and judge it with
complete objectivity. Nature exceeds the human mind....
The proper response to nature ... is awe, not just from its
magnitude and power, but from the mystery that ... is part
of the essential poetry of the natural world.[12]

Thus, both models are wedded to the view that proper aesthetic appreciation
requires a regard toward natural objects that involves letting them be what
they are and admitting that what they are remains forever beyond human
knowledge. I think it hardly matters whether one thinks of this as inviting an
acentric perspective or an engaged one.

It must be admitted that the epistemological underpinnings of both
views are somewhat suspect. It is hard to see, for example, how a person
could *really* take a position independent of any point of view or become so
immersed in nature as to lose all awareness of subject and object and still be
in a position to make an appreciative judgment about a natural object.[13] If we
put such epistemological reservations aside, the real strength of the aloofness
and engagement models lies in their shared emphasis on defending nature's
integrity against both man-made physical intrusions (roads, dams, and the
like) and the imposition by aesthetic observers of framing devices alien to
the natural environment. Their insistence that nature is ultimately aloof or
mysterious is, I think, a way of repudiating the stock notion of appreciation as
a two-sided enterprise in which we rely on what we humans know (on this side)
to identify and evaluate what nature presents (on the other side). By asserting
the primacy of environmental integrity and nature's ultimate unknowability,
both models reinforce the importance in our aesthetic experience of natural
objects of what is just *there*, unnamed, unconceptualized, and therefore beyond
the cognizance of science. In doing so, however, they appear to sacrifice any
secure basis for critical reflection beyond personal, emotive response. Mystery
is mystery; and the truly incomprehensible provides no point of purchase for
communicable appreciation.[14]

The four remaining models have yet to be developed in a way that would
make them serious competitors to the models we have now considered. The
non-aesthetic model claims that the aesthetic appreciation of natural objects
is impossible because aesthetic appreciation is by its very nature limited to
man-made objects.[15] Such a view entails a radical rethinking of the standard

conception of aesthetics, imposing a limit on the discipline few would endorse. The postmodern model similarly refuses to regard nature *per se* aesthetically, focusing instead on meanings which humans have attached to natural objects and undertaking to interpret them as one might interpret a multi-layered literary text.[16] This way of approaching nature purchases theoretical versatility at too high a cost to natural integrity. Natural beauty isn't just whatever we've put there to find. The metaphysical imagination model is a close cousin to the postmodern model, taking interpretation in the direction of a range of sweeping metaphysical claims (about experience itself, the meaning of life, etc.).[17] Here again the worry is that there is nothing in the natural objects being appreciated that reins in speculation about these subjects. Natural beauty isn't a doorway to every deep truth.

Finally, there is the so-called pluralist model, a position that has yet to be fully worked out and defended. It is presented as a response to the recognition that "neither nature or we are one unitary thing," and that therefore "not all of humankind's cultural deposit is aesthetically significant either to all parts of nature or for all of humankind."[18] As Carlson describes it,

> A pluralist model would accept the diversity and richness of the cultural overlay in which a postmodern model delights. However, such a model would also recognize, first, that for any particular part of nature only a small part of that cultural overlay is really relevant to serious, appropriate appreciation, and second, that for any particular appreciator only a small part of the overlay can truly be claimed as his or her own. A pluralist model would endorse diversity, but yet would hold that in appropriate aesthetic appreciation, not all nature either can be or should be all things to all human beings.[19]

There are at least two ways to read this description. First, we might regard pluralism as chiefly a matter of respecting cultural diversity. Understood in this way, the chief thrust of the model is to provide room for different cultures to contribute different elements to the (serious, appropriate) appreciative manifold and for different individuals within those cultures to rely on those elements in making aesthetic judgments regarding a natural object. I see inclusiveness of this sort as an important, and indeed inevitable, aspect of any credible natural aesthetic. It goes to the heart of the reflective response to an aesthetic culture's descriptive judgments and to their evolution through corrective and affirmative judgments that emerge from the reflective response. Second, we might regard pluralism as a model in which the "cultural overlay" contains elements of various kinds within a given culture. Here, the idea would seem to be that appreciating nature as what it is for the participants in a culture entails multiple interpretive layers, that some of these layers are relevant and serious, while others are not, that some are more fundamental than others, and that a range of the relevant, serious, fundamental ones can contribute meaningfully to judgments of natural beauty.

On the second reading, the key question for the pluralist model is: Are we to understand "cultural overlay" to include just any thoughts and associations that might be attached to natural objects in a given culture? If so, then what winnows them down to the serious and relevant ones? Is that the job of the models of appreciation? And if the pertinent elements of cultural overlay are those that show up in the various models, does this last model aim to supplant all the others by including *all* the preferred evaluative factors? It is clear that the pluralist model, as it has been presented, is not impartially inclusive of the notions of appreciation presented in its nine rivals. For one thing, several of these models insist that some elements in the appreciative manifold are simply "more basic" than others. And, for another, the modes of appreciation presented in certain models (notably the arousal model and the natural environmental model) occupy a more prominent place than others as guides to the appropriate appreciation because they "concentrate on the most fundamental layers of human overlay, those constituting the very foundations of our experience and understanding of nature."[20] But this way of putting things begs the very questions these models were meant to answer. What is basic and fundamental from the point of view of one model may look anything but basic and fundamental from another.

THE PLACE OF SYNCRETIC THEORY

This brief survey of approaches to the aesthetic appreciation of nature has shown that, while many of the models have apparent strengths, none of them is free from shortcomings. Three responses suggest themselves. First, one might simply endorse whichever model appears strongest overall. This is Carlson's approach. After offering some charitable gestures in the direction of the pluralist and arousal models, he makes it clear that he thinks this is a contest with a clear winner, and that the winner is the natural-environmental model. Second, one may conclude that the identified flaws are serious enough to disqualify *all* models, and that aesthetic appreciation of nature is better understood as a freer sort of enterprise in which models provide no guidelines. This is Budd's approach. Faced with inadequacies in all the proposed models, he suggests that we should simply appreciate aesthetically whatever is available in nature for appreciation, and do so in whatever manner makes that appreciation possible.[21] Third, one may try to glean from the several models those elements that seem to be plausible contributors to aesthetic value in our experience of natural objects and weld them together into an account that is stronger than any one model on its own. This has been my approach in articulating the syncretic theory presented in this book. It may be appropriate to call mine a pluralist theory, but only if one recognizes that it hardly resembles the pluralist model in Carlson's inventory. It is neither wide open to all manner of content and response nor so constrained by doctrinal commitment as to preclude different elements from weighing in differently in different cases. It is instead pluralist in the grand tradition of political, scientific, and epistemological pluralisms. It insists that, because no one theory has all the truth while many, if not most, have some of it, the best we can do is to draw together the strongest elements from all into an approach that respects both a diversity of subject matter and a diversity of response to it.

By centering the theory on our *experience* of natural beauty and by taking stock of the many disparate factors observers report as playing into this experience, the account I have developed draws upon several of the rival theories without collapsing into any of them. I believe it is as great a mistake to suppose that certain factors—design features, say, or typal exemplariness—*always* count toward a natural object's beauty as to suppose that they *never* do. And I believe that if lines separating the various models prevent observers from taking stock of one set of elements in one case and another in another, then those lines have to be crossed or dissolved. There is no one correct way of appreciating natural objects.[22] And just as there is no one correct way of appreciating natural objects, there is no one way that they *are*. It is a familiar (Davidsonian) ontological axiom that every factual condition or event can be truly described in a limitless number of propositions, an axiom which, if it is to be useful to us at all, implies that the propositions in question are to be sorted for relevance according to the purposes (epistemic, normative, evaluative, etc.) they are meant to serve.

If we think of aesthetic appreciation as an enterprise in which we are concerned with how things are *for us*, then the claim that we should appreciate natural objects as they are supports any or all of the models of natural appreciation. It is apparent that the ways natural things are for us—i.e., are taken by us to be this or that—are as numerous as they are diverse. Among these ways, aesthetic experience selects those that are closely related to sensory response. Within this more restricted set of phenomena, it is manifestly apparent that the variety of ways natural things are for us, together with the ways they interact, demands a philosophical account that goes beyond the focus of any one model. It demands an account that invokes the various models we have reviewed severally and jointly in a comprehensive appreciation of natural objects.

In order to see how this process might play itself out, let us consider again the seashore episode I mentioned in chapter 2. Walking along a desolated stretch of Oregon shoreline, I came upon a scene[23] that captivated my attention and rewarded it with intense pleasure. It was, on the face of it, nothing extraordinary. Just a little, multi-stranded rivulet, wandering its way across the beach toward the sea. As the twining streams of water shifted slightly this way and that, they ate away at their shallow banks, causing the peripheral sands to tumble and slide into the current. These sands were of various hues—black, grey, rust brown, ochre, and various intermediary shades. It was, as it happens, a rare sunny afternoon. So as the running water pulled strands of sand down into itself, their color intensified and changed kaleidoscopically. The multitude of sand particles glittered as they tumbled along. Long, sinuous lines of varicolored sand emerged and disappeared, emerged and disappeared, over and over, in a rhythmic, ever-changing process of unfolding.[24]

As I knelt, then sat, silently watching this spectacle, I was at first simply absorbed with what I was observing, smitten with its loveliness. Then, as time passed, I became aware of a rift in my attention. Part of me was lost in the sand and the water; part of me was aware of the pleasure that was creeping over me in response to what I was observing as well as to the reflections that it began to stir in my mind. Part of me wanted to stay riveted to the spot for as long as the light conditions could sustain the spectacle. Part of me wanted to run off to summon my wife and daughter over to share in the delight. I saw what was there as wonderfully, purely unmade and accidental. Then, after a while, I began to recognize similarities between the lines, colors, and movements before me and lines, colors, and movements that had earlier impressed me in works of art I admire. As more time passed, I came to think of the twining flow of patterns as suggestive of the systole and diastole of sentient life itself. At no time did my attention wander from the frame of the stream-in-the-sand. Still, my thoughts kept reaching out to concepts, comparisons, and contrasts. And these fed the sense of beauty I was experiencing. In coming to think that the thing I was observing was beautiful, I was conscious of paying close attention to the phenomenal objects before me and equally close attention to the elements of consciousness that adhered to them. Although there was something intractably simple and uncomplicated about the object of my awareness, there was nothing simple or uncomplicated about my response to it.

Was it beautiful? It unquestionably was. This was a conclusion I reached within the first minute of my response. It was a conclusion reached independently of any reflection on aesthetic theory at all, let alone the array of models for the aesthetic appreciation of natural objects mentioned above. I am certain that subscription to the aptness of any model or combination of models would neither have created nor have destroyed this initial conviction.[25] But in what ways *would* the various models have helped inform (ratify, rationalize, or ramify) the impression of beauty this seaside experience gave me? It doesn't seem to me that any one of the models provides such compelling guidance that I should have relied on it alone. Instead, as I subsequently reflected on the experience, it seemed obvious that there was no way short of drawing on their several insights that would accommodate the multiplicity of factors that contributed to its beauty.

To begin with, as I sat there on that Oregon beach, I was deeply aware of the confluence of aesthetic ingredients as *natural*. I knew that what I was observing wasn't a clever earthwork/performance piece mounted by one of the local environmental artists. My delight in what I saw was tightly connected to the fact that the aesthetic object I enjoyed was detached from human enterprise. To that extent, I felt the force of the natural-environmental model's insistence on regarding natural things as natural and not artifactual. I realized, moreover, that what I saw as an attractive, evolving patterning was—in a way—reducible in its elements to sand and water, sun and sky. And I admitted to myself that if I were trying to explain these ingredients to my very young daughter, I would surely turn to the accounts provided by natural science. Thus, even though I believe that natural categories and their commonsense counterparts played a minor role in relation to the beauty of this experience, that role was a significant part of the rationalization element involved in the appreciative process.

On the beach, I was vaguely conscious of drawing the range of my attention down to just this rivulet, stretching from a cliff to the shore. But within that sphere of attention, I became much more conscious of forming local and informal frames around various constellations of objects—e.g., just this arrangement of flowing lines, fading out there; just these contours of sand cliffs, and not all the others nearby. The frames moved as I moved or moved the focus of my awareness. But as long as I was paying attention to the beach-stream-phenomenon, I never found my attention utterly unbounded or unframed.

Within one attentional conspectus after another, pattern and design features played a substantial role in making the complex object (sand and water, shift and glitter, and so on) beautiful. To take stock of the beauty-within-conspectus element that played prominently into my aesthetic appreciation of this phenomenon, it is useful to turn to the object and landscape models, which highlight arrangement, pattern, and design elements framed or contextually organized. My beach experience wasn't beautiful simply because it involved the patterning of component ingredients. But, equally, it wasn't beautiful simply because it was water and sand.

If there is any one thing about my response to the beach-stream that is beyond doubt, it is that I emphatically responded emotively to what I observed. The arousal model puts emotive response at the fore. Even if the question of how *much* emotional arousal is required to qualify a natural object as beautiful remains unanswered, the pertinence of emotional arousal to the judgment that a natural object is beautiful seems unassailable. When I was powerfully moved by the water-and-sand phenomenon, the fact that I was so moved must count toward ratification of my initial beauty judgment. What is beautiful about the sand and stream phenomenon is partly a matter of its being natural sand-and-stream and partly a matter of its being the sort of thing (like a waterfall) that, just because of its configuration in the rest of the natural world, arouses our affirmative responses for reasons we will never know.

As I sat on the sand, absorbed in the scene before me, I was intensely engaged with the peculiarities of this particular natural phenomenon. On the one hand, the consciousness-directing demand entailed by the engagement model was, I think, satisfied by my being fully immersed in the natural presentation that lay before me. On the other hand, my being so immersed didn't preclude my taking stock of other factors—even factors outside the perceptual frame—that bore upon its beauty. In a way, the same thing can be said about the pertinence of the aloofness model in this context. I did, undeniably, see what I saw as remarkable and outside normal bounds of descriptive comprehension. There was something about this whole encounter that struck me as wanting to stay outside explanation. Explanation generally requires words. But there are no words to name the tumbling, rippling, sparkling sand-and-water episode I saw. This isn't, of course, because the thing was weird and otherworldly. It was instead because we have no way of using our available stock of concepts to capture all of what is evident to the senses in this kind of situation. This means that nature will always be aloof, even as it is right at hand.

To the degree that my experience of the beach stream drew upon the insights developed in the remaining models—the non-aesthetic model, the postmodern model, the metaphysical imagination model, and the pluralist model—it is because, in different ways, these models direct attention to the ramifications of our aesthetic experience of natural objects. They say that our contemplation of the aesthetic object neither terminates in an initial emotive response nor ends the moment a beauty judgment regarding it has been reached. They aim to show how an aesthetic object can instead reveal a range of ways in which it can reward continuing attention. The important common point these models embrace is that appreciation is a process that takes time and that runs on long after an initial impression. The models differ over where they think the trajectory of appreciation might lead. But they agree on the importance of following appreciation's trajectory beyond its launching.

My sense of the beauty of the beach stream was not contained within the present-time frame of that experience. Instead, I found myself reflecting on the similarity of the lines, colors, and motions here to lines, colors, and motions I had previously experienced. Some of these, as I have mentioned, were elements I had become acquainted with in works of art. ("That curve is reminiscent of curves that impart a certain sensuousness to mannerist paintings.")[26] Some of them were elements that resonated with other events. ("The way those sand fragments keep falling into the flow and coursing on is, in a way, quite like the history of higher education.") There were other lines of reflection as well. Most of them seemed pertinent to the beach-stream experience and complementary to its beauty. Some did not. And when they didn't, I had a sense of losing the experience itself, accompanied by a desire to return.

What this series of theoretical reflections on a homely anecdote tells us is that there is no compelling reason to choose among identified models of natural appreciation. The more we look at the phenomenological details of actual aesthetic response, the more driven we are to think that any open-minded and informed response must draw upon several of the models described in Carlson's inventory, and not just one. In a way, Malcolm Budd has preceded me in this judgment. In *The Aesthetic Appreciation of Nature*, he attacks Carlson's taxonomy of models of nature appreciation by pointing out, as I have, that there is nothing wrong with admitting the relevance of *some* design elements, for instance, together with other elements in appraising natural beauty. But, in the end, he denies that there is *any* principled solution to the problem for which he takes it all these models were devised.

> [T]he fact that the aesthetic appreciation of nature is endowed with a freedom denied to the appreciation of art renders the search for a model of the aesthetic appreciation

of nature (in particular, the natural environment) that will indicate what is to be appreciated and how it is to be appreciated—something we have a good grasp of in the case of works of art—a chimerical quest.... The answer to the question, 'In the case of nature (i) what is to be aesthetically appreciated and (ii) how is it to be aesthetically appreciated?' is just this: (i) Whatever is available in nature for aesthetic appreciation (as nature), (ii) in whatever manner or manners it is possible to appreciate it aesthetically (as nature).[27]

Budd and I share the view that no *one* model of appreciation can stand on its own. We differ over whether shortcomings in the several models render them useless as a whole.[28] The quest for a reasonable policy for aesthetically appreciating natural objects need not be chimerical if we a) acknowledge the fact that people are powerfully responsive to some such objects and accept that there need be no philosophical accounting for *that* fact,[29] b) agree that various modes of awareness (typal beauty, formal beauty, intensity, etc.) play into and amplify these initial responses, c) agree that drawing on different models can help to bring out different features of various natural aesthetic objects, and d) bear in mind that it is the enrichment of the aesthetic experience itself that is the ultimate objective of the combinatory policy.

Think of the way people, young and old, begin to appreciate *art*. They don't have to be introduced to beauty as to a total stranger. They generally come into the field with firmly-held, if naïve, basic aesthetic ideas, and they want help in learning how to size up the art objects presented to them so as to build upon those ideas in a way that will make their experience of them as rich and rewarding as it can be. The payoff they are seeking is not some theoretically clarified concept of art-beauty, but an *aesthetic experience* in which art-beauty plays a central and instrumental part. They want art to make a positive difference in their lives, and they want beauty in art to be a major vector in this difference.

The story is, I believe, much the same in regard to the aesthetic appreciation of natural objects.[30] People start out with pre-reflective aesthetic notions and want to learn how to develop and extend them. If and when they turn to models of nature appreciation, they do so not to acquaint themselves with what they already know, but to find ways in which they can refine and clarify (and perhaps correct) those intuitions. As we have seen, various models of natural aesthetics emphasize different aspects of attention and awareness, many of which can fruitfully be combined. Ultimately, the point of drawing ideas from more than one model is, as I have urged, to create a responsive context in which awareness is enhanced as it is sustained, bringing together both cognitive and emotive effects. And the point of having experiences of that sort is not only that they are goods in themselves (although they are). It is instead that the qualities we come to appreciate in such experiences spread across the lines we draw between parts of our lives and pull these parts together.

This last remark may seem far-fetched, or even mystical. But it isn't, really. Instead, it reflects a plain truth about the way people habitually thread values together in their lives.[31] Our reasons for finding a mossy rock outcropping beautiful may be similar to finding the angular array of interlocking lines and patches of color in a Kandinsky painting beautiful. And these reasons may be similar to those we have for finding beauty in an array of lines and colors in an exuberantly designed herb garden. In a given culture, at a given time, certain patterns emerge as significant, impressive, pleasing, or resonant with others and for those reasons (among others) rewarding to attention. A few pages back, I mentioned that I once found the beauty of a line of sand tumbling in a rivulet to be similar to the beauty of curvilinear strokes in mannerist paintings. A certain shape in space, framed in a certain way, may reach deep into the repository of our acquired ideas about such shapes. Seeing that disparate things share aesthetic qualities and that the beauty of one can help us see the beauty of the others is a major part of the general enterprise of aesthetic appreciation. It is the very quality that positions aesthetic attention in the middle of life's business, rather than on the margin. Just as it is important to keep in mind that natural objects are non-artifactual, and hence free from human design, it is important to keep in mind that the *beauty* of natural objects is connected to beauty in all that we make and do.

GROWING UP AESTHETICALLY

I have been describing only a few of the many means available to us as we seek to apprehend natural beauty and to make sense of it when we find it. The account spread out over the last few chapters may make it seem as though the aesthetic experience of natural objects is so complicated and demanding as to make it unavailable to anyone but adults, and perhaps only sophisticated adults at that. But accepting that conclusion would be a serious mistake. When we take youngsters to an art museum and, to our delight (and perhaps relief), they tell us that they find some of the works on display beautiful, we don't admonish them that they lack the maturity and wisdom to make such judgments. Instead, we applaud and encourage their appreciation. We know it's rudimentary—that it may be based on little more than an agreeable juxtaposition of colors or the transparent coziness of a domestic scene—but it's probably genuine. And it's the beginning of something that, like most of our capacities for judgment—aesthetic, moral, political, social, and so on—will likely evolve and deepen over the course of their lives.

Likewise, when youngsters express aesthetic delight in natural objects—a pine cone, a birdsong, or the starry splendor of a night sky—we are pleased and encouraged that these simple emotive judgments will grow and mature as the youngsters themselves do. We don't discount their claims that the things they observe are beautiful. But we expect that the initial grasp of natural beauty that they have developed will be extended and amplified throughout their lives. And what do we suppose will be the source of this extension and amplification? It seems to me that the components of natural aesthetic experience I have traced above *are* that source. I do not deny that other components can be usefully added to the inventory I have presented. But I believe that I have identified the major elements that lead from youthful to mature impressions of natural beauty.

Children start out with big, bold likes and dislikes. Tactile qualities in the fur of a dog might well make a deeper aesthetic impression than the visible qualities of a mountain cascade. Increments that follow from that beginning can be serious increments or stale, trite, and unproductive ones. In chapters 7 and 8 I have spelled out some of the ingredients that contribute to the development of natural aesthetic appreciation by conducing to the enrichment of aesthetic experience and thereby to the attainment of a wider normative maturity. Over time, young observers are likely to find that natural objects engage their senses and their thoughts more emphatically when they put aside distracting concerns. They may find that certain elements of natural beauty appear when the ingredients of attention are framed and ordered in some way, so that patterns and design features emerge. They may find that their appreciation of certain natural objects is intensified when they regard them through a category provided by natural science, and thus contemplate them in relation to other elements of an environmental matrix. And they may find, to their relief, that they don't have to do this alone. Instead, they develop means of appreciating natural beauty within communities of appreciation. And it is within these same communities that they develop means of communicating their experiences to others. In the course of reflecting on their own experiences regarding natural objects, and through discussing their reflections with others in their aesthetic community, they may come to realize that they have a *stake* in natural beauty. That is, they may find that the aesthetic qualities they have found in natural objects make enough of a difference in their lives to warrant a commitment of attention and responsive effort regarding them. It is in this way that they become participants in what I have called the "natureworld," the framework of natural objects essentially equivalent to Danto's "artworld," as the basis for their eventual natural beauty judgments. In the natureworld context, patterns of appreciation reviewed earlier in this chapter serve as useful positioning devices, locating emerging aesthetic commitments on a map of possibilities.

Whether in the domain of art or that of nature, the process of growing up aesthetically is neither steady nor certain. Some folks become so preoccupied with other concerns or so alienated from the value of beauty in their lives that they remain aesthetic infants. But for others, the process of aesthetic growth parallels other processes of maturation. Just as we expect that a teenager doesn't need the kind of autocratic parental guidance that a pre-schooler does, we expect that the teenager will have acquired a range of responsiveness to the beauty in natural objects that the pre-schooler could not have mastered. And just as we rightly think of teenage opinions about most things as at best preliminary, we anticipate that they will mature in time and eventually become moral, political, social, and aesthetic adults.

So, what is the goal? What is it to be an aesthetic grownup? There is no single, straightforward answer to that question. This is clear from the fact that intelligent, informed, and sensitive people differ markedly on the features they deem most pertinent to the formation of aesthetic judgments. Still, at least within the institutional setting of the artworld, it seems possible to identify some generally-accepted markers of reflective awareness that distinguish mature from immature appreciation. When Michael Parsons, a prominent art education scholar, was asked to consider what qualities might count toward being an aesthetic adult (in the way that certain qualities of thought count toward moral maturity in Kant's ethics), he responded that

> [a]esthetic adulthood ... means being able to respond appropriately to the art of one's society. This includes being able to interpret artworks meaningfully and to respond to them relevantly, to place them in context, to understand their kinds, to value some for relevant reasons, to discuss them in a critical way.... Responding relevantly might well include responding with marked emotion ... [reflecting] the current general consensus in philosophy that aesthetic response, and emotion in general, is cognitively structured and interpretive in character.[32]

This statement presents a plausible, broad-brush picture of the interplay of objective and subjective, cognitive and non-cognitive factors in the responsive capacity of a person who has an adult sense of what is going on in her aesthetic culture as well as in her own mind. If we substitute "nature" for "art" and "natural objects" for artworks in Parson's statement, we have at least the beginnings of an answer to the question of what qualities are demanded of aesthetic adulthood in regard to the appreciation of natural beauty.

We grow up learning how to respond appropriately to natural and artifactual objects both within and in reaction to a given social context. We learn how to regard things in relation to their kinds, to value them, or their aspects, for relevant reasons, and how to discuss them with others in a thoughtful and critical way. In our critical perspective, we incorporate elements of emotion, cognition, and interpretation. And the more ably and extensively we are able to do this, the more our appreciation of beauty transcends its simple, emotive beginnings. The key idea is that the attainment of aesthetic maturity is, like the attainment of moral, political, or social maturity, the crossing of a threshold of reflection. Beyond this threshold, one is aware of having adopted one's own judgments and of being willing to defend them against a background of other judgments that both inform and rival them. Growing up is, among other things, a process of growing into and through one's culture, a gradual process of both adopting and amending what gets handed down.[33]

Young people's first acquaintance with natural beauty is generally an untutored enjoyment of observable things—what I have called "simple emotive judgments." They take pleasure in the plain, unadorned sensory appearance of things—the fragrance of the plumeria, the taste of wild strawberry, the feel of the moss, the brilliant palette of the rainbow, and so on. Children's early aesthetic responses are like ancient philosophical views in that distinctions between nature and artifact are not distinctly drawn. Things are things, and they appeal or they don't appeal to tender sensibilities. Once the notion of context assumes prominence, the notion of framing, or contextual limit, is inevitable. Youngsters on a walk through a meadow who are invited at a certain point to say whether they find it beautiful might be inclined to ask, "how much?" or "which part?" In this way, the idea that beauty has to do with the comprehension of elements within some bounding or framing conditions begins to take hold.

There is frequently a period in the young person's developing awareness in which the value of natural beauty is emblematically connected with a host of other values—and maybe all other values—much as it was in certain historical periods in the West. It may come to be seen as inextricably caught up with spirituality, environmental concerns, romantic sensibility, or even with virtue, sanctity, and justice, all rolled into one. This stage is usually succeeded by one in which values propounded by other people come to the fore. It cannot but occur to the attentive young mind that the person next to him doesn't sense natural things in just the way he does, and so will not have quite the same take on natural beauty that he does. In one way or another, the progressive breakdown of the egocentric perspective inevitably opens young minds to fundamental questions regarding the relations of self to others that lie at the threshold not only of aesthetic maturity, but of moral, political, and social maturity as well. To what extent can I see through another's eyes (or, more generally, sense through another's senses)? Is it reasonable to expect convergent value judgments because of our essential human commonalities? What confidence can I have in my own convictions in the face of divergent convictions in my community? Answering, or least seriously addressing, such questions as these is one of the most formidable tasks young people face on the path to aesthetic maturity.

The "subjective turn," as a familiar feature of late adolescence, need not be a regression into self-absorption. Instead, it can signal an awakening of reflective capacities in the perceiving subject—the basis of what I have called "reflective judgment." Having taken stock of the received wisdom of one's culture and the various opinions of one's fellows, the young adult may set out to rethink, rationalize, and defend the judgments that she thinks most plausible. Here is where a sense of one's own place in the natureworld begins to form. There is no denying that one's capacities for awareness, let alone appreciation, are greatly molded by one's cultural heritage. But, equally, the move to adulthood demands that one make one's own contribution to that heritage by espousing (and possibly advocating) corrective or affirmative judgments.[34] Introspection is one of the key talents developed in the process of growing up. Very young people simply *have* whatever experiences of natural beauty they have. It is only in young adulthood that people not only *have* experiences but *reflect* on them to the point of having the experience of having an experience. In order to be cognizant of such aspects of responsiveness as these, one must draw on gradually developed imaginative and cognitive repertoires, as well as on a sense of their interconnections.

Cultural maturity—whether it's aesthetic, moral, political, or social—is marked by the conscious adoption of cognitive principles and responsive styles as one's *own*, after the growing-up process of examining and sampling the principles and styles of others and after having positioned oneself in relation to a given normative heritage. Cultural maturity is marked by commitment.

To be a moral adult, for example, is to make a personal decision to live one's life one way rather than another after having sorted through the normative cards spread out on the table. To be an aesthetic adult, as I see it, is to be similarly committed to a course of valuation (which may entail appreciation, preservation, protection, encouragement, among other involvements) regarding both artifactual and natural objects. It is to have worked one's way through the various levels of objective and subjective valuation that one's aesthetic culture presents to the point where one determines that these things count enough to have established a stake in one's life. Stakeholders in artifactual beauty enter the artworld. Stakeholders in natural beauty enter the natureworld.

How does the process of aesthetic maturation into natureworld commitment play out in a typical cultural community in the West? To this question there can be no easy answer. The realization that there can't be goes straight to the heart of my theoretical approach. Different people come to aesthetic maturity with differing sets of skills and sensibilities; they need to draw on a variety of resources to cultivate worthwhile aesthetic experiences; and they compose experiences that are rewarding in different ways. It is precisely because of these differences that any useful theory of the aesthetic appreciation of natural beauty must be syncretic. Differences among mature aesthetic experiences of natural beauty should not, however, blind us to their shared features. These are, I believe, the very features that link the aesthetic element to other value elements in the life of the cultural grownup. To the degree that the experience of natural beauty involves close attention to sensible features of the world, it cultivates an appreciation of facts and details that is an essential capacity in reckoning value in all aspects of life. To the degree that it involves disinterestedness, or disengagement from immediate and practical concerns, it cultivates a vital ability to appreciate things, persons, and events without having a personal stake in them. To the degree that it involves an affinity for what is rare, it cultivates an appreciation of the uncommon features in life, intensifying our enjoyment of whatever elements of the world about us are irreplaceable. To the degree that it involves constructive interpretation, seeing X's as Y's, it cultivates an essential element in moral and political appraisal, the capacity to see things, people, and events, first as this, then as that, and possibly as both. To the degree that it involves framing, or the capacity to draw disparate elements into a conspectus, it cultivates an appreciation of the interplay of parts and wholes, a central element of understanding the relations of people, institutions, and the objects they survey. To the degree that it involves mirroring, the reflective awareness of one's own thought processes in the activity of appreciating natural beauty, it cultivates self-reflection and self-appraisal, capacities that conduce to the recognition that in making choices we are always at the same time choosing the persons we shall be.

A person seeking to become an aesthetic adult need not set out in the dark. Although there is no one right way to grow up aesthetically, and no one right form of aesthetic experience of natural objects, there *are* known ways of enhancing and deepening aesthetic awareness. These ways are reflected in the "fundamental elements," "general factors," and "patterns of appreciation" I have described above. Far from being a haphazard collection of values and personal preferences, the various elements I have presented are a distillate of cumulative Western cultural attention to beauty in natural things. We live our aesthetic lives in cultural contexts, and it is therefore not surprising that we should be guided by the modes of awareness and reflection that come to us from our social settings. At the same time, as aesthetic adults we should understand that we have an imperative to contribute to this ongoing legacy by turning past and present renditions of aesthetic experience into something that is personal and possibly new.

At the beginning of this book I said that I wanted to articulate a view of natural beauty that makes sense of common perceptions while it justifies a philosophical position that renders these perceptions intelligible and coherent. The account I have sketched here of the process of aesthetic maturation does just that. No one thinks that relatively naïve assessments of natural beauty are worthless. No one thinks that so-called-expert opinions are decisive. Most folks are willing to admit that natural beauty judgments can be cultivated and improved by appropriate guidance. Most folks are unwilling to concede that that guidance should come in just one form rather than another. The syncretic approach aims to respect all of these convictions while making good use of philosophical theory to put them into a cogent array. As I have told the story, the most recent stages of natural aesthetic theory separate on the divide between conceptualists and non-conceptualists. It seems to me that the business of growing up aesthetically inevitably lands the thoughtful adult in the center of this controversy. There is undeniably a substantial role for categories and classifications in our awareness of many natural objects. There are also many natural objects which, as I have argued, may best be appreciated apart from these conceptual limits. Certain parts of the aesthetically mature apprehension of natural objects require substantial knowledge about natural things, a knowledge that is predictably acquired in the process of growing up culturally. Other parts of aesthetically mature apprehension of natural objects require a familiarity with such natural elements as shape, color, and composition, a knowledge that is equally essential in the process of growing up culturally.

Much of the current turmoil in the theory of natural aesthetics concerns efforts to separate or reconcile these parts. So, the conceptual predicament of the standard adult observer of natural beauty may be fraught with tension between competing ideals of aesthetic attention and competing models of appreciation. But this leaves aesthetic adulthood just where it should be. There are, and can be, no easy answers here. That is the general condition of thoughtful adulthood. We are all in the business of trying to make order out of the messy display of human experience, knowing that the providers of that experience—sense and intelligence—are themselves hostages to competing philosophical theories.

NOTES

1 Carlson, *Aesthetics and the Environment*. The same inventory is presented in only slightly different form in Carlson's essay, "Nature: Contemporary Thought," *Encyclopedia of Aesthetics*, vol. 3 (Oxford University Press, 1998), 346-49.

2 Carlson, *Aesthetics and the Environment*, p. 6.

3 Ibid.

4 Budd, *Aesthetic Appreciation of Nature*, p. 136.

5 Ibid., pp. 136-38. See also Michael Pollan's discussion of the implications of relying on a "wilderness ethic" versus a "garden ethic" in determining whether Cathedral Pines (a small Connecticut stand of old-growth) should be cleared of storm debris or left as it was. What the town folk took to be virgin growth—that is, untrammeled nature—had in fact been logged and otherwise altered by human intervention, just not (noticeably) during the lives of folks then living. *Second Nature: A Gardener's Education* (New York: Atlantic Monthly Press, 1991), pp. 176-201.

6 Carlson, *Aesthetics and the Environment*, p. 6.

7 Here again, I am in agreement with Budd, who points out that "to appreciate the wonderful smoothness of a rock as an effect of erosion by the sea ... it is not necessary for it still to be in the sea or washed up on the shore." *Aesthetic Appreciation of Nature*, p. 132.

8 Carroll, "On Being Moved by Nature," in Kemal and Gaskell, eds. *Landscape, Natural Beauty, and the Arts*, pp. 245, 258-59. As was mentioned earlier, Carroll supposes that the problem of "framing" an object of aesthetic attention independently of categories provided by natural science is easily overcome. He takes it that the focus of emotional arousal

in relation to natural objects is predicated on natural closure and natural salience. This position allows Carroll to maintain that the arousal model is "objective" in a sense distinct from scientific objectivity.

9   To be sure, we might scale down the model's apparent requirement that we be moved positively and strongly to warrant a beauty judgment in such a way as to qualify the mental acts described in these instances. But it would be very hard to define an arousal that wouldn't trivialize the overall account or make it collapse into one of the other models.

10   Godlovitch, "Icebreakers," p. 111.

11   Ibid., p. 123.

12   Berleant, *Aesthetics of Environment*, p. 169.

13   I do think that we sometimes lose ourselves in aesthetic experience. We sometimes (as T.S. Eliot observed) hear music so deeply that we are the music while it lasts. We sometimes suspend our sense of ourselves in the darkened theater. And we can, equally, become so absorbed in a spectacular sunset that we are truly unaware of this or that point of view, or of being in or outside the phenomenon. But Kant was right about this one. When the moment comes (and it may come long after the experience itself) at which we are asked for an aesthetic appraisal, we express a value judgment that imputes that same judgment to all similarly situated rational observers. That is to say, a decision that this particular sunset is beautiful cannot be a *private* mystery. However divorced from perspective, however lost in the experience we may have been, when it comes to asserting an aesthetic judgment, we are inevitably forced to invoke a position which others in the relevant social context can be expected to embrace.

14   Carlson alleges that the engagement model, by denying the object-subject distinction, tends to trivialize the enterprise of nature appreciation, while the aloofness model, by opening an irreparable breach between object and subject, displaces appreciation with a form of respect that verges on worship (*Aesthetics and the Environment*, pp. 6, 8).

15   Carlson identifies Don Mannison and Robert Eliot as the primary expositors of this view. See "A Prolegomenon to a Human Chauvinistic Aesthetic," in Don Mannison, Michael McRobbie, and Richard Routley, eds., *Environmental Philosophy* (Canberra: Australian National University Press, 1980), and Robert Elliot, "Faking Nature," *Inquiry* 25 (1982) pp. 81-93.

16   Carlson takes George Santayana to be the father of the point of view espoused in this model.

17   Carlson identifies Ronald Hepburn as the leading exponent of this model.

18   Carlson, *Aesthetics and the Environment*, p. 10. Carlson points out that some elements of this model are suggested in the work of Yrjo Sepanmaa (see *The Beauty of Environment* (Denton, TX: Environmental Ethics Books, 1993), and that he endorses some aspects of it himself in chapter 14 of *Aesthetics and the Environment*.

19   Carlson, *Aesthetics and the Environment*, p. 10.

20   Ibid.

21   Budd, *Aesthetic Appreciation of Nature*, p. 147.

22   Carlson is fond of quoting a lovely remark of Paul Ziff about aspection in the art world: "[T]o study, observe, survey, inspect, examine, scrutinize, etc. are ... acts of aspection. ... I survey a Tintoretto, while I scan an H. Bosch. Thus I step back to look at the Tintoretto, up to look at the Bosch. Different actions are involved. Do you drink brandy in the way you drink beer?" (from "Reasons in Art Criticism," *Philosophical Turnings: Essays in Conceptual Appreciation* (Cornell University Press, 1966), p. 71, cited in *Aesthetics and the Environment*, p. 41. But of course the same point holds for aspective appreciation with regard to natural objects. I regard a daffodil as a beautiful representative of its variety; I admire the glossy smoothness of the river rock; I am struck by the way the light on the lake water brings out beautiful patterns similar to the patterns in Monet's lily pond paintings. Do you look at one as you look at the other? No more than you drink brandy the way you drink beer.

23   In saying that what I observed was a scene, I am not conceding to Carlson's objection that non-conceptualists convert episodes of appreciation in natural environments into scenes—meaning by that that they regard them as quasi-artworks, quasi-postcards, or quasi-snapshots. Instead, I am simply saying that what presented itself to me was not an endless, or arbitrarily limited congeries of natural elements. It presented itself to me as a conspectus, a limited (though not imperviously bounded) body of attention.

24   I don't want to suggest that the only aesthetic elements playing into this experience were visual. I was certainly aware of the pungent, ambient sea smell, as well as of the tactile pleasure of the mild breeze brushing sand around my ankles. But the heart of the experience, as it struck me, lay in the visible qualities I describe. A more comprehensive account of the same experience might well take into account the full sensory panoply. But it wouldn't change the point I am making.

25   This is hardly surprising, since, properly understood, the role of these models is not to *bring about* beauty judgments. Rather, it is to *ratify*, *rationalize*, and *ramify* those judgments. They ratify them by providing a

basis for holding the initial judgment to be valid. They rationalize them by giving reasons for that judgment that ought to be acceptable to other reasonable observers. And they ramify those judgments by suggesting ways in which the initial impression may be sustained and enriched by being linked to reflections that carry appreciation substantially beyond it. Surely proponents of the various appreciation models have no intention of denigrating or denying powerful, positive aesthetic responses people have to natural objects despite their being oblivious of aesthetic theory. Instead, they want to be understood as offering advice for focusing attention one way or another so as to affirm and extend the initial positive impression in reasonable and productive ways.

26 This thought popped into my mind because I had been talking about Cranach's work in my class, and had shown a slide of his 1506 woodcut of St. Christopher, in which the leg of the saint makes a dramatic curve of this sort.

27 Budd, *Aesthetic Appreciation of Nature*, p. 147.

28 Budd's own critique demonstrates the value of capturing fragments of one model as complements (or antidotes) to fragments of other models. In the end, it is a Kantian sense of centrality of judgmental freedom that leads him to the conclusion that *nothing* should take the place of the discredited models. To the contrary, it seems to me that Kant's twin commitments to the profundity of natural beauty and the importance of definitive beauty judgments should warn us away from that conclusion.

29 Any more than, as David Hume observed, human beings are disposed to be pleased by certain forms or qualities "from the original structure of the internal fabric." "Of the Standard of Taste," pp. 233-34.

30 Here again the caveat is necessary that the art and art appreciation being discussed are located in the Western aesthetic tradition.

31 This is one of those points where aesthetic and other normative values work their way into alignment. We have to choose which way to go. And in making life choices, we draw upon all of our various appreciative capacities. A decision to spend time looking at, and thinking about, a beach stream affects the other value-based decisions in one's life. It might inspire an invention. It might get one fired for showing up late for work. And, then again, it might suggest how many of the things one cares about might be brought together in a comprehensive pattern.

32 Michael J. Parsons, "Can Children Do Aesthetics? A Developmental Account," in *Aesthetics for Young People*, ed. Ronald Moore (Reston, MD: National Art Education Association, 1995), p. 35.

33   This handing-down process may be subtler and more pervasive than is
usually supposed. According to a well-known slogan in the biological
sciences, ontogeny recapitulates philogeny—which is to say that the
development of the individual retraces the steps whereby the species
came to evolve that individual. The slogan may be more-or-less sound
as it applies to organic evolution. There is no pretending that the same
principle applies straightforwardly to aesthetic evolution. Clearly the development of natural aesthetic appreciation in modern-day individuals
does not simply recapitulate, one after another, the historical stages of
philosophical reflection on natural beauty. Still, patterns of growth and
maturation in the individual and in the culture are often strikingly similar. This shouldn't be too surprising. After all, a good deal of the development of aesthetic sensibilities that occurs in the advance toward aesthetic
maturity in today's natureworld draws upon features of awareness and
reflection that gained ascendancy, one after another, in the evolution of
theories of natural beauty I have described earlier.

34   Literature is perhaps the commonest context in which young people appreciate this point. Nothing, they come to realize, that is written is altogether new. Neither is it altogether old. They come to see that what "rose"
means depends not only on what the poet saw when he looked outside
his window, but also what it had come to mean by the accumulation of
usage over centuries. The key transitional point comes when they realize
that the poet's latest use remakes the tradition itself, so that new keeps
absorbing and changing the old. This is the point at which young people
often come to recognize that their own impressions and judgments can
make an important contribution to the development of the world they
live in.

CHAPTER 10

Theoretical Implications and Conclusion

LAYERS OF RESPONSE

*I*t is a sign of maturity in general—moral, political, and social no less than aesthetic—that feelings and thoughts stratify. Instead of just feeling this or that and thinking this or that, we normally have feelings *about* our feelings, thoughts *about* our thoughts. And, in time, we go on to have thoughts about that, too. Moreover, in the ongoing course of reflection about things of value, we are often aware of socially inherited ideas as a substratum upon which our ideas are mounted. We may also become aware of antagonistic ideas as a superstratum against which our feelings and thoughts may have to contest. And if we step back to evaluate the relation between our critical ideas and the ideas against which they are posed, yet another layer of response appears. A significant part of maturity is coming to appreciate—for both its positive and its negative effects—this inevitable, productive layering of normative response.

The first-order response to natural beauty is a pleased reaction to a natural object. It is normally the pleasure of "felt immediacy," pleasure in the sensory apprehension of features of natural objects sustained long enough to savor this response. Here the sensory element is dominant. The child's open and unrehearsed delight in the horn-sounds and V-formation of a flight of passing geese is a good example of first-order beauty response.[1]

The second-order response to natural beauty is reflective awareness. It involves a cognitive reaction to, or exploration of, the first-order response. Part of this response should be acknowledgment that the thing observed is natural rather than artifactual (the appreciation I described in chapter 2 of natural beauty as natural).[2] It may also involve *framing* the object (as discussed in chapter 6) in one or another way. One way might be aimed at making the relation of its parts to its whole intelligible so that its formal characteristics can properly be appreciated (as discussed in chapter 8). Another might be aimed at showing a natural object to qualify at some level as an exemplar of its type. Second-order responses are frequently dynamic, involving a series of reframings (taking stock of what one has found appealing from a shifted perspective or in a different light) and a continuing series of reflective inquiries. "Why is this beautiful?" "What is it about this that pleases me so?" "How does this object, which came into being independent of human design, cause me to have a response that is so like those that I have to artworks?" And so on.

The third-order response to natural beauty is a matter of measuring first and second order responses in relation to prevailing ideas or standards of beauty in a given cultural community. This is, of course, one way of laying the groundwork for potential aesthetic judgment. Not all natural beauty response emanates in beauty judgment, nor should it. But, as layered reflection on an original, emotive beauty response evolves, the grounds for making a reasonable beauty judgment regarding it are usually clarified. Here, aesthetic response moves beyond felt pleasure into the arena of informed commitment, and welcomes, as a basis of communicating with others, consideration of whatever contrasting thoughts and feelings they may have.

There are many ways in which layers of additional higher-order responses may attach to layers beneath them. One familiar form of fourth-order response is analogical extension. I have previously described ways in which "trains of thought" may be motivated by natural objects found to be beautiful. Associative connections of this kind typically involve imaginative and conceptual linkages that are independent of the kinds of evidentiary considerations prominent in third-order responses. And yet there are, as we have seen, reasonable constraints that can be imposed on the elaborative process. Clearly, not every associative connection is as apt as the next. To make apt and revealing connections, one must rely upon a practiced sense of how different ideas inform one another, a sense of what details count in aesthetic comparisons, and a flair for spotting non-obvious but telling similarities and differences. In short, one needs to have in the realm of natural beauty a set of aesthetic sensibilities quite like those that Hume presented as requisite for judgments of taste in the realm of art. It is in the fourth layer that connections between aesthetic values and other values are most likely to emerge. The basis of this connection was addressed in chapters 8 and 9.

The layering of response I have described is not a metaphysical nicety. Rather, it is an account of how simple emotive judgments may evolve into reflective judgments and thus emerge as the basis for dispositive reaction to the beauty we find in natural things.[3] When, earlier, I asserted that natural aesthetic judgments are dispositive, I implied that they both declare a person's personal judgments and express that person's disposition to act in one way rather than another in regard to the objects in question. A person making a reflective beauty judgment is doing more than staking a claim about a fact.[4] He makes (or takes himself to be prepared to make) a move in regard to that object. It may be a move to protect it, to encourage its sustenance, to draw attention to it, to sing or write about it, as well as many other things. One conspicuous exhibition of the dispositive character of natural aesthetic judgments is the inclination of one generation to pass on the basis of these judgments to the next generation. It is a rare parent who, delighting in the splendor of a brilliant sunset, doesn't at the same time wish to bring his or her children into that same arena of delight. And, of course, the dispositive character I attach to aesthetic judgments need not attach to family members alone. It is, instead, an imperative for communion between an entire aesthetic community and its successor communities. The judgment that a natural object is beautiful begins in the personal, immediate experience of pleasure, but it cannot mature unless it accretes elements of reflection and association that connect this experience to the thoughts and feelings of others. Initial reactions simply are what they are. Mature aesthetic responses link individuals and their communities in a creative way, advancing the normative interests of both.

HARD QUESTIONS

The account I have presented is sufficiently unconventional to invite some hard questions. Before concluding, I want to address some of the most obvious ones. One possible line of objection is that my account is *circular*. I take the view that people come into possession of the tools of aesthetic appreciation of natural objects by growing up in a setting in which the various cognitive and non-cognitive capacities for making natural beauty judgments are already on display. But this presupposes a prior cultural acceptance of what counts in making such judgments. Natural beauty judgments are predicated on individual appraisals. Individual appraisals are, in turn, based on factors that have emerged in the evolution of aesthetic reflection. But aesthetic reflection is predicated on some form of recognition of natural beauty. There *is* an undeniable circularity in all of this. But, there are circles and circles. Although philosophers rightly eschew *vicious* circles, as necessarily frustrating to reason, not all circles in the theory of aesthetic appreciation are, in the disqualifying way, vicious.

Hume's account of beauty judgment is arguably circular in a similar way. What beauty is depends on the judgments of true judges. But the true judges are qualified on the basis of their capacity to identify beauty. So it seems that beauty enters the decision process both as objective and as qualifier, and this makes the process circular. Hume's defenders have pointed out that his account of the qualifications of true judges doesn't really depend on antecedent recognition of beauty. Rather, it depends on the identification of those capacities a community interested in beauty judgments would deem appropriate. Similarly, George Dickie's formulation of the definition of "art" in the institutional theory of art (revised version) is self-avowedly circular. Dickie points out that an account of identifying judgments in the artworld need not exclude all elements of the defined. "What philosophical definitions of 'work of art' are really attempting to do," he says, "is … to make clear to us in a self-conscious and explicit way what we already in some sense know."[5] The account I present here is non-viciously circular in just the way Hume's and Dickie's theories are. A good part of what we "in some sense know" about natural beauty is built into the inexplicable pleasure we take in some of our contacts with things around us—a pleasure whose evolutionary basis is lost to us. Another part comes about through our having grown up in one aesthetic culture or another, learning the notions of natural beauty prevailing in it much as we learn a language by living in a linguistic culture—gradually, incrementally, and unselfconsciously. Does the fact that we can't pry the concept of natural beauty we deploy regarding present-day objects free from this unconscious and cultural context fatally undercut its use?

It seems to me that the circularity problem is linked to the developmental issue we considered above. Growing up in any sense is a business of working out individual ideas against a backdrop of established ideas. This is certainly true as regards growing up aesthetically. My theory says that natural beauty is best apprehended in a way that reflects the aesthetic experiences of those who have, in various ways, come to appreciate natural beauty. Because they come to do so in a cultural context in which natural beauty judgments are already being made, their sense of what counts in the experience supporting those judgments is bound to be dependent on that context. But, the aesthetic experience *itself* has to be their own, a product of their own particular take on the natural object or objects at hand. My claim that natural beauty is a product of the aesthetic experience of natural things is not viciously circular unless all reflective judgments collapse into descriptive judgments—that is, unless aesthetic experience is so tightly tied to the established norms of appraisal in one's cultural community that the reflective franchise becomes a hollow mandate for conformity. But the analysis I have offered above is an extended demonstration that it doesn't.

Another hard question strikes at the heart of my theory. Why, it might be asked, should an account that selects this piece from theory A, that piece from theory B, another piece from theory C, and so on down the line, be thought more convincing than A, B, C, or any other stand-alone theory? To begin with, no one of the currently prominent stand-alone theories addresses *all* of the elements that I have argued are pertinently involved in forming beauty judgments regarding natural objects. Of course, any theory could be amended to absorb pertinent features it now omits. But, deploying a series of amendments to incorporate the features a series seems to lack threatens to undercut that theory's dominant theme—the perspective absent the features in question—and it was this theme that made the theory appealing in the first place. This situation is a familiar one in ethical theory, where efforts to rescue utilitarianism, for example, from its evident shortcomings are sometimes undertaken by adding exceptions and side-constraints to it such as: "No punishment of the innocent is to be tolerated." It is clear, however, that in short order the exceptions begin to swallow up the rule and the theory ceases to be distinctively utilitarian. For this reason, models and theories, by their very nature, don't welcome the haphazard accretion of amendments. Where each of a variety of approaches has a positive contribution to make to the overall enterprise of understanding natural beauty judgment, however, it is pointless to foreclose the prospect of their useful combination. A syncretic theory aims to weld together useful insights from all available sources by giving each its due, rather than by attaching them as amendments to a single polemical position. It draws upon a very wide range of sources—some of them (e.g., the theory of educational development) lying well outside the perimeter of usual aesthetic consideration. But it draws these sources together by focusing on the historically evolved notion of aesthetic experience, a plain enough idea, yet one powerful enough to affirm various connections between the theory of natural beauty judgment and the larger business of leading a good and rewarding life.

It might be argued that a syncretic theory is a loose and amorphous jumble of ideas, incapable of focusing clearly on its topic. It is, one might allege, a little of this and a little of that wrapped up in a promise that everything in it will somehow add up to a way of determining that some natural object is or is not beautiful. But syncretic theory is not a random jumble. To be sure, it rejects the time-honored methodology of definition *per genus et differentiam* as inappropriate to this context.

243

But it is not the only theory to decline to articulate a set of necessary and sufficient conditions for determining a natural thing's beauty. All the other theories we have reviewed do the same. This should not surprise us. Beauty judgments—whether in nature or in art—simply aren't algorithmic. There is no one series of thoughts, sensory responses, or emotive conditions that can conclusively establish a thing's beauty in the way a yardstick can (relatively) conclusively establish a thing's length. And this is because natural beauty judgments are, like the aesthetic experiences that support them, ultimately *sorites* determinations. There are lots of features we can agree upon as natural-beauty-contributors. But there is no one of them that is necessary, nor is there any specifiable set of them that is jointly sufficient to establish a natural thing's beauty.

A whorl of grain on the weathered root of a fallen oak may be beautiful simply because of its sinuous, curving pattern, a pattern that is beautiful in much the way waving, windblown hair can be beautiful. The upturned tangle of oak roots may be beautiful in an entirely different way, perhaps involving the contrapuntal rhythm of silvery dead projections against the backdrop of verdant, living forest. The surface of the root may be beautifully soft and smooth to the touch. If we train our attention exclusively on the natural objects themselves, it may seem impossible to find a clear way of singling out the features that count aesthetically, determining how they will count in relation to each other, or measuring how many and how prominent they must be to make the object beautiful. If, however, we focus attention on the aesthetic experience the observer of such natural objects has, we may find it far less difficult to draw informative distinctions. The grain whorl, the play of dead roots against the living forest, and the feel of the wood itself may all strike us a beautiful in different and incommensurable ways. Nevertheless we are conscious of as quality and depth in our experience of one of these that the others lack. The counterpoint of silvery roots against dark green, living forest affects us more powerfully than the other experiences because of its evocation of powerful forces in the broader sweep of life experience. Or the tactile quality of the weathered root is so rare, so extraordinarily smooth and sensuous that it produces an aesthetic response that eclipses whatever other responses the root may arouse. My point isn't that turning from the qualities experienced to the experience itself will automatically identify all winners and losers in some grand natural beauty contest. It's rather that we *do* routinely and unproblematically recognize some of our experiences of natural objects as richer, more powerful, more lasting, more affecting, and therefore more worthwhile than others. In saying that these are beautiful experiences, or experiences of beauty, we are really saying that they are experiences worth seeking, worth cultivating, worth sustaining, worth trying to bring to others. Here we can recognize a discernible better and worse, a more and a less intense. A reasonable objective for a theory of natural beauty is to identify ingredients that play into these aesthetic experiences and take stock of the way they add up. That is what this theory does.

Another potential line of objection would take syncretic theory to be unduly *subjective*. A theory in which natural beauty judgments turn on the comparative quality of aesthetic experiences of natural objects might seem destined to resolve itself into an endless battle over personal value preferences. Suppose that Smith is positively affected by the smell of lavender exactly as much as Jones is positively affected by the look of towering waterfalls. Does this mean that the one is just as beautiful as the other? If so, the theory seems to be in trouble, because it may be possible to find Smiths and Joneses whose experiences range over the features of any natural objects you please and whose equivalence of aesthetic experience renders conflicts among natural beauty judgments irresolvable. But, of course, this is not what the theory means at all.

Aesthetic experiences may be equally intense, equally impressive, and equally positive without being equal. Consider what we think of comparative beauty judgments in the world of art. A schoolchild at his first classical concert may be very powerfully impressed by what he sees and hears, may regard the event as a rare and wonderful aesthetic experience, and may therefore (rightly) regard it as emphatically beautiful. We shouldn't denigrate his beauty judgment because it is naïve and simplistic. His experience was powerful and positive and the beauty he found in it real. But, equally, we shouldn't regard his experience as having the same standing in settling the question of whether the concert was beautiful as the experience of the veteran music critic who was sitting behind him. It wouldn't matter if both of them filled in the same number in an exit poll asking for a numerical indication of the overall strength of their aesthetic experiences. We, like Mill, will want to reckon quality of experience along with quantity. We will probably be inclined to say something like this: The schoolchild found beauty in the concert because the causal conditions conducive to a strong, sustained, positive aesthetic experience were there. We would hope that he continues to develop his aesthetic sensitivities and his musical awareness so that his later concert experiences will incorporate some of the features involved in the music critic's finding the concert beautiful. We also hope that the music critic will not, in the course of making a lifetime of judgment calls, have lost that spark of freshness and untrammeled enthusiasm that marked the schoolchild's experience.

Much the same conditions obtain in our experience of natural beauty. Natural beauty appears wherever there are sincere, positive aesthetic experiences of the kind we have described. It is deepened and rendered more important in our lives as it is more fully integrated with other values, more reflected upon, more productive of pertinent and informative "trains of thought." As I have said, syncretic theory tries to walk the same fine line that Hume's theory of taste did. Hume wanted to recognize the importance of making every person's beauty judgment count while insisting that practice, alertness to distracting prejudice, cultivated sensibilities, and capacity for drawing comparisons of experienced beauty judges provide them and all of us with a way of making them count more substantially. Earlier, I observed that it is not the role of models of appreciation of natural beauty to *bring about* beauty judgments (i.e., to provide a means of directing attention toward natural objects that would insure their being sources of aesthetic reward) but rather it is their role to ratify, rationalize, and ramify those judgments. The point can now be generalized across syncretic theory as a whole. Ratification is the provision of a conceptual framework required to confirm an initial judgment that something is (to some degree) beautiful. It describes aesthetic experience in such a way as to permit the ascription of beauty to natural objects when that experience is positive, sustained, and generally consistent with a culture's mode of beauty-ascription.[6] Rationalization is the provision of concepts and cognitive strategies for comparing aesthetic experiences with others. This involves the identification of grounds for thinking that certain features of natural objects or constellations of such objects count toward their beauty and that others don't. And it involves interpersonal comparisons of claims that given sets of features in given contexts do add up to a basis for beauty judgment by reasonable observers.[7] Ramification is the development of ingredients in a natural beauty judgment beyond their present experiential status. It draws upon a broad spectrum of aesthetic concepts and modes of appreciation to extend the initial beauty judgments in productive ways.

It may be that the syncretic theory I have offered makes it appear that natural aesthetic judgments start out looking hopelessly subjective and undisciplined. If they start out that way, that is not how they end up. The elements of regard I described in chapters 7 and 8 inform the business of rationalization, and the models of appreciation I surveyed earlier in this chapter inform the business of ramification. They do so in ways that provide a sensible basis for determining which of two natural beauty judgments is more developed, more productive of sustained and enriched attention, and in that sense, deeper and more informative.

Along the same line, it might be objected that syncretic theory, in its effort to make room for so many strands of disparate thought, is *conceptually over-generous*. It is surely a fatal weakness of an account of judgment to have no way of showing that a given judgment is mistaken. And it might be thought that I have opened so many roads to showing that a natural object might sustain the kind of aesthetic experience that warrants a positive beauty judgment that I provide no means of showing that such a judgment might be wrong. It is certainly true that I want my account to be conceptually generous. Its view of beauty is meant to be compatible with the widest range of theories as to beauty's nature. Its account of natural beauty-making features is meant to include all, or almost all, of the features acknowledged in rival accounts. But I don't think it is so conceptually generous that it has no way of finding any natural beauty judgments mistaken.

What is it, after all, to make a mistake in aesthetic judgment? The simplest and most easily remedied kind of mistake is a simple misuse of terms, or category mistake. A child or newcomer to a linguistic community might say that a natural thing is beautiful meaning that it is tasty, or fragrant, or amusing. A person wishing to make a descriptive, objective beauty judgment by reporting whether a given natural object is taken to be beautiful in her aesthetic community can simply get the facts wrong. The way I connect natural beauty to a certain kind of aesthetic experience is meant to insure that reflective, corrective, and affirmative judgments are free of these elementary kinds of mistakes. Serious theoretical challenges arise when we ask whether a mature, informed observer, one who knows what the word "beauty" means, and is prepared to reach his own reflective judgment, can be mistaken in declaring a natural object to be beautiful. One way he can be mistaken is by inaccurately or dishonestly reporting the experience he has had or would have had under normal perceptual circumstances. It is conceivable that a person whose attention is trained on a non-beautiful natural object could have taken a drug that would cause her to have an experience she wrongly takes to be a natural beauty experience, and thus makes the wrong judgment call. Or that, in an effort to impress someone with her taste in natural beauty, she overstates her response. In both these instances, I think we should call the beauty judgment mistaken. The first is an accidental mistake, the second a deliberate (or fraudulent) one. Another way she can be mistaken is in thinking that the thing she finds beautiful is *natural* when it's not. (Perhaps it's one of those pesky glass flowers, again.) This last kind of mistake gets ruled out *ab initio* in my theory by the stipulation that the account given is one of beauty in objects that are taken to be natural and are in fact natural.

What, however, about the honest, informed, and undeluded appreciator? He hears, say, the song of the mourning dove and says it's beautiful. Could he be mistaken? The answer to this question will hinge entirely on what is implied in saying that an aesthetic experience is honest, informed, and undeluded. Conceptualists insist on a cognitive understanding of this requirement. They say that judging a natural object to be beautiful is partly a matter of knowing what it is—i.e., what natural category it belongs to. And thus to regard a birdsong one has heard as beautiful when one supposes it to be that of a mourning dove and it turns out to have been that of a meadowlark is to make a mistaken beauty judgment. In arguing against conceptualism I have insisted on the legitimacy of a non-cognitive understanding of some aspects of natural beauty judgment. In my view, an observer can be honest, informed, and undeluded with respect to the (non-conceptual) contents of his aesthetic experience—the pattern of birdsong he hears, say; to that extent he is free from the kind of mistake conceptualists describe. The account I've given does not make room for his being mistaken *altogether* in such an observation. If he is actually affected in the way I have described as peculiar to natural aesthetic experience and he is making an honest, accurate declaration of that experience, he is bound to be right. The song *is* beautiful. But, his being right about there being beauty here leaves plenty of room for his being wrong about what that beauty *amounts to*, as it is elaborated and reflected upon. If we think of the experienced beauty in this instance as setting in motion a train of associations, some of those associations may be shown to be mistaken or inapt. The birdsong may have called to mind a certain Puccini soprano aria which, if rightly remembered, would have enhanced appreciation of the birdsong by underscoring tonal features that would otherwise have gone unnoticed. But, the hearer might misremember the opera or the aria, and thus confuse rather than clarify his auditory experience. That would be a mistake in what is made of the beauty judgment (or the way in which it is extended and developed) rather than in the beauty judgment itself. And, of course, similar mistakes can occur in the application of any of the various models of appreciation I have considered.

CONCLUSION

Behind my house I maintain a humble urban flower garden. It is certainly a far cry from the grand masterworks created by historically renowned garden-artists and modern master gardeners. But it brings together into an agreeable configuration a considerable variety of flowering trees, rhododendrons, camellias, bamboo, roses, dahlias, various sturdy perennials and a few colorful annuals, interspersed with plantings of fruit and vegetables, a few patches of grass, and a fair smattering of weeds. As I walk through this garden, I find it surprisingly easy to let down my intellectual guard and simply let the garden give me what beauty it has to give. When I do so, I refuse to let any of the many claims about appropriate appreciation I have been considering here at my keyboard interfere with my relaxed enjoyment. This isn't simply a matter of deliberately trying to take natural objects on their own terms, as the aesthetic attitude theorists urged we should do. Nor is it a matter of freeing attention in order to see the garden elements as components of a living ecosystem, as natural environmentalists have urged we should do. It is rather, as I engage the experience, a matter of holding all theoretical imperatives aside and just wandering around the garden attentively and responsively.

When I do this, I find myself doing just what I have done in this book. I gather important elements of response from this corner and that, sometimes calling upon my knowledge of the things I am observing and sometimes responding to aspects of these things that I can't capture in words or concepts. I certainly don't concentrate my attention on the names of things. Nor do I concentrate it on the whole garden as a formal array. I admire the intensity of some colors in some flowers and the leafy patterning in others. I like the way the wisteria hangs its blossoms in a waterfall-like manner off my deck. And I admire that particular iris as a beautiful exemplar of its type. I can think of no way to say what it is about the interplay of the twisted arms of the empress tree in the middle of the garden with the gladiate leaves of the bamboo behind them that strikes me as beautiful. But it *is* beautiful, and obviously so. There are parts of the garden that evoke other things or constellations of things, both natural and artifactual. And there are other parts that assert themselves for what they are in their sensory simplicity—sweet fragrances, leafy rustling sounds, the furry feel of wisteria seedpods. Just as we find a rich diversity of pleasures in a stroll through an art gallery, so we find that the pleasures we experience in our gardens are endlessly various and richly compounded, as our responses build layer upon layer. Just as we don't look at artworks through a single mode of appreciation, we don't enjoy the beauty in our gardens in a single way.

This backyard garden of mine is both a congeries of natural components in an artificial environment and an artifact composed, as all artifacts ultimately are, of natural ingredients. It is not nature. But its ingredients are natural in the sense that they are not man-made, however much control and design may have cooperated in their propagation, cultivation, and arrangement. Backyard gardeners don't aim to produce art in the way the Sunday painters do. They aim to make evident and comprehensible precisely those features of their artifice they *haven't* made. This feature of the garden world works powerfully against claims some philosophers have made about the independence of beauty appreciation in art and nature.

The status of gardens as artworks or not is a topic fraught with controversy in recent philosophical literature.[8] But, putting that controversy aside, it is easy to see that gardens are, by design and tradition, places where we are invited to join our appreciation of natural beauty with our appreciation of art. This row of roses is natural in the sense that its components are all non-man-made. But it is positioned just here, to stay long enough in the sunlight to repel mildew and to provide a colorful contrast to the vegetation on either side. And it is juxtaposed to other garden elements in a way that accentuates its aesthetic virtues. How much of what we find beautiful in the rose is attributable to its roseate nature? How much is attributable to its contrived presentation? These are unanswerable questions. We see what is beautiful in the rose *because* it has been presented in a way that makes it vividly available to our senses. We see at the same time that thoughtful reorganization of natural ingredients has provided the conditions for that vivid availability.[9] Artistic influence frames and makes available to our senses those features of aesthetic delectation art cannot create. And yet, part of what we enjoy in our delectation of the natural ingredients of the garden is the fact that they appear the way they do by artful decision.

This same point is evident in the wider scope of our experience. Everything, or almost everything, we encounter in our lives has the garden-like quality of combining natural process with human influence. If we count as artifactual elements our decisions to intrude or refrain from intrusion into various domains, then the scope of the garden-like hybridization of aesthetic perspective widens considerably. On the one hand, everything we experience is natural because nature provides the only components we have to regard or manipulate, including ourselves. On the other hand, everything we experience is artifactual because we humans have cognized and strategized everything there is to experience.

The gardener positions the rose in such a way as to make its beauty evident. There are countless ways in which we position other natural objects to make their beauty evident. Some of them involve physical actions (as when we open up a vista on the lake by cutting back brambles, or when we adjust a lens to see a planetary ring). Some of them involve cognitive actions (as when we relieve someone of a morbid association affixed to lilies by showing how lilies can brighten a dark corner). And some involve emotive actions (as when we counteract an immediate, negative olfactory response by revealing that its source is an extremely rare and otherwise admirable plant). As the gardener shows us, to experience natural objects as beautiful is far more than just to observe them with one's mind and senses turned on. It is to develop and deploy a wide variety of means of calling them into a comprehensible array. In the garden we frame things using concepts and categories. But, as we do so, we intentionally restrict our attention to one field or facet of awareness or another. In particular, we pay attention to aspects of the sensory display that resonate with other elements in our experience. We exercise our imagination in connecting these objects to others to which they seem analogous.

It seems to me that the various models of appreciation philosophers have devised are, in the end, nothing more than elaborate descriptions of rival intentional-positioning strategies. They are like colored glasses one might decide to try on, one pair after another, to see how they change the way the world looks. When one looks through one set of lenses, certain features of the natural world come forward as beautiful and others recede. When one looks through the next, some of the same features stand out, but some don't, and others emerge as well. Put on formalist glasses and patterns in the array of wildflowers as well as details in a particular open bud may emerge. Put on typal glasses and the bamboo becomes beautiful as a splendid example of its variety. All colored glasses filter, and therefore alter, the visual field in some way. So it might be tempting to think that we could acquaint ourselves with a natural world as replete with untrammeled beauty as possible simply by taking *off* the glasses. That is to say, it might be tempting to suppose that we could see natural objects for what they are simply by refusing to try on *any* pattern of aesthetic appreciation. But this is impossible. It is just as impossible to experience beauty free from any mode of appreciation as it is to think without concepts. To see natural beauty, we must see *through* whatever mechanisms we have for turning the sensory panorama into aesthetic experiences. Where there is no focus there is no experience. Where there is no experience, there is no beauty.

The chief advantage of the syncretic theory I have presented is that it declines to accept any one pattern as exclusively appropriate. It says: If we can't help wearing colored glasses, we make the most of what we observe by trying them all on. If there *were* convincing grounds for supposing that just one way of regarding natural objects is appropriate to appreciation of their beauty, we should of course adopt that mode of appreciation just as we should wear properly prescribed eyeglasses, rather than just a preferred set of colored glasses, in the interest of perceiving natural objects as clearly as possible. But, as I have argued, there are no such grounds. Each of the general factors I have reviewed makes an important contribution to the overall appraisal of natural beauty. Each of the patterns of appreciation I have reviewed plays valuably into a comprehensive account of natural beauty. Each aesthetic experience of natural beauty is inherently free and open-ended. We can attend to things, features of things, arrays of things, contrasts between some of these elements, harmonies among them, perceived relations to elements formerly experienced, to artifactual objects, and so on. There is no imperative to limit this appreciative freedom in the interest of perceiving things as clearly as possible.

Malcolm Budd was quite right to insist on the ultimate freedom at work in the aesthetic appreciation of natural objects.[10] But he draws the wrong inference from that claim of freedom. He concludes that natural aesthetic appreciation is entirely unbounded, i.e., that "there is no such thing as the appropriate foci of aesthetic significance" in natural appreciation, so that no more guidance is available to us than the advice that we should appreciate whatever is appreciable in nature in whatever manner works for us.[11] As I see it, aesthetic appreciation of natural objects is not an enterprise where anything goes and everything counts. Rather, it is one where we can draw from a variety of approaches, pay attention to a variety of features, and call upon a variety of framing and associative devices to bring about a result in which there is an aesthetic experience of a certain kind. Admittedly, the account I give does not draw lines of demarcation in such a way that a person who is uncertain as to whether the experience he is having is certifiably an aesthetic experience of natural beauty can turn to a credential list to settle the issue. But indefiniteness of this kind is inevitable in aesthetic contexts. Aristotle warned us, long ago, that we should never expect more precision in our analyses than is permitted by the nature of the untidy subjects we undertake to analyze. Moreover indefiniteness in this context is asset, rather than a liability. We must, at the end of the day, remind ourselves that the general objective of a proper theory of natural beauty is not to nullify or undercut ways in which people normally and habitually appreciate natural objects, but to make clear (or clearer) how these ways and other ways may cooperate in conducing to the most rewarding experience of these objects.

If aesthetic experience is, as it should be, the central focus of our theory, and if we are convinced that reference to this field of awareness is neither mystical nor incoherent, then the point of the project is neither to vindicate one mode of appreciative approach over another nor to deny the prospect of any worthwhile approach altogether. It is instead to establish a rationale for taking stock of what people can find rewarding in their engagement with natural objects, what can sustain their attention, what can deepen their awareness of these objects as they contemplate them, as well as what these engagements reveal to them about themselves, and others, including relations of these objects to other objects, natural and artifactual.

I began with a discussion of the apparent conflation of art and nature in our appreciation of glass flowers. I end with reflections on the inter-penetration of art and nature in our appreciation of real flowers in backyard gardens. When we leave the world of getting and spending behind and walk down the steps into our gardens, we expect to be affected in a way that both gratifies our senses and enlarges our reflections. It is in such places that we deploy a familiar and easy basis of beauty judgment equally dependent on recognition of natural factors for what they are and of human contrivance for what it has provided. In backyard gardens, the manufactured and the spontaneous are harmonized. We gardeners contrive to impose some order on natural things. And yet these things continue to delight us with ever new, unplanned aspects. In engaging in the gardening enterprise, we become aware of little ways in which we can interject planned patterns on natural objects even as we learn about the habits of these objects and how limited our control over them is. We can make rose beds. We can't make a rose. Yet we *can* make it possible to see, smell, and feel roses for the wonderful things they are.

We create gardens so that we can have an aesthetic experience of a certain kind—one that lets us move relatively freely and instructively from art to nature and back again. And this experience, when we really think about it, is a constant leitmotif in our growing up aesthetically. We are *in* nature and *of* nature. We are also—in an important way—our own artworks. Surely the lessons we learn from natural beauty and from artistic beauty should inform each other as they guide us in the larger project that is their mutual goal, the project of living a good life.

NOTES

1   The first response need not always be a pleased reaction, of course. In many cases, children respond to unfamiliar things with questions. Questions about the nature or basis of beauty claims take the discussion from the plane of emotive response to initial approaches to descriptive and reflective judgments. How things play out in particular circumstances is likely to depend on such factors as the privileges of siblings and the availability of lunch.

2   My locating the recognition of a natural object's naturalness in this second layer indicates that I allow that a person who doesn't know some object is natural can nevertheless have a correct first-order beauty response to it. This will happen when she takes the thing to be beautiful, thinking that it is an artifact, and it turns out that it is a natural object. It doesn't seem to me that the conception that the thing is natural or not has to be present prior to the point where reflective awareness mediates the raw beauty response.

3   It is obvious that what I say about the layering of response here is closely connected to what I said earlier about the process of growing up aesthetically. That is because the conceptual structure of appreciation largely mirrors the developmental structure of an aesthetically attentive

life. Among other similarities, both processes are dynamic, involving the unfolding of awareness upon an informed base, and both are deeply conscious of the relation between individuals and their communities.

4 What I have called "descriptive beauty judgment" may be said to do just that. A descriptive judgment is non-dispositive because it makes a claim about the location of an object on an aesthetic culture's value map rather than one's own affirmative response to that object.

5 George Dickie, *The Art Circle* (New York: Haven Publications, 1984), p. 79.

6 I don't want to rule out anomalous beauty ascriptions (such as the surprising discovery on the part of an observer that she finds a partly decayed squirrel carcass "strangely beautiful"). But I want to avoid confusing beauty ascriptions with other sustained, positive aesthetic qualifications, such as "comical," or with qualifications that are sustained and positive, yet not aesthetic at all, such as "yielding a high rate of return on investment."

7 Again, the "adding up" must be understood as a sorites-style accumulation (as described in chapter 5) rather than the invocation of either necessary or sufficient conditions for beauty ascription.

8 On this controversy, see Mara Miller, *The Garden as Art* (State University of New York Press, 1993), and "Gardens as Art," in vol. 2. *Encyclopedia of Aesthetics*, pp. 274-80; and Stephanie Ross, *What Gardens Mean* (University of Chicago Press, 1998).

9 And that is, in the end, all we are capable of doing. In one important sense, all humans can ever do to make non-natural objects is to rearrange natural materials. And since both what is rearranged and what does the rearranging are non-man-made, it is not preposterous to claim that everything is ultimately natural, and that the only sensible aesthetic approach to the world is therefore a natural aesthetic. But, the difference between what people have made through rearranging natural materials (say, in creating the ceiling of the Sistine Chapel) and what those materials, taken as natural things, amount to is what makes a people a civilization.

10 Budd, *Aesthetic Appreciation of Nature*, pp. 146-48.

11 Ibid., p. 147. It is as much part of my account of natural beauty as it is part of Budd's that people should be free to appreciate it in whatever ways reward their attention. But I disagree with his view that deficiencies of the several models of appreciation leave us with no useful theoretical guidance. Instead, I believe we can retrieve from all of these models useful and instructive components that can be coordinated around a notion of aesthetic experience that makes sense of the way people's lives profit from their attention to natural things.

RefeRences

Apppleton, Jay. *The Experience of Landscape*. New York: Wiley, 1975.

Aristotle. *Basic Works*. Edited by Richard McKeon. New York: Random House, 1941.

Beardsley, Monroe C. "Aesthetic Experience Regained." *Journal of Aesthetics and Art Criticism* 28 (1969), pp. 3-11.

_____. *The Aesthetic Point of View: Selected Essays*. Edited by Michael J. Wreen and Donald M. Callen. Ithaca: Cornell University Press, 1982.

_____. *Aesthetics from Classical Greece to the Present*. New York: Macmillan, 1966.

_____. *Aesthetics: Problems in the Philosophy of Criticism*. New York: Harcourt, Brace & World, 1958.

Bell, Clive. *Art*. London: Chatto and Windus, 1914.

Berleant, Arnold. *The Aesthetics of Environment*. Philadelphia: Temple University Press, 1992.

_____. *Living in the Landscape: Toward an Aesthetics of Environment*. Lawrence, Kansas: University Press of Kansas, 1997.

Brady, Emily. "Imagination and the Aesthetic Appreciation of Nature." *Journal of Aesthethics and Art Criticism* 56 (1998), pp. 139-47.

Budd, Malcolm. *The Aesthetic Appreciation of Nature*. Oxford: Oxford University Press, 2002.

Bullough, Edward. "Psychical Distance as a Factor in Art and as an Aesthetic Principle." *British Journal of Psychology* 5 (1912), pp. 87-98.

Burke, Edmund. *A Philosophical Enquiry into the Origin of Our Ideas of the Sublime and Beautiful*. Edited by James T. Boulton. London: Routledge & Kegan Paul, 1958.

Carrier, David. "Art Without Its Objects?" *British Journal of Aesthetics* 19 (1979), pp. 53-62.

Carlson, Allen. "Aesthetic Appreciation of Nature." In *Routledge Encyclopedia of Philosophy*. London: Routledge, 1998.

_____. *Aesthetics and the Environment: The Appreciation of Nature, Art, and Architecture*. London: Routledge, 2000.

_____. "Appreciation and the Natural Environment." *Journal of Aesthetics and Art Criticism* 37 (1978), pp. 267-75.

———. "Formal Qualities in the Natural Environment." *Journal of Aesthetic Education* 13 (1979), pp. 99-114.

———. "Nature, Aesthetic Judgment, and Objectivity." *Journal of Aesthetics and Art Criticism* 40 (1981), pp. 15-27.

Carlson, Allen and Arnold Berleant, eds. *The Aesthetics of Natural Environments.* Peterborough, ON: Broadview Press, 2004.

Carroll, Noël. *Beyond Aesthetics: Philosophical Essays.* Cambridge: Cambridge University Press, 2001.

———. "On Being Moved by Nature: Between Religion and Natural History." In *Landscape, Natural Beauty, and the Arts.* Edited by Salim Kemal and Ivan Gaskell. Cambridge: Cambridge University Press, 1993.

———. *Philosophy of Art: A Contemporary Introduction.* London: Routledge, 1999.

Clark, Kenneth. *Landscape Into Art.* New. ed. New York: Harper and Row, 1976.

Collingwood, R.G. *Essays in the Philosophy of Art.* Edited by Alan Donagan. Bloomington: Indiana University Press, 1964.

Crawford, Donald. "Comparing Natural and Artistic Beauty." In *Landscape, Natural Beauty, and the Arts.* Edited by Salim Kemal and Ivan Gaskell. Cambridge: Cambridge University Press, 1993.

———. *Kant's Aesthetic Theory.* Madison: University of Wisconsin Press, 1974.

———. "Nature and Art: Some Dialectical Relationships." *Journal of Aesthetics and Art Criticism* 42 (1983), pp. 49-58.

Danto, Arthur. "The Artworld," *Journal of Philosophy* 61 (1964), pp. 571-584.

Davies, Stephen. *Definitions of Art.* Ithaca: Cornell University Press, 1991.

Dewey, John. *Art as Experience.* New York: Putnam, 1934.

———. *Experience and Nature.* Reprinted in *John Dewey, The Later Works,* Vol. 1. Edited by Jo Ann Boydston. Carbindale: Southern Illinois University Press, 1981.

Dickie, George. *Art and the Aesthetic: An Institutional Analysis.* Ithaca: Cornell University Press, 1974.

———. "Bullough and the Concept of Psychical Distance." *Philosophy and Phenomenological Research* 22 (1961), pp. 233-38.

Diffey, T.J. "Arguing about the Environment." *British Journal of Aesthetics* 40 (2000), pp. 133-48.

Eaton, Marcia. *Aesthetics and the Good Life.* Madison, NJ: Fairleigh Dickinson University Press, 1989.

———. "Beauty and Ugliness In and Out of Context." In *Contemporary Debates in Aesthetics and the Philosophy of Art.* Edited by Matthew Kieran. Malden, MA: Blackwell, 2006.

———. *Merit, Aesthetic and Ethical.* Oxford: Oxford University Press, 2001.

Eaton, Marcia and Ronald Moore. "Aesthetic Experience: Its Revival and Its Relevance to Aesthetic Education." *Journal of Aesthetic Education* 36 (2002), pp. 9-23.

Feagin, Susan. "Imagination: Contemporary Thought." *Encyclopedia of Aesthetics*, Vol. 3. Edited by Michael Kelly. Oxford: Oxford University Press, 1998.

Fisher, John Andrew. "The Value of Natural Sounds." *Journal of Aesthetic Education* 33 (1999), pp. 26-42.

Fry, Roger. *Vision and Design*. London: Chatto and Windus, 1920.

Godlovitch, Stan. "Creativity in Nature." *Journal of Aesthetic Education* 33 (1999), pp. 17-26.

———. "Icebreakers: Environmentalism and Aesthetics." In *The Aesthetics of Natural Environments. Journal of Applied Philosophy* II (1994), pp. 15–30.

Goodman, Nelson. *Languages of Art: An Approach to a Theory of Symbols*. Indianapolis: Hackett, 1976.

Gracyk, Theodore. "Kant on Nature and Art." In *Encyclopedia of Aesthetics*, Vol. 3. Edited by Michael Kelly. Oxford: Oxford University Press, 1998.

Guyer, Paul. *Kant and the Claims of Taste*. 2d ed. Cambridge: Cambridge University Press, 1997.

Hepburn, Ronald W. "Aesthetic Appreciation of Nature." In *Aesthetics in the Modern World*. Edited by Harold Osborne. New York: Weybright & Talley, 1968.

———. "Contemporary Aesthetics and the Neglect of Natural Beauty." In *The Aesthetics of Natural Environments*. Edited by Allen Carlson and Arnold Berleant. Peterborough, ON: Broadview Press, 2004.

———. "Nature in the Light of Art." In *Royal Institute of Philosophy Lectures: Philosophy and the Arts*. Vol. 6 (1971-72). New York: St. Martin's Press, 1973.

———. "Trivial and Serious in Aesthetic Appreciation of Nature." In *Landscape, Natural Beauty, and the Arts*. Edited by Salim Kemal and Ivan Gaskell. Cambridge: Cambridge University Press, 1993.

Hume, David. *Of the Standard of Taste and Other Essays*. Edited by J.W. Lenz. Indianapolis: Bobbs-Merrill, 1965.

Hutcheson, Francis. *Philosophical Writings*. Edited by R.S. Downie. London: Everyman, 1994.

Kant, Immanuel. *Critique of Judgment*. Translated by J.C. Meredith. Oxford: Oxford University Press, 1952.

Kemal, Salim and Ivan Gaskell, eds. *Landscape, Natural Beauty, and the Arts*. Cambridge: Cambridge University Press, 1993.

Kivy, Peter. *The Seventh Sense: A Study of Francis Hutcheson's Aesthetics and Its Influence on Eighteenth-Century Britain*. New York: Franklin, 1976.

Korsmeyer, Carolyn. "Terrible Beauties." In *Contemporary Debates in Aesthetics and the Philosophy of Art*. Edited by Matthew Kieran. Malden, MA: Blackwell, 2006.

Langfeld, Herbert Sidney. *The Aesthetic Attitude*. New York: Harcourt, Brace, 1920.

Levinson, Jerrold. "Schopenhauer, Arthur." In *Encyclopedia of Aesthetics*. Vol. 4. Edited by Michael Kelly. Oxford: Oxford University Press, 1998.

Matthews, Patrick. "Aesthetic Appreciation of Art and Nature." *British Journal of Aesthetics* 41 (2001), pp. 395-410.

Miller, Mara. *The Garden as an Art*. Albany: State University of New York Press, 1993.

Moore, Ronald. "Ugliness." In *Encyclopedia of Aesthetics*. Vol. 4. Edited by Michael Kelly. Oxford: Oxford University Press, 1998.

Mothershill, Mary. *Beauty Restored*. Oxford: Oxford University Press, 1984.

Nicholson, Marjorie Hope. *Mountain Gloom and Mountain Glory: The Development of the Aesthetics of the Infinite*. Ithaca: Cornell University Press, 1959.

Parsons, Glenn and Allen Carlson. "New Formalism and the Aesthetic Appreciation of Nature." *Journal of Aesthetics and Art Criticism* 62 (2004), pp. 363-76.

Pepper, Stephen C. *Principles of Art Appreciation*. New York: Harcourt, Brace, 1949.

Plato. *The Collected Dialogues*. Edited by Edith Hamilton and Huntington Cairns. Princeton: Princeton University Press, 1961.

Rader, Melvin and Bertram Jessup. *Art and Human Values*. Englewood Cliffs: Prentice-Hall, 1976.

Rolston III, Holmes. *Philosophy Gone Wild*. Buffalo: Prometheus, 1986.

Ross, Stephanie. *What Gardens Mean*. Chicago: University of Chicago Press, 1998.

Ross, Stephen David. "Beauty: Conceptual and Historical Overview." In *The Encyclopedia of Aesthetics*. Vol. 4. Edited by Michael Kelly. Oxford: Oxford University Press, 1998.

Sadler, Barry and Allen Carlson, eds. *Environmental Aesthetics: Essays in Interpretation*. Victoria, BC: Department of Geography, University of Victoria, 1982.

Saito, Yuriko. "Is There a Correct Aesthetic Appreciation of Nature?" *Journal of Aesthetic Education* 18 (1984), pp. 35-46.

Savile, Anthony. *The Test of Time*. Oxford: Oxford University Press, 1982.

Schopenhauer, Arthur. *The Works of Schopenhauer*. Abr. ed. Edited by Will Durant. New York: Frederick Ungar, 1928.

Shaftesbury, Earl of (Anthony Ashley Cooper). *Characteristics of Men, Manners, Opinions, Times*. Edited by John M. Robertson. Indianapolis: Bobbs-Merrill, 1964.

Sircello, Guy. *A New Theory of Beauty*. Princeton: Princeton University Press, 1975.

Smith, R.A. and C.M. Smith. "Aesthetics and Environmental Education." *Journal of Aesthetic Education* 4 (1970), pp. 125-40.

Sparshott, Francis E. *The Theory of the Arts*. Princeton: Princeton University Press, 1982.

Stecker, Robert. *Aesthetics and the Philosophy of Art*. New York: Rowman and Littlefield, 2005.

Stolnitz, Jerome. *Aesthetics and Philosophy of Art Criticism: A Critical Introduction*. Boston: Houghton Mifflin, 1960.

_____. "Of the Origins of Aesthetic Disinterestedness." *Journal of Aesthetics and Art Criticism* 20 (1960), pp. 131-33.

Summers, David. *The Judgment of Sense: Renaissance Naturalism and the Rise of Aesthetics.* Cambridge: Cambridge University Press, 1987.

Tatarkiewicz, Wladyslaw. *History of Aesthetics.* Vols. 1-3. The Hague: Mouton, 1970, 1974.

Townsend, Dabney. "The Interaction of Art and Nature: Shifting Paradigms in Eighteenth-Century Philosophy." In *The Reasons of Art: Artworks and the Transformations of Philosophy.* Edited by Peter McCormick. Ottawa: University of Ottawa Press, 1985.

Tuan, Yi-fu. *Topophilia: A Study of Environmental Perception, Attitudes, and Values.* Englewood Cliffs: Prentice-Hall, 1974.

Vivas, Elisio. *Creation and Discovery: Essays in Criticism and Aesthetics*, Chicago: Henry Regnery Co., 1955.

Walton, Kendall L. "Categories of Art." *Philosophical Review* 79 (1970), pp. 334-67.

Warnke, Martin. *Political Landscape: The Art History of Nature.* Cambridge, MA: Harvard University Press, 1995.

Warnock, Mary. *Imagination.* Berkeley: University of California Press, 1976.

Weitz, Morris. "The Role of Theory in Aestheticism." *Journal of Aesthetics and Art Criticism* 15 (1956), pp. 27-35.

Zangwill, Nick. *The Metaphysics of Beauty.* Ithaca: Cornell University Press, 2001.

Ziff, Paul. *Antiaesthetics: An Appreciation of the Cow with the Subtile Nose.* Dordrecht: D. Reidel, 1984.

Index

Recycled
Supporting responsible use
of forest resources
www.fsc.org Cert no. SGS-COC-003153
© 1996 Forest Stewardship Council

100%